CLIFFSCOMPLETE

Shakespeare's

Macbeth

Edited by Sidney Lamb

Associate Professor of English

Sir George Williams University, Montreal

Complete Text + Commentary + Glossary

Commentary by Christopher L. Morrow

WILEY

Wiley Publishing, Inc.

CLIFFSCOMPLETE

Shakespeare's

Macbeth

About the Author

Christopher L. Morrow is currently a doctoral student at Texas A&M University where he is working on a dissertation in Early Modern drama. Morrow received his Bachelor of Arts from the University of Wyoming in 1996 and his Master of Arts from Texas A&M University in 1998. He is also currently a graduate assistant with the *World Shakespeare Bibliography* as well as a volunteer graduate assistant with the *Seventeenth-Century News*.

Publisher's Acknowledgments

Editorial

Project Editor: Joan Friedman

Acquisitions Editor: Gregory W. Tubach

Copy Editor: Billie A. Williams

Editorial Manager: Kristin A. Cocks

Illustrator: DD Dowden

Special Help: Patricia Yuu Pan

Composition

Indexer: Sharon Hilgenberg

Proofreader: Rachel Garvey

Wiley Indianapolis Composition Services

CliffsComplete Macbeth

Published by:

Wiley Publishing, Inc.

111 River Street

Hoboken, NJ 07030-5774

www.wiley.com

Copyright © 2005 Jerry Bobrow, Ph.D.

Published simultaneously in Canada

Library of Congress Control Number: 00-01102

ISBN: 978-0-7645-8572-2

Printed in the United States of America

15 14 13

1O/RV/RQ/QY/IN

WILEY

CLIFFSCOMPLETE

Shakespeare's

Macbeth

CONTENTS AT A GLANCE

CLIFFSCOMPLETE

Shakespeare's

Macbeth

TABLE OF CONTENTS

Shakespeare's
MACBETH

INTRODUCTION TO WILLIAM SHAKESPEARE

William Shakespeare, or the "Bard" as people fondly call him, permeates almost all aspects of our society. He can be found in our classrooms, on our televisions, in our theatres, and in our cinemas. Speaking to us through his plays, Shakespeare comments on his life and culture, as well as our own. Actors still regularly perform his plays on the modern stage and screen. The 1990s, for example, saw the release of cinematic versions of *Romeo and Juliet, Hamlet, Othello, A Midsummer Night's Dream,* and many more of his works.

In addition to the popularity of Shakespeare's plays as he wrote them, other writers have modernized his works to attract new audiences. For example, *West Side Story* places *Romeo and Juliet* in New York City, and *A Thousand Acres* sets *King Lear* in Iowa corn country. Beyond adaptations and productions, his life and works have captured our cultural imagination. The twentieth century witnessed the production of a play and film about two minor characters from Shakespeare's *Hamlet* in *Rosencrantz and Guildenstern are Dead* and a fictional movie about Shakespeare's early life and poetic inspiration in *Shakespeare in Love.*

Despite his monumental presence in our culture, Shakespeare remains enigmatic. He does not tell us which plays he wrote alone, on which plays he collaborated with other playwrights, or which versions of his plays to read and perform. Furthermore, with only a handful of documents available about his life, he does not tell us much about Shakespeare the person, forcing critics and scholars to look to historical references to uncover the true-life great dramatist.

Anti-Stratfordians — modern scholars who question the authorship of Shakespeare's plays — have used this lack of information to argue that William Shakespeare either never existed or, if he did exist, did not write any of the plays we attribute to him. They believe that another historical figure, such as Francis Bacon or Queen Elizabeth I, used the name as a cover. Whether or not a man named William Shakespeare ever actually existed is ultimately secondary to the recognition that the group of plays bound together by that name does exist and continues to educate, enlighten, and entertain us.

An engraved portrait of Shakespeare by an unknown artist, ca. 1607.
Culver Pictures, Inc./SuperStock

Family life

Though scholars are unsure of the exact date of Shakespeare's birth, records indicate that his parents — Mary and John Shakespeare — baptized him on April 26, 1564, in the small provincial town of Stratford-upon-Avon — so named because it sat on the banks of the Avon river. Because common practice was to baptize infants a few days after they were born, scholars generally recognize April 23, 1564 as Shakespeare's birthday. Coincidentally, April 23 is the day of St. George, the patron saint of England, as well as the day upon which Shakespeare would die 52 years later. William was the third of Mary and John's eight children and the first of four sons. The house in which scholars believe Shakespeare to have been born stands on Henley Street and, despite many modifications over the years, you can still visit it today.

Shakespeare's father

Prior to William Shakespeare's birth, John Shakespeare lived in Snitterfield, where he married Mary Arden, the daughter of his landlord. After moving to Stratford in 1552, he worked as a glover, a money-lender, and a dealer in agricultural products such as wool and grain. He also pursued public office and achieved a variety of posts including bailiff, Stratford's highest elected position — equivalent to a small town's mayor. At the height of his career, sometime near 1576, he petitioned the Herald's Office for a coat of arms and thus the right to be a gentleman. But the rise from the middle class to the gentry did not come right away, and the costly petition expired without being granted.

About this time, John Shakespeare mysteriously fell into financial difficulty. He became involved in serious litigation, was assessed heavy fines, and even lost his seat on the town council. Some scholars suggest that this decline could have resulted from religious discrimination. The Shakespeare family may have supported Catholicism, the practice of which was illegal in England. However, other scholars point out that not all religious dissenters (both Catholics and radical Puritans) lost their posts due to their religion. Whatever the cause of his decline, John did regain some prosperity toward the end of his life. In 1596, the Herald's Office granted the Shakespeare family a coat of arms at the petition of William, by then a successful playwright in London. And John, prior to his death in 1601, regained his seat on Stratford's town council.

Childhood and education

Our understanding of William Shakespeare's childhood in Stratford is primarily speculative because children do not often appear in the legal records from which many scholars attempt to reconstruct Shakespeare's life. Based on his father's local prominence, scholars speculate that Shakespeare most likely attended King's New School, a school that usually employed Oxford graduates and was generally well respected. Shakespeare would have started *petty school* — the rough equivalent to modern preschool — at the age of 4 or 5. He would have learned to read on a *hornbook*, which was a sheet of parchment or paper on which the alphabet and the Lord's Prayer were written. This sheet was framed in wood and covered with a transparent piece of horn for durability. After two years in petty school, he would have transferred to grammar school, where his school day probably lasted from 6 or 7 o'clock in the morning (depending on the time of year) until 5 o'clock in the evening, with only a handful of holidays.

While in grammar school, Shakespeare would have primarily studied Latin, reciting and reading the works of classical Roman authors such as Plautus, Ovid, Seneca, and Horace. Traces of these authors' works can be seen in his dramatic texts. Toward his last years in grammar school, Shakespeare probably acquired some basic skills in Greek as well. Thus the remark made by Ben Jonson, Shakespeare's well-educated friend and contemporary playwright,

Shakespeare's birthplace in Stratford-upon-Avon.
SuperStock

pregnancy, and *Measure for Measure* includes this kind of premarital contract.) Two years later, in February 1585, Shakespeare baptized his twins Hamnet and Judith. Hamnet would die at the age of 11 when Shakespeare was primarily living away from his family in London.

For seven years after the twins' baptism, the records remain silent on Shakespeare. At some point, he traveled to London and became involved with the theatre, but he could have been anywhere between 21 and 28 years old when he did. Though some have suggested that he may have served as an assistant to a schoolmaster at a provincial school, it seems likely that he went to London to become an actor, gradually becoming a playwright and gaining attention.

that Shakespeare knew "small Latin and less Greek" is accurate. Jonson is not saying that when Shakespeare left grammar school he was only semiliterate; he merely indicates that Shakespeare did not attend University, where he would have gained more Latin and Greek instruction.

Wife and children

When Shakespeare became an adult, the historical records documenting his existence began to increase. In November 1582, at the age of 18, he married 26-year-old Anne Hathaway from the nearby village of Shottery. The disparity in their ages, coupled with the fact that they baptized their first daughter, Susanna, only six months later in May 1583, has caused a great deal of modern speculation about the nature of their relationship. However, sixteenth-century conceptions of marriage differed slightly from our modern notions. Though all marriages needed to be performed before a member of the clergy, many of Shakespeare's contemporaries believed that a couple could establish a relationship through a premarital contract by exchanging vows in front of witnesses. This contract removed the social stigma of pregnancy before marriage. (Shakespeare's plays contain instances of marriage prompted by

The plays: On stage and in print

The next mention of Shakespeare comes in 1592 by a university wit named Robert Greene when Shakespeare apparently was already a rising actor and playwright for the London stage. Greene, no longer a successful playwright, tried to warn other university wits about Shakespeare. He wrote:

> For there is an upstart crow, beautified with our feathers, that with his "Tiger's heart wrapped in a player's hide" supposes he is as well able to bombast out a blank verse as the best of you, and, being an absolute Johannes Factotum, is in his own conceit the only Shake-scene in a country.

This statement comes at a point in time when men without a university education, like Shakespeare, were starting to compete as dramatists with the university wits. As many critics have pointed out, Greene's statement recalls a line from *3 Henry VI*, which reads, "O tiger's heart wrapped in a woman's hide!" (I.4.137). Greene's remark does not indicate that Shakespeare was generally disliked. On the contrary, another university wit, Thomas Nashe, wrote of the great theatrical success of *Henry VI*, and Henry Chettle, Greene's publisher, later printed a flattering apology to Shakespeare. What Greene's statement does show us is that Shakespeare's reputation for poetry had reached enough prominence to provoke the envy of a failing competitor.

In the following year, 1593, the government closed London's theatres due to an outbreak of the bubonic plague. Publication history suggests that during this closure, Shakespeare may have written his two narrative poems, *Venus and Adonis*, published in 1593, and *The Rape of Lucrece*, published in 1594. These are the only two works that Shakespeare seems to have helped into print; each carries a dedication by Shakespeare to Henry Wriothesley, Earl of Southampton.

A ground plan of London after the fire of 1666, drawn by Marcus Willemsz Doornik.
Guildhall Library, London/AKG, Berlin/SuperStock

Stage success

When the theatres reopened in 1594, Shakespeare joined the Lord Chamberlain's Men, an acting company. Though uncertain about the history of his early dramatic works, scholars believe that by this point he had written *The Two Gentlemen of Verona, The Taming of the Shrew,* the *Henry VI* trilogy, and *Titus Andronicus*. During his early years in the theatre, he primarily wrote history plays, with his romantic comedies emerging in the 1590s. Even at this early stage in his career, Shakespeare was a success. In 1597, he was able to purchase New Place, one of the two largest houses in Stratford, and secure a coat of arms for his family.

In 1597, the lease expired on the Lord Chamberlain's playhouse, called The Theatre. Because the owner of The Theatre refused to renew the lease, the acting company was forced to perform at various playhouses until the 1599 opening of the now famous Globe theatre, which was literally built with lumber from The Theatre. (The Globe, later destroyed by fire, has recently been reconstructed in London and can be visited today.)

Recent scholars suggest that Shakespeare's great tragedy *Julius Caesar* may have been the first of Shakespeare's plays performed in the original playhouse. When this open-air theatre on the Thames River opened, financial papers list Shakespeare's name as one of the principal investors. Already an actor and a playwright, Shakespeare was now becoming a "Company Man." This new status allowed him to share in the profits of the theatre rather than merely getting paid for his plays, some of which publishers were beginning to release in quarto format.

Publications

A *quarto* was a small, inexpensive book typically used for leisure books such as plays; the term itself indicates that the printer folded the paper four times. The modern day equivalent of a quarto would be a paperback. In contrast, the first collected works of Shakespeare were in folio format, which means that the printer folded each sheet only once. Scholars call the collected edition of Shakespeare's works the *First Folio*. A folio was a larger and more prestigious book than a quarto, and printers generally reserved the format for works such as the Bible.

No evidence exists that Shakespeare participated in the publication of any of his plays. Members of Shakespeare's acting company printed the First Folio seven years after Shakespeare's death. Generally, playwrights wrote their works to be performed on stage, and publishing them was a novel innovation at the time. Shakespeare probably would not have thought of them as books in the way we do. In fact, as a principal investor in the acting company (which purchased the play as well as the exclusive right to perform it), he may not have even thought of them as his own. He would probably have thought of his plays as belonging to the company.

For this reason, scholars have generally characterized most quartos printed before the First Folio as "bad" by arguing that printers pirated the plays and published them illegally. How would a printer have received a pirated copy of a play? The theories range from someone stealing a copy to an actor (or actors) selling the play by relating it from memory to a printer. Many times, major differences exist between a quarto version of the play and a folio version, causing uncertainty about which is Shakespeare's true creation. *Hamlet*, for example, is almost twice as long in the Folio as in quarto versions. Recently, scholars have come to realize the value of the different versions. The *Norton Shakespeare*, for example, includes all three versions of *King Lear* — the quarto, the folio, and the *conflated* version (the combination of the quarto and folio).

Prolific productions

The first decade of the 1600s witnessed the publication of additional quartos as well as the production of most of Shakespeare's great tragedies, with *Julius Caesar* appearing in 1599 and *Hamlet* in 1600–1601. After the death of Queen Elizabeth in 1603, the Lord Chamberlain's Men became the King's Men under James I, Elizabeth's successor. Around the time of this transition in the English monarchy, the famous tragedy *Othello* (1603–1604) was most likely written and performed, followed closely by *King Lear* (1605–1606), *Antony and Cleopatra* (1606), and *Macbeth* (1606) in the next two years.

Shakespeare's name also appears as a major investor in the 1609 acquisition of an indoor theatre known as the Blackfriars. This last period of Shakespeare's career, which includes plays that considered the acting conditions both at the Blackfriars and the open-air Globe theatre, consists primarily of romances or tragicomedies such as *The Winter's Tale* and *The Tempest*. On June 29, 1613, during a performance of *All is True*, or *Henry VIII*, the thatching on top of the Globe caught fire and the playhouse burned to the ground. After this incident, the King's Men moved solely into the indoor Blackfriars theatre.

Final days

During the last years of his career, Shakespeare collaborated on a couple of plays with contemporary dramatist John Fletcher, even possibly coming out of retirement — which scholars believe began sometime in 1613 — to work on *The Two Noble Kinsmen* (1613–1614). Three years later, Shakespeare died on April 23, 1616. Though the exact cause of death remains unknown, a vicar from Stratford in the mid-seventeenth-century wrote in his diary that Shakespeare, perhaps celebrating the marriage of his daughter, Judith, contracted a fever during a night of revelry with fellow literary figures Ben Jonson and Michael Drayton. Regardless, Shakespeare may have felt his death was imminent in March of that year because he altered his will. Interestingly, his will mentions no book or theatrical manuscripts, perhaps indicating the lack of value that he put on printed versions of his dramatic works and their status as company property.

Seven years after Shakespeare's death, John Heminge and Henry Condell, fellow members of the King's Men, published his collected works. In their preface, they claim that they are publishing the true versions of Shakespeare's plays partially as a response to the previous quarto printings of 18 of his plays, most of these with multiple printings. This Folio contains 36 plays to which scholars generally add *Pericles* and *The Two Noble Kinsmen.* This volume of Shakespeare's plays began the process of constructing Shakespeare not only as England's national poet but also as a monumental figure whose plays would continue to captivate imaginations at the end of the millenium with no signs of stopping. Ben Jonson's prophetic line about Shakespeare in the First Folio — "He was not of an age, but for all time!" — certainly holds true.

Chronology of Shakespeare's plays

1590–1591	*The Two Gentlemen of Verona*
	The Taming of the Shrew
1591	*2 Henry VI*
	3 Henry VI
1592	*1 Henry VI*
	Titus Andronicus
1592–1593	*Richard III*
	Venus and Adonis
1593–1594	*The Rape of Lucrece*
1594	*The Comedy of Errors*
1594–1595	*Love's Labour's Lost*
1595	*Richard II*
	Romeo and Juliet
	A Midsummer Night's Dream
1595–1596	*Love's Labour's Won*
	(This manuscript was lost.)
1596	*King John*

1596–1597	*The Merchant of Venice*
	1 Henry IV
1597–1598	*The Merry Wives of Windsor*
	2 Henry IV
1598	*Much Ado About Nothing*
1598–1599	*Henry V*
1599	*Julius Caesar*
1599–1600	*As You Like It*
1600–1601	*Hamlet*
1601	*Twelfth Night, or What You Will*
1602	*Troilus and Cressida*
1593–1603	*Sonnets*
1603	*Measure for Measure*
1603–1604	*A Lover's Complaint*
	Othello
1604–1605	*All's Well That Ends Well*
1605	*Timon of Athens*
1605–1606	*King Lear*
1606	*Macbeth*
	Antony and Cleopatra
1607	*Pericles*
1608	*Coriolanus*
1609	*The Winter's Tale*
1610	*Cymbeline*
1611	*The Tempest*
1612–1613	*Cardenio* (with John Fletcher; this manuscript was lost.)
1613	*All is True (Henry VIII)*
1613–1614	*The Two Noble Kinsmen* (with John Fletcher)

This chronology is derived from Stanley Wells' and Gary Taylor's *William Shakespeare: A Textual Companion,* which is listed in the "Works consulted" section in this introduction.

A note on Shakespeare's language

Readers encountering Shakespeare for the first time usually find Early Modern English difficult to understand. Yet rather than serving as a barrier to Shakespeare, the richness of this language should form part of our appreciation of the Bard.

One of the first things readers usually notice about the language is the use of pronouns. Like the King James Version of the Bible, Shakespeare's pronouns are slightly different from our own and can cause confusion. Words like "thou" (you), "thee" and "ye" (objective cases of you), and "thy" and "thine" (your/yours) appear throughout Shakespeare's plays. You may need a little time to get used to these changes. You can find the definitions for other words that commonly cause confusion in the glossary column on the right side of each page in this edition.

Iambic pentameter

Though Shakespeare sometimes wrote in prose, he wrote most of his plays in poetry, specifically blank verse. Blank verse consists of lines in unrhymed *iambic pentameter. Iambic* refers to the stress patterns of the line. An *iamb* is an element of sound that consists of two beats — the first unstressed (da) and the second stressed (DA). A good example of an iambic line is Hamlet's famous line "To be or not to be," in which you do not stress "to," "or," and "to," but you do stress "be," "not," and "be." *Pentameter* refers to the *meter* or number of stressed syllables in a line. *Penta*-meter has five stressed syllables. Thus, Romeo's line "But soft, what light through yonder window breaks?" (II.2.2) is a good example of an iambic pentameter line.

Wordplay

Shakespeare's language is also verbally rich because he, along with many dramatists of his period, had a fondness for wordplay. This wordplay often takes the forms of double meanings, called *puns*, where a word can mean more than one thing in a given context. Shakespeare often employs these puns as a way of illustrating the distance between what is on the surface — *apparent* meanings — and what meanings lie underneath. Though recognizing these puns may be difficult at first, the glosses in the right-hand column point many of them out to you.

If you are encountering Shakespeare's plays for the first time, the following reading tips may help ease you into the text. Shakespeare's lines were meant to be spoken; therefore, reading them aloud or speaking them should help with comprehension. Also, though most of the lines are poetic, do not forget to read complete sentences — move from period to period as well as from line to line. Although Shakespeare's language can be difficult at first, the rewards of immersing yourself in the richness and fluidity of the lines are immeasurable.

Works consulted

For more information on Shakespeare's life and works, see the following:

Bevington, David, ed. *The Complete Works of Shakespeare.* New York: Longman, 1997.

Evans, G.Blakemore, ed. *The Riverside Shakespeare.* Boston: Houghton Mifflin Co., 1997.

Greenblatt, Stephen, ed. *The Norton Shakespeare.* New York: W.W. Norton and Co., 1997.

Kastan, David Scott, ed. *A Companion to Shakespeare.* Oxford: Blackwell, 1999.

McDonald, Russ. *The Bedford Companion to Shakespeare: An Introduction with Documents.* Boston: Bedford-St. Martin's Press, 1996.

Wells, Stanley and Gary Taylor. *William Shakespeare: A Textual Companion.* New York: W.W. Norton and Co., 1997.

INTRODUCTION TO EARLY MODERN ENGLAND

William Shakespeare (1564–1616) lived during a period in England's history that people have generally referred to as the English Renaissance. The term *renaissance,* meaning rebirth, was applied to this period of English history as a way of celebrating what was perceived as the rapid development of art, literature, science, and politics: in many ways, the rebirth of classical Rome.

Recently, scholars have challenged the name "English Renaissance" on two grounds. First, some scholars argue that the term should not be used because women did not share in the advancements of English culture during this time period; their legal status was still below that of men. Second, other scholars have challenged the basic notion that this period saw a sudden explosion of culture. A rebirth of civilization suggests that the previous period of time was not civilized. This second group of scholars sees a much more gradual transition between the Middle Ages and Shakespeare's time.

Some people use the terms *Elizabethan* and *Jacobean* when referring to periods of the sixteenth and seventeenth centuries. These terms correspond to the reigns of Elizabeth I (1558–1603) and James I (1603–1625). The problem with these terms is that they do not cover large spans of time; for example, Shakespeare's life and career span both monarchies.

Scholars are now beginning to replace Renaissance with the term Early Modern when referring to this time period, but people still use both terms interchangeably. The term *Early Modern* recognizes that this period established many of the foundations of our modern culture. Though critics still disagree about the exact dates of the period, in general, the dates range from 1450 to 1750. Thus, Shakespeare's life clearly falls within the Early Modern period.

Shakespeare's plays live on in our culture, but we must remember that Shakespeare's culture differed greatly from our own. Though his understanding of human nature and relationships seems to apply to our modern lives, we must try to understand the world he lived in so we can better understand his plays. This introduction helps you do just that. It examines the intellectual, religious, political, and social contexts of Shakespeare's work before turning to the importance of the theatre and the printing press.

Intellectual context

In general, people in Early Modern England looked at the universe, the human body, and science very differently from the way we do. But while we do not share their same beliefs, we must not think of people during Shakespeare's time as lacking in intelligence or education. Discoveries made during the Early Modern period concerning the universe and the human body provide the basis of modern science.

Cosmology

One subject we view very differently than Early Modern thinkers is cosmology. Shakespeare's contemporaries believed in the astronomy of Ptolemy, an intellectual from Alexandria in the second century A.D. Ptolemy thought that the earth stood at the center of the universe, surrounded by nine concentric rings. The celestial bodies circled the earth in the following order: the moon, Mercury, Venus, the sun, Mars, Jupiter, Saturn, and the stars. The entire system was controlled by the *primum mobile*, or Prime Mover, which initiated and maintained the movement of the celestial bodies. No one had yet discovered the last three planets in our solar system, Uranus, Neptune, and Pluto.

In 1543, Nicolaus Copernicus published his theory of a sun-based solar system, in which the sun stood at the center and the planets revolved around it. Though this theory appeared prior to Shakespeare's birth, people didn't really start to change their minds until 1610, when Galileo used his telescope to confirm Copernicus's theory. David Bevington asserts in the general introduction to his edition of Shakespeare's works that during most of Shakespeare's writing career, the cosmology of the universe was in question, and this sense of uncertainty influences some of his plays.

Universal hierarchy

Closely related to Ptolemy's hierarchical view of the universe is a hierarchical conception of the earth (sometimes referred to as the Chain of Being). During the Early Modern period, many people believed that all of creation was organized hierarchically. God existed at the top, followed by the angels, men, women, animals, plants, and rocks. (Because all women were thought to exist below all men on the chain, we can easily imagine the confusion that Elizabeth I caused when she became queen of England. She was literally "out of order," an expression that still exists in our society.) Though the concept of this hierarchy is a useful one when beginning to study Shakespeare, keep in mind that distinctions in this hierarchical view were not always clear and that we should not reduce all Early Modern thinking to a simple chain.

Elements and humors

The belief in a hierarchical scheme of existence created a comforting sense of order and balance that carried over into science as well. Shakespeare's contemporaries generally accepted that four different elements composed everything in the universe: earth, air, water, and fire. People associated these four elements with four qualities of being. These qualities — hot, cold, moist, and dry — appeared in different combinations in the elements. For example, air was hot and moist; water was cold and moist; earth was cold and dry; and fire was hot and dry.

In addition, people believed that the human body contained all four elements in the form of *humors* — blood, phlegm, yellow bile, and black bile — each of which corresponded to an element. Blood corresponded to air (hot and moist), phlegm to water (cold and moist), yellow bile to fire (hot and dry), and black bile to earth (cold and dry). When someone was sick, physicians generally believed that the patient's humors were not in the proper balance. For example, if someone were diagnosed with an abundance of blood, the physician would bleed the patient (using leeches or cutting the skin) in order to restore the balance.

Shakespeare's contemporaries also believed that the humors determined personality and temperament. If a person's dominant humor was blood, he was considered light-hearted. If dominated by yellow bile (or choler), that person was irritable. The dominance of phlegm led a person to be dull and kind. And if black bile prevailed, he was melancholy or sad. Thus, people of Early Modern England often used the humors to explain behavior and emotional outbursts. Throughout Shakespeare's plays, he uses the concept of the humors to define and explain various characters.

Religious context

Shakespeare lived in an England full of religious uncertainty and dispute. From the Protestant Reformation to the translation of the Bible into English, the Early Modern era is punctuated with events that have greatly influenced modern religious beliefs.

The Reformation

Until the Protestant Reformation, the only Christian church in Europe was the Catholic, or "universal," church. Beginning in the early sixteenth century, religious thinkers such as Martin Luther and John Calvin, who claimed that the Roman Catholic Church had become corrupt and was no longer following the word of God, began what has become known as the Protestant Reformation. The Protestants ("protestors") believed in salvation by faith rather than works. They also believed in the primacy of the Bible and advocated giving all people access to reading the Bible.

Many English people initially resisted Protestant ideas. However, the Reformation in England began in 1527 during the reign of Henry VIII, prior to Shakespeare's birth. In that year, Henry VIII decided to divorce his wife, Catherine of Aragon, for her failure to produce a male heir. (Only one of their children, Mary, survived past infancy.) Rome denied

She remained unmarried throughout her 45-year reign, partially by styling herself as the Virgin Queen whose purity represented England herself. Her refusal to marry and her habit of hinting and promising marriage with suitors both foreign and domestic helped Elizabeth maintain internal and external peace. Not marrying allowed her to retain her independence, but it left the succession of the English throne in question. In 1603, on her deathbed, she named James VI, King of Scotland and son of her cousin Mary, as her successor.

James I

When he assumed the English crown, James VI of Scotland became James I of England. (Some historians refer to him as James VI and I.) Like Elizabeth, James was a strong believer in the divine right of kings and their absolute authority. Some critics believe that *Macbeth,* written three years after James ascended to the throne, is a tribute to the king, in part because of its many affirmations of divine right.

Upon his arrival in London to claim the English throne, James made his plans to unite Scotland and England clear. However, a long-standing history of enmity existed between the two countries. Partially as a result of this history and the influx of Scottish courtiers into English society, anti-Scottish prejudice abounded in England. When James asked Parliament for the title of "King of Great Britain," he was denied.

As scholars such as Bevington have pointed out, James was less successful than Elizabeth was in negotiating between the different religious and political factions in England. Although he was a Protestant, he began to have problems with the Puritan sect of the House of Commons, which ultimately led to a rift between the court (which also started to have Catholic sympathies) and the Parliament. This rift between the monarchy and Parliament eventually escalated into the civil war that would erupt during the reign of James's son, Charles I.

In spite of its difficulties with Parliament, James's court was a site of wealth, luxury, and extravagance. James I commissioned elaborate feasts, masques, and pageants, and in doing so he more than doubled the royal debt. Stephen Greenblatt suggests that Shakespeare's *The Tempest* may reflect this extravagance through Prospero's magnificent banquet and accompanying masque. Reigning from 1603 to 1625, James I remained the King of England throughout the last years of Shakespeare's life.

Social context

Shakespeare's England divided itself roughly into two social classes: the aristocrats (or nobility) and everyone else. The primary distinctions between these two classes were ancestry, wealth, and power. Simply put, the aristocrats were the only ones who possessed all three.

Aristocrats were born with their wealth, but the growth of trade and the development of skilled professions began to provide wealth for those not born with it. Although the notion of a middle class did not begin to develop until after Shakespeare's death, the possibility of some social mobility did exist in Early Modern England. Shakespeare himself used the wealth gained from the theatre to move into the lower ranks of the aristocracy by securing a coat of arms for his family.

Shakespeare was not unique in this movement, but not all people received the opportunity to increase their social status. Members of the aristocracy feared this social movement and, as a result, promoted harsh laws of apprenticeship and fashion, restricting certain styles of dress and material. These laws dictated that only the aristocracy could wear certain articles of clothing, colors, and materials. Though enforcement was a difficult task, the Early Modern aristocracy considered dressing above one's station a moral and ethical violation.

The status of women

The legal status of women did not allow them much public or private autonomy. English society functioned on a system of patriarchy and hierarchy (see "Universal hierarchy" earlier in this introduction), which means that men controlled society beginning with the individual family. In fact, the family metaphorically corresponded to the state. For example, the husband was the king of his family. His authority to control his family was absolute and based on divine right, similar to that of the country's king. People also saw the family itself differently than today, considering apprentices and servants part of the whole family.

The practice of *primogeniture* — a system of inheritance that passed all of a family's wealth through the first male child — accompanied this system of patriarchy. Thus, women did not generally inherit their family's wealth and titles. In the absence of a male heir, some women, such as Queen Elizabeth, did. But after women married, they lost almost all of their already limited legal rights, such as the right to inherit, to own property, and to sign contracts. In all likelihood, Elizabeth I would have lost much of her power and authority if she had married.

Furthermore, women did not generally receive an education and could not enter certain professions, including acting. Society relegated women to the domestic sphere of the home. In *Macbeth*, Shakespeare explores questions about the roles of women through the character of Lady Macbeth, who is not content to take the traditional subjugated role of a wife. Lady Macbeth plays a very assertive and active role in her marriage and in the plot of the play.

Daily life

Daily life in Early Modern England began before sun-up — exactly how early depended on one's station in life. A servant's responsibilities usually included preparing the house for the day. Families usually possessed limited living space. Even among wealthy families, multiple family members tended to share a small number of rooms, suggesting that privacy may not have been important or practical.

Working through the morning, Elizabethans usually had lunch about noon. This midday meal was the primary meal of the day, much like dinner is for modern families. The workday usually ended around sundown or 5 p.m., depending on the season. Before an early bedtime, Elizabethans usually ate a light repast and then settled in for a couple of hours of reading (if the family members were literate and could bear the high cost of books) or socializing.

Mortality rates

Mortality rates in Early Modern England were high compared to our standards, especially among infants. Infection and disease ran rampant because physicians did not realize the need for antiseptics and sterile equipment. As a result, communicable diseases often spread very rapidly in cities, particularly London.

In addition, the bubonic plague frequently ravaged England, with two major outbreaks — from 1592–1594 and in 1603 — occurring during Shakespeare's lifetime. People did not understand the plague and generally perceived it as God's punishment. (We now know that the plague was spread by fleas and could not be spread directly from human to human.) Without a cure or an understanding of what transmitted the disease, physicians could do nothing to stop the thousands of deaths that resulted from each outbreak. These outbreaks had a direct effect on Shakespeare's career, because the government often closed the theatres in an effort to impede the spread of the disease.

London life

In the sixteenth century, London, though small compared to modern cities, was the largest city of Europe, with a population of about 200,000 inhabitants in the city and surrounding suburbs.

London was a crowded city without a sewer system, which facilitated epidemics such as the plague. In addition, crime rates were high in the city due to inefficient law enforcement and the lack of street lighting.

Despite these drawbacks, London was the cultural, political, and social heart of England. As the home of the monarchy and most of England's trade, London was a bustling metropolis. Not surprisingly, a young Shakespeare moved to London to begin his professional career.

The theatre

Most theatres were not actually located within the city of London. Rather, theatre owners built them on the South bank of the Thames River (in Southwark) across from the city in order to avoid the strict regulations that applied within the city's walls. These restrictions stemmed from a mistrust of public performances as locations of plague and riotous behavior. Furthermore, because theatre performances took place during the day, they took laborers away from their jobs. Opposition to the theatres also came from Puritans who believed that they fostered immorality. Therefore, theatres moved out of the city, to areas near other sites of restricted activities, such as dog fighting, bear- and bull-baiting, and prostitution.

The recently reconstructed Globe theatre.
Chris Parker/PAL

Despite the move, the theatre was not free from censorship or regulation. In fact, a branch of the government known as the Office of the Revels attempted to ensure that plays did not present politically or socially sensitive material. Prior to each performance, the Master of the Revels would read a complete text of each play, cutting out offending sections or, in some cases, not approving the play for public performance.

Performance spaces

Theatres in Early Modern England were quite different from our modern facilities. They were usually open-air, relying heavily on natural light and good weather. The rectangular stage extended out into an area that people called the *pit* — a circular, uncovered area about 70 feet in diameter. Audience members had two choices when purchasing admission to a theatre. Admission to the pit, where the lower classes (or *groundlings*) stood for the performances, was the cheaper option. People of wealth could purchase a seat in one of the three covered tiers of seats that ringed the pit. At full capacity, a public theatre in Early Modern England could hold between 2,000 and 3,000 people.

The stage, which projected into the pit and was raised about five feet above it, had a covered portion called the *heavens*. The heavens enclosed theatrical equipment for lowering and raising actors to and from the stage. A trapdoor in the middle of stage provided theatrical graves for characters such as Ophelia in *Hamlet* and also allowed ghosts, such as Banquo in *Macbeth*, to rise from the earth. A wall separated the back of the stage from the actors' dressing room, known as the *tiring house*. At each end of the wall stood a door for major entrances and exits. Above the wall and doors stood a gallery directly above the stage, reserved for the wealthiest spectators. Actors occasionally used this area when a performance called for a difference in height — for example, to represent Juliet's balcony or the walls of a besieged city. A good example of this type of

Shakespeare in Love *shows how the interior of the Globe would have appeared.*
Everett Collection

theatre was the original Globe theatre in London in which Shakespeare's company, The Lord Chamberlain's Men (later the King's Men), staged its plays. However, indoor theatres, such as the Blackfriars, differed slightly because the pit was filled with chairs that faced a rectangular stage. Because only the wealthy could afford the cost of admission, the public generally considered these theatres private.

Actors and staging

Performances in Shakespeare's England do not appear to have employed scenery. However, theatre companies developed their costumes with great care and expense. In fact, a playing company's costumes were its most valuable items. These extravagant costumes were the object of much controversy because some aristocrats feared that the actors could use them to disguise their social status on the streets of London.

Costumes also disguised a player's gender. All actors on the stage during Shakespeare's lifetime were men. Young boys whose voices had not reached maturity played female parts. This practice no doubt

influenced Shakespeare's and his contemporary playwrights' thematic explorations of cross-dressing.

Though historians have managed to reconstruct the appearance of the Early Modern theatre, such as the recent construction of the Globe in London, much of the information regarding how plays were performed during this era has been lost. Scholars of Early Modern theatre have turned to the scant external and internal stage directions in manuscripts in an effort to find these answers. While a hindrance for modern critics and scholars, the lack of detail about Early Modern performances has allowed modern directors and actors a great deal of flexibility and room to be creative.

The printing press

If not for the printing press, many Early Modern plays may not have survived until today. In Shakespeare's time, printers produced all books by *sheet* — a single large piece of paper that the printer would fold in order to produce the desired book size. For example, a folio required folding the sheet once, a quarto four times, an octavo eight, and so on. Sheets would be printed one side at a time; thus, printers had to simultaneously print multiple nonconsecutive pages.

In order to estimate what section of the text would be on each page, the printer would *cast off* copy. After the printer made these estimates, *compositors* would set the type upside down, letter by letter. This process of setting type produced textual errors, some of which a proofreader would catch. When a proofreader found an error, the compositors would fix the piece or pieces of type. Printers called corrections made after printing began *stop-press* corrections because they literally had to stop the press to fix the error. Because of the high cost of paper, printers would still sell the sheets printed before they made the correction.

Printers placed frames of text in the bed of the printing press and used them to imprint the paper. They then folded and grouped the sheets of paper into gatherings, after which the pages were ready for sale. The buyer had the option of getting the new play bound.

The printing process was crucial to the preservation of Shakespeare's works, but the printing of drama in Early Modern England was not a standardized practice. Many of the first editions of Shakespeare's plays appear in quarto format and, until recently, scholars regarded them as "corrupt." In fact, scholars still debate how close a relationship exists between what appeared on the stage in the sixteenth and seventeenth centuries and what appears on the printed page. The inconsistent and scant appearance of stage directions, for example, makes it difficult to determine how close this relationship was.

We know that the practice of the theatre allowed the alteration of plays by a variety of hands other than the author's, further complicating any efforts to extract what a playwright wrote and what was changed by either the players, the printers, or the government censors. Theatre was a collaborative environment. Rather than lament our inability to determine authorship and what exactly Shakespeare wrote, we should work to understand this collaborative nature and learn from it.

Shakespeare wrote his plays for the stage, and the existing published texts reflect the collaborative nature of the theater as well as the unavoidable changes made during the printing process. A play's first written version would have been the author's *foul papers*, which invariably consisted of blotted lines and revised text. From there, a scribe would recopy the play and produce a *fair copy*. The theatre manager would then copy out and annotate this copy into a playbook (what people today call a *promptbook*).

At this point, scrolls of individual parts were copied out for actors to memorize. (Due to the high cost of paper, theatre companies could not afford to provide their actors with a complete copy of the play.) The government required the company to send the playbook to the Master of the Revels, the government official who would make any necessary changes or mark any passages considered unacceptable for performance.

Printers could have used any one of these copies to print a play. We cannot determine whether a printer used the author's version, the modified theatrical version, the censored version, or a combination when printing a given play. Refer back to the "Publications" section of the "Introduction to William Shakespeare" for further discussion of the impact printing practices have on our understanding of Shakespeare's works.

Passing through many of the stages explained above, *Macbeth* was not published until the 1623 First Folio — seven years after Shakespeare's death. The published play is thought to be a revision of the original 1606 version penned by Shakespeare. Scholars have asserted that a fellow playwright, very possibly Thomas Middleton, added at least two songs and some dialogue to the work. See the following "Introduction to *Macbeth*" for a more detailed account of these additions.

Works cited

For more information regarding Early Modern England, consult the following works:

Bevington, David. "General Introduction." *The Complete Works of William Shakespeare*. Updated Fourth edition. New York: Longman, 1997.

Greenblatt, Stephen. "Shakespeare's World." *Norton Shakespeare*. New York: W.W. Norton and Co., 1997.

Kastan, David Scott, ed. *A Companion to Shakespeare*. Oxford: Blackwell, 1999.

McDonald, Russ. *The Bedford Companion to Shakespeare: An Introduction with Documents*. Boston: Bedford-St. Martin's Press, 1996.

INTRODUCTION TO *MACBETH*

Macbeth is among the shortest and most intense of Shakespeare's plays, as well as one of the best known and most widely recognized. *Macbeth* is generally viewed as one of Shakespeare's four great tragedies, in addition to *Hamlet, Othello,* and *King Lear*. The play's penetrating exploration of human nature, ambition, evil, gender, human relationships, and kingship — along with the periodic appearance of supernatural forces — has captivated audiences and critics for centuries.

Like all of Shakespeare's works, *Macbeth* is an incredibly rich and rewarding play to read and study. It was written more than 400 years ago, so this introduction provides cultural, theatrical, and publication contexts. The introduction also highlights many of the themes and concepts that Shakespeare explores.

Shakespeare's tragedies

Although Shakespeare wrote many comedies and history plays, he seems to be best known for his tragedies. A tragedy usually depicts the fall of a man of high station or class, such as a king, a prince, or a general. Occasionally, as in *Romeo and Juliet*, it portrays the fall of a couple. Main characters in a tragedy can fall from power or fall from happiness, but they almost always die by the end of the play.

In a good tragedy, such as *Macbeth*, readers and audience members get pulled into the play by identifying with the protagonist, who is painted as a great and admirable person wielding considerable influence in society. Having established this point of identification, Shakespeare then leads his audience through the downfall of this character, involving the audience in the hero's pain and suffering, as well as his or her mistakes. This identification slowly separates as, through the course of the play, the audience gains more knowledge of the situation than the hero does. This distance and enlarged view allows the audience to foresee the hero's demise. Though no longer identifying with the hero, the audience is still trapped in the tension of the play and released only by the protagonist's death.

In most tragedies, the decline of the character arises from circumstances of the protagonist's own creation. Because tragic heroes are almost always responsible for their demise, critics and scholars sometimes identify their mistakes as stemming from some sort of *tragic flaw*, be it indecision, ambition, pride, or jealousy. Though Shakespeare's tragic heroes are complex and cannot be easily reduced to one abstract principle, identifying a character's tragic flaw can provide a wonderful place to begin studying the play.

The rise and fall of Macbeth

Macbeth is one of Shakespeare's fastest and most straight-forward tragedies in its portrayal of the rise and fall of Macbeth, a nobleman of Scotland who is also a successful military leader. Early in the play, he encounters three "weird sisters," usually referred to as witches. These witches refer to him by his current title, Thane of Glamis; then by a title that he is not yet aware of, Thane of Cawdor; and finally by a title that he does not yet possess, King of Scotland.

When Macbeth later learns that he has been named Thane of Cawdor, he begins to believe that the weird sisters have the gift of prophecy. He then must decide between waiting patiently for the prophecy to come true or killing the current king, Duncan, and forcing it to come true. Prompted by his wife (and by the announcement that Malcolm, Duncan's son, is the heir to throne), Macbeth kills Duncan and becomes the King of Scotland.

Unfortunately for Macbeth, the witches' prophecy also indicated that although he would be king, his friend Banquo's descendents would establish a line of kings after Macbeth. (An apparition that Macbeth sees in Act IV, Scene 1 of the play indicates that Banquo's line stretches all the way to King James VI of Scotland, who became King James I of England during Shakespeare's lifetime.)

Threatened by Banquo's prophecy, Macbeth begins to behave like a tyrant, killing Banquo and trying to kill his son, Fleance. His paranoia takes over, and he begins to kill anyone who seems to pose a threat to his reign. Literally haunted by apparitions, Macbeth continues his horrific behavior until Malcolm returns with the help of Macduff, another Scottish nobleman, and support from England. Macbeth is killed, and at the play's end, Malcolm becomes king and restores Duncan's line to the Scottish throne. We do not see the witches' prophecy for Banquo come true, but because Fleance survives the attempt against his life, the possibility exists that Banquo's line will someday assume the throne.

A scene from a 1997 production at the Savonlinna Opera Festival.
Clive Barda/PAL

Historical sources of the story

Though *Macbeth* is not considered a history play, the title character is a Scottish historical figure. As we shall see when we look at its cultural context, this play also has intimate links with Early Modern England. Historically, Macbeth ruled as King of Scotland for 17 years, from 1040 to 1057. The accounts of this period in Scottish history vary. They all agree, however, that Macbeth gained the throne by killing King Duncan and lost the throne to Malcolm by being killed. Shakespeare relied upon these histories as well as other sources in the composition of this play. Specifically, he drew heavily from Raphael Holinshed's *Chronicles of England, Scotland, and Ireland* (1587), but he may also have been familiar with George Buchanan's *Rerum Scoticarum Historae* (1582).

Shakespeare deviates from these historical sources a great deal in his exploration of the themes of kingship, human nature, and evil. These alterations to the story include portraying the tragic hero in a more evil manner while painting Banquo (King James I's ancestor) in a more sympathetic light. For example, Holinshed's and Shakespeare's depictions of Duncan differ wildly. Historically, Duncan is described as a young, weak, and ineffective king. But Shakespeare's Duncan is an older, benevolent, influential, and virtuous king, whose murder is a crime against nature itself.

Furthermore, in Holinshed's account, Banquo figures more prominently in Macbeth's ascension to the throne because he serves as Macbeth's accomplice in Duncan's murder. Shakespeare's Banquo maintains his loyalty to Duncan, telling Macbeth that he will help as long as it does not compromise this loyalty: "So I lose none / In seeking to augment it, but still keep / My bosom franchis'd and allegiance clear, / I shall be counsell'd" (II.1.26–29).

In Shakespeare's play, Macbeth's descent into tyranny occurs over what seems a matter of weeks, and there is no mention of the ten years of peaceful rule that Scotland enjoyed under Macbeth. The final major alteration concerns Lady Macbeth, who figures very little in the historical accounts but is quite prominent in Shakespeare's play. Lady Macbeth appears only once in Holinshed's *Chronicles,* and her only action is to persuade her husband to commit *regicide* (the murder of a king). Critics have speculated that Shakespeare's depiction of Duncan's murder and Lady Macbeth's active and ambitious role (drugging the servants and smearing them with blood) may be borrowed from Holinshed's account of Captain Donwald and his wife's murder of King Duffe. As we can see, in addition to revising historical sources, Shakespeare frequently integrated various accounts to construct one coherent story.

The revisions to the historical accounts of Macbeth are more easily understood when we understand the culture in which Shakespeare was writing. Pinpointing the date of composition for this tragedy will allow us to get a better glimpse at the play's immediate context.

The birth of the play

The earliest published version of *Macbeth* appears in the First Folio in 1623, though many critics feel that this edition of the play is modified from the lost original. The first reference to a production of *Macbeth* pushes the play's date back to 1611. A Jacobean playgoer named Simon Forman recorded in his *Book of Plays* that he saw this work performed on April 20, 1611 at the Globe theatre.

Upon examining references to contemporary events and people, however, critics have concluded that *Macbeth* was most likely written and first performed in 1606. In the intervening 17 years, the play was revised (around 1609), most likely by dramatist Thomas Middleton, who added some of the witches' songs in Act III, Scene 5 and Act IV, Scene 1. Middleton may also be responsible for other lines in the play, though we cannot be certain. Keep in mind, as explained in the "Introduction to Early Modern

England," that a play belonged to the theatre company. Therefore, revisions by other playwrights were common. Middleton's additions to *Macbeth* do not detract from the quality of Shakespeare's work; rather, they provide scholars and critics with opportunities to learn more about the ways in which plays were produced in Early Modern England.

The ascension of James I

The event that had the biggest impact on the 1606 production of *Macbeth* — and which may have been responsible for Shakespeare writing this play — is the ascension of King James VI of Scotland to the English throne, thus becoming King James I of England. In May 1603, shortly after he became king, James became the personal patron of Shakespeare's acting company, causing it to change names from the Lord Chamberlain's Men to the King's Men. This patronage provided many benefits to the theatrical company, including increased opportunities to perform at court and financial assistance when the theatres were closed because of plague. Because of this, some critics view the production of *Macbeth* a mere three years after James's ascension to the English throne as Shakespeare's tribute to his company's patron. Others have argued the opposite — that this play is more a criticism of King James than a tribute to him.

Divine right versus elected kingship

Regardless of Shakespeare's intentions toward the king, James and his beliefs play a large part in this play. James was supposedly a direct descendent of Banquo, and critics assert that in Macbeth's apparition of Banquo's royal descendents (in Act IV, Scene 1), James is the last king portrayed in the vision. As discussed in the "Introduction to Early Modern England," King James believed in the divine right of kings, which is the assertion that the king is God's emissary on Earth and that kingship is passed patrilineally through the father. This belief system led to the practice of *primogeniture*, which meant that a king's eldest son inherited the throne.

In the eleventh century, Scotland changed the way it selected its kings. Prior to that time, kings were elected by a council of noblemen (or thanes). In the eleventh century, Scotland adopted the patrilineal system, so the throne was passed from father to eldest son. This historical information is important to our understanding of the play. After Macbeth kills Duncan, Malcolm and Donalbain fear for their lives and flee the country. Thus, Duncan's sons are suspected of playing an active role in their father's death. This implication and their absence leaves the throne available to Macbeth. In Act II, Scene 4, Macduff tells fellow nobleman Ross that Macbeth "is already nam'd, and gone to Scone / To be invested." That Macbeth is *named* king implies a reversion to the process of election to the throne.

These questions of kingship could be found in Shakespeare's England as well. Because Elizabeth did not marry, she never produced a male heir. This fact prompted anxieties and questions over succession in the minds of many people in Early Modern England. Without a male heir, Elizabeth named James VI of Scotland (who could trace his lineage to Henry VII, Elizabeth's grandfather) as King of England on her deathbed. Though James's succession did not face much opposition, Shakespeare is clearly grappling with questions of kingship that were raised during James's succession of Elizabeth.

The Gunpowder Plot

Macbeth also mirrors a plot to assassinate King James that had been discovered in 1605 — a year before Shakespeare's play appeared on stage. This curtailed attempt at James's life is commonly referred to as the Gunpowder Plot, because officials found a large amount of gunpowder and iron bars in a basement below Parliament the day before King James was to personally open a new session. Under divine right, regicide was the worst crime possible. It is no coincidence that one of the most striking references to early seventeenth-century England in *Macbeth* appears directly after Macbeth kills Duncan.

At the beginning of Act II, Scene 3, Macbeth's porter answers the knocking at Macbeth's gate that began in the previous scene. While complaining about the incessant pounding, the porter refers to the person knocking as an "equivocator, that could swear in both the scales against either scale" (II.3.8–10). Modern editors and scholars, such as Stephen Greenblatt and David Bevington, assert that this line is a direct reference to the Jesuit thinker Henry Garnet. In addition to being executed for his participation in the Gunpowder Plot, Garnet wrote *A Treatise of Equivocation,* which provided a justification for lying. The treatise argued that a statement was not a lie if it could possibly be true from another perspective. Consequently, this reference is one of the ways in which modern editors have placed *Macbeth's* composition in 1606.

Macbeth and the weird sisters in a 1993 National Theatre production
Fritz Curzon/PAL

Focus on the supernatural

In addition to exploring theories of kingship in the play, Shakespeare also capitalized on James's interest in the supernatural. Though interest in witches and the supernatural existed during Elizabeth's reign, James's fascination extended to a personal interaction with these forces.

News from Scotland (1591) recounts the trial of Scottish witches from the town of Forres. The witches allegedly had attempted to kill James while he was king of Scotland by trying to cause a shipwreck during his voyage to Denmark. The publication includes a woodcut of James, who had presided over the trial, personally interrogating the witches.

The weird sisters in *Macbeth* resemble these witches in their activity. Before Banquo and Macbeth encounter them in Act I, Scene 3, the weird sisters discuss sending tempestuous storms to a sailor's ship because his wife would not share her chestnuts with one of them. In addition, Banquo, just before he sees the weird sisters, asks Macbeth, "How far is't call'd to Forres?" (I.3.39). Thus, these weird sisters are linked to the witches in *News from Scotland* both by their behavior and their geographical location.

James himself wrote a work about witches called *Daemonologie* (1597). In this work, James discusses not only how witches operate and the extent of their power, but also their relationship to the Devil. According to James, the purpose of witches was to harm the king; thus, witchcraft was considered treason. Certainly, the witches in *Macbeth* wield considerable influence over the regicide of Duncan.

James also believed that witches were agents of the Devil who could bestow prophecies. Witches would use these prophecies to tempt the faith and virtue of men. Interestingly, the weird sisters tempt both Banquo and Macbeth in the play. Macbeth succumbs to his desires and ambitions while Banquo (supposedly James's ancestor) remains loyal and virtuous.

However, the presentation of the witches may not be as flattering to James as it appears. In his Bedford Cultural edition of the play, William C. Carroll notes that under James's influence, the Scottish people believed in and hunted witches. The English, on the other hand, were slightly more skeptical about the existence of witches. Obviously, the presence of a king who believed in witches caused a stir in England.

The controversy over the existence of witches may be reflected in this play. As Greenblatt points out in his introduction to *Macbeth* in the *Norton*

Shakespeare, while these weird sisters seem to figure prominently, only Banquo and Macbeth see them or know of their existence and their role in the rise of Macbeth to the throne of Scotland. This obscurity, some critics argue, pushes them to the margins of the play. Thus, Shakespeare presents their influence and even existence ambiguously. Some modern critics have even speculated that they might be a psychic projection by Macbeth, though this would not explain why Banquo sees them as well.

Themes explored

Though *Macbeth* may be one of Shakespeare's most topical plays, with its strong links to current events in Jacobean England, it also explores a wide variety of themes that do not necessarily relate to specific events. For instance, Shakespeare explores a great number of dichotomies — or paired opposites — such as good and evil, order and disorder, reason and emotion, and reality and illusion. Using these dichotomies, he investigates themes related to human nature, ambition, gender, and the family.

Virtue versus evil

Many of the major characters in this play are virtuous; the major exceptions are the Macbeths. Macbeth begins as an admirable character whose loyalty to Duncan and military prowess gain him the title of Thane of Cawdor. However, upon hearing the prophecy of the weird sisters, he begins to contemplate the murder of Duncan. His thoughts turn to "horrible imaginings" (I.3.139).

By using the word "horrible" to describe his thoughts of regicide, Macbeth alerts us that he is acutely aware of the nature of his actions. He acknowledges more than once that Duncan does not deserve to die. In his first true soliloquy, Macbeth imagines that Duncan's "virtues / Will plead like angels trumpet-tongu'd against / The deep damnation of his taking-off" (I.7.18–20).

After killing Duncan, Macbeth initially is haunted by the horror of his actions and regards himself with repugnance. But he soon becomes more callous as his murder of innocents continues with Macduff's family. By the end of the play, his tyranny has reached its peak as he continues to destroy anyone who opposes him, including Young Siward. Through Macbeth's descent into tyranny, Shakespeare explores the power of evil and illustrates how it can use human ambition to consume a person.

Lady Macbeth presents a slightly different case study of evil. Like her husband, she clearly is not a virtuous character. But while Macbeth becomes increasingly evil and less sympathetic as the play progresses, Lady Macbeth moves in the opposite direction.

In the early stages of the play, when Macbeth hedges about whether to kill Duncan, Lady Macbeth convinces her indecisive husband to follow through with his plans. Greenblatt notes in his introduction to *Macbeth* in the *Norton Shakespeare* that she accomplishes this in two primary ways. First, she questions his masculinity by connecting his ability to murder Duncan with his manhood. She taunts her husband by asking him if he would prefer to "live a coward in thine own esteem" (I.7.43).

Second, Lady Macbeth is rhetorically much more vicious than her husband in her beliefs and her determination. In a statement that is often cited to demonstrate the evil nature of Lady Macbeth, she claims that she would willingly sacrifice her own child if she had sworn to do so. Despite their atrocity, these are only words. And despite being the primary force behind Macbeth's actions, Lady Macbeth ultimately seems to be more haunted by their deeds than Macbeth is. Unlike Macbeth, she cannot descend fully into evil.

After many murders have taken place, Lady Macbeth repeatedly sleepwalks, rubbing her hands in a vain effort to wash off a spot of blood that she sees continually. In exasperation, she asks, "[W]ill these hands ne'er be clean?" (V.1.38). Her mental struggles escalate, and Lady Macbeth eventually commits suicide, suggesting that her conscience provides her with a sort of redemption that Macbeth could never find.

Reason versus passion

During their debates over which course of action to take, Macbeth and Lady Macbeth use different persuasive strategies. Macbeth is very rational, contemplating the consequences and implications of his actions. He recognizes the political, ethical, and religious reasons why he should not commit regicide. In addition to jeopardizing his afterlife, Macbeth notes that regicide is a violation of Duncan's "double trust" that stems from Macbeth's bonds as a kinsman and as a subject (I.7.12).

Lady Macbeth, on the other hand, has a more passionate way of examining the pros and cons of killing Duncan. She is motivated by her feelings and uses emotional arguments to persuade her husband to commit the evil act. Interestingly, though she uses her zeal to convince her husband to kill Duncan, she adopts a detached and pragmatic view of their crimes after they are committed, while Macbeth becomes emotionally gripped with horror and repugnance. Lady Macbeth even returns the daggers to the king's bedchamber and smears blood on his servants to implicate them in the crime. From her perspective, "what's done is done" and need not be regretted (III.2.12).

Despite this initial detachment from guilt, Lady Macbeth ultimately is unequipped to deal with the consequences of their actions. Conversely, Macbeth initially reacts emotionally with repugnance and remorse but later reasons that "blood will have blood" (III.4.122). Macbeth coldly deduces that he must continue to act villainously in order to maintain his crown. His continued villainy is accompanied by a deadening of emotions. Macbeth realizes that he will be unable to clean himself of the crime of regicide, saying that his hands could turn the green seas red (II.3.61–63). He reasons that, having chosen his course of action, "returning [would be] as tedious as go[ing] over" (III.4.138). The deadening of his emotions culminates in Act V when Macbeth greets news of his wife's death with no outward grief, saying that "[s]he should have died hereafter" (V.5.17).

Gender roles

Lady Macbeth is the focus of much of the exploration of gender roles in the play. As Lady Macbeth propels her husband toward committing Duncan's murder, she indicates that she must take on masculine characteristics. Her most famous speech addresses this issue. In Act I, Scene 5, after reading Macbeth's letter in which he details the witches' prophecy and informs her of Duncan's impending visit to their castle, Lady Macbeth indicates her desire to lose her feminine qualities and gain masculine ones. She cries, "Come, you spirits / That tend on mortal thoughts! unsex me here, / And fill me from the crown to the toe top full / Of direst cruelty" (I.5.38–41).

This request is part of what David Bevington, in his introduction to *Macbeth* in the fourth edition of the *Complete Works of Shakespeare*, sees as "sexual inversion" in the play. Clearly, gender is out of its traditional order. This disruption of gender roles is also presented through Lady Macbeth's usurpation of the dominant role in the Macbeth's marriage; on many occasions, she rules her husband and dictates his actions.

The disruption of gender roles is also represented in the weird sisters. Their very status as witches is a violation of how women were expected to behave in Early Modern England. The trio is perceived as violating nature, and despite their designation as sisters, the gender of these characters is also ambiguous. Upon encountering them, Banquo says, "You should be women, / And yet your beards forbid me to interpret / That you are so" (I.2.45–47). Their facial hair symbolizes their influence in the affairs of the male-dominated warrior society of Scotland. William C. Carroll, in his Bedford Cultural edition of *Macbeth,* sees the witches and the question of their gender as a device Shakespeare uses to criticizes the male-dominated culture, where titles are acquired through what Carroll describes as "murderous violence."

Nature out of order

The disorder of nature, as well as gender, is a major theme in this play. The hierarchical view of the universe described in the "Introduction to Early Modern England" is violated and disrupted at almost every turn. The unnatural and disruptive death of the monarch is paralleled by equally violent disruptions in nature itself.

The weird sisters in a Savonlinna Opera Festival production, 1997.
Clive Barda/PAL

On the night of Duncan's death, the nobleman Lennox claims there were "Lamentings heard i' the air; strange screams of death / And prophecying with accents terrible / Of dire combustion and confus'd events / New hatch'd to the woeful time" (II.3.61–64). Many critics see this parallel between Duncan's death and disorder in nature as an affirmation of the divine right theory of kingship. As we witness in the play, Macbeth's murder of Duncan and his continued tyranny extends the disorder to the entire country.

Timeless tragedy

Though *Macbeth* is firmly rooted in the contexts of Early Modern England, this play remains timeless for its penetrating and extensive portrait of the evils that humans can commit. It depicts Macbeth's conscious decision to descend into evil and tyranny in the name of personal ambition, and it illustrates the disorders in politics, gender, nature, and religion that this decision causes.

Unlike many of Shakespeare's other tragic heroes, Macbeth feels the agony of his decision in the beginning rather than the end of his fall. Emotionally deadened by his actions, Macbeth ends the play with a terrible determination to fight against fate and die in the process. Moments before he dies offstage, he tells his foe, "Lay on, Macduff, / And damn'd be him that first cries, 'Hold enough!'" (V.8.33–34). Shakespeare's play reveals a great deal about the political, social, and theatrical beliefs and practices of Early Modern England. It also reveals a great deal about being human.

CHARACTERS IN THE PLAY

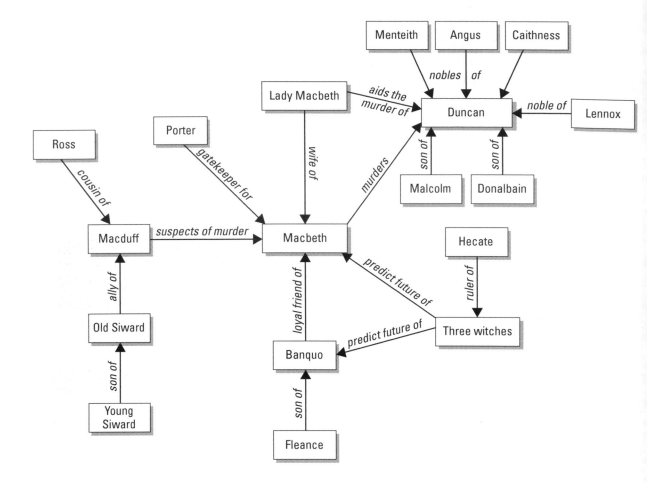

CLIFFSCOMPLETE

MACBETH
ACT I

Lady Macbeth *To beguile the time,*
Look like the time; bear welcome in your eye,
Your hand, your tongue: look like the innocent flower,
But be the serpent under 't. He that's coming
Must be provided for. . . .

Act I, Scene 1

This short scene establishes the supernatural element in the play and introduces the three witches (or weird sisters). During the disorderly scene, the witches reveal their plan to meet Macbeth.

ACT I, SCENE 1
A desert heath.

[Thunder and lightning. Enter three Witches]

First Witch When shall we three meet again
  In thunder, lightning, or in rain?

Second Witch When the Hurlyburly's done,
  When the battle's lost and won.

Third Witch That will be ere the set of sun.   5

First Witch Where the place?

Second Witch   Upon the heath.

Third Witch There to meet with Macbeth.

First Witch I come, Graymalkin!

Second Witch Paddock calls.

Third Witch Anon.   10

All Fair is foul, and foul is fair:
  Hover through the fog and filthy air. *[Exeunt]*

NOTES

1–2.   *When . . . rain?*. Witches and demons were supposed to be particularly active in stormy weather.

This play opens in the midst of a violent storm.

3.   *Hurlyburly:* the noise and confusion of battle. The battle described in the next scene is now raging.

6.   *heath:* a waste tract of land.

8.   *Graymalkin:* a gray cat, but commonly used as the name of any cat.

9.   *Paddock:* a toad. Witches were supposed to have attendant spirits that call them when it's time to go on an evil errand.

11.   *Fair is foul,* etc.. Fair weather and good deeds are foul, and only foul things are beautiful to the Witches.

COMMENTARY

The opening scene of *Macbeth* not only introduces the audience to the supernatural element that will be carried throughout the play, but it also establishes a theme of disorder through the presence of the witches, the stormy weather, and the bleak landscape. The witches (or weird sisters) probably would have been portrayed on the stage — as they have been in modern cinematic productions — as grotesque and ugly creatures.

Audience members in Early Modern England viewed witchcraft differently than audiences do today. At that time, many people, including King James I, believed in the presence of witches and their ability to harm and destroy virtuous people.

The witches agree that they will meet Macbeth at a particular time and place, suggesting the importance of that encounter, which will occur in Act I, Scene 3.

Macbeth and the Witches *by Joseph Anton Koch.*
SuperStock

Act I, Scene 2

After hearing a report about the battle against the traitors, which includes an account of Macbeth's glorious feats on the battlefield, Duncan orders that the title of Thane of Cawdor, which currently belongs to one of the traitors, be given to Macbeth.

ACT I, SCENE 2
A camp near Forres.

[Alarum within. Enter KING DUNCAN, MALCOLM, DONALBAIN, LENNOX with Attendants, meeting a bleeding Sergeant]

Duncan What bloody man is that? He can report,
As seemeth by his plight, of the revolt
The newest state.

Malcolm This is the sergeant
Who, like a good and hardy soldier, fought
'Gainst my captivity. Hail, brave friend!   5
Say to the king the knowledge of the broil
As thou didst leave it.

Sergeant Doubtful it stood;
As two spent swimmers, that do cling together
And choke their art. The merciless Macdonwald —
Worthy to be a rebel, for to that   10
The multiplying villanies of nature
Do swarm upon him — from the western isles
Of kerns and gallowglasses is supplied;
And fortune, on his damned quarrel smiling,
Show'd like a rebel's whore: but all's too weak;   15
For brave Macbeth, — well he deserves that name, —
Disdaining fortune, with his brandish'd steel,
Which smok'd with bloody execution,
Like valour's minion carv'd out his passage
Till he fac'd the slave;   20
Which ne'er shook hands, nor bade farewell to him,
Till he unseam'd him from the nave to the chaps,
And fix'd his head upon our battlements.

NOTES

s.d. *Alarum:* a trumpet call to attack or to congregate.

1–3. *He can . . . state:* To judge by his condition (weak and covered with blood), he can give the latest report of the rebellion.

3. *sergeant:* an officer of the guard who held much higher rank than a modern sergeant.

4. *hardy:* stout, valiant.

5. *my captivity:* Malcolm has been in the thick of battle and would've been captured if not for the Sergeant.

8. *spent:* exhausted.

9. *choke their art:* hamper each other's movements so that neither can use his swimming skill.

10. *to that:* for that purpose, i.e., to be a rebel.

11. *villanies:* evil qualities.

12. *western isles:* the Hebrides, small islands to the west of Scotland.

13. *kerns and gallowglasses:* lightly armed soldiers from Ireland.

14. *his ... quarrel:* his cause.

15. *Show'd . . . whore:* appeared to have taken Macdonwald as her lover.

19. *minion:* darling, favorite.

20. *slave:* villain, rascal.

21. *Which:* i.e., Macbeth. Shakespeare often uses 'which' for 'who' in his works.

22. *nave:* navel.

  chaps: jaws.

Duncan O valiant cousin! worthy gentleman!

Sergeant As whence the sun 'gins his reflection   25
Shipwracking storms and direful thunders break,
So from that spring whence comfort seem'd to come
Discomfort swells. Mark, King of Scotland, mark:
No sooner justice had with valour arm'd
Compell'd these skipping kerns to trust their heels,   30
But the Norweyan lord, surveying vantage,
With furbish'd arms and new supplies of men
Began a fresh assault.

Duncan   Dismay'd not this
Our captains, Macbeth and Banquo?

Sergeant   Yes;
As sparrows eagles, or the hare the lion.   35
If I say sooth, I must report they were
As cannons overcharg'd with double cracks;
So they doubly redoubled strokes upon the foe:
Except they meant to bathe in reeking wounds,
Or memorize another Golgotha,   40
I cannot tell —
But I am faint, my gashes cry for help.

Duncan So well thy words become thee as thy wounds;
They smack of honour both. Go, get him surgeons.
[Exeunt SERGEANT, attended]
[Enter ROSS]
Who comes here?   45

Malcolm The worthy Thane of Ross.

Lennox What a haste looks through his eyes! So should he look
That seems to speak things strange.

Ross   God save the king!

Duncan Whence cam'st thou, worthy thane?

Ross   From Fife, great king;
Where the Norweyan banners flout the sky   50
And fan our people cold. Norway himself.
With terrible numbers,
Assisted by that most disloyal traitor,
The Thane of Cawdor, began a dismal conflict;
Till that Bellona's bridegroom, lapp'd in proof,   55

---

24.   *cousin:* Macbeth's mother and Duncan's mother were sisters.

25–28.   *whence . . . swells:* The sun rises in the east, but so do storms. Also refers to the bad news of the Norwegian king's invasion after a victory over Macdonwald.

25.   *reflection:* return.

31.   *Norweyan:* Norwegian, i.e., Sweno, king of Norway.

   vantage: advantage.

32.   *furbish'd:* freshly polished, implying that they hadn't been in battle yet.

34.   *Yes:* ironical, as the following line shows.

36.   *sooth:* truth.

   cracks: charges. (This is an anachronism; cannons were used in Shakespeare's day but not in Macbeth's.)

39.   *Except:* unless.

40.   *memorize . . . Golgotha:* make this battlefield as famous as Golgotha.

41.   *I cannot tell:* He becomes faint here and doesn't finish the sentence. He was probably going to say: I cannot tell what their purpose was.

46.   *Thane:* an old title of nobility in Scotland almost equal to that of earl.

47.   *What . . . eyes!:* What an expression of haste there is in his eyes!

48.   *seems to speak:* looks as if he were about to speak.

50.   *flout:* mock.

51.   *fan . . . cold:* Their banners now serve merely to cool off our victorious soldiers.

54.   *dismal:* threatening disaster.

55.   *Bellona's bridegroom:* Macbeth. Bellona was the Roman goddess of war.

   lapp'd in proof: clad in well-tested armor.

Confronted him with self-comparisons,
Point against point, rebellious arm 'gainst arm,
Curbing his lavish spirit: and, to conclude,
The victory fell on us. —

Duncan   Great happiness!

Ross   That now
Sweno, the Norways' king, craves composition;   60
Nor would we deign, him burial of his men
Till he disbursed, at Saint Colme's Inch,
Ten thousand dollars to our general use.

Duncan No more that Thane of Cawdor shall deceive
Our bosom interest. Go pronounce his present death,   65
And with his former title greet Macbeth.

Ross I'll see it done.

Duncan What he hath lost noble Macbeth hath won.

[Exeunt]

56.	*Confronted . . . comparisons:* met him in single combat and made him compare himself with Macbeth.
57.	*Point . . . point:* sword against sword.
58.	*lavish:* insolent.
59.	*That:* so that.
60.	*craves composition:* begs for terms of peace.
62.	*Inch:* Celtic for island.
63.	*dollars:* these Danish silver coins were first minted in 1518.

COMMENTARY

The location of this scene stands in stark contrast to the opening scene. While Act I, Scene 1 took place on a deserted heath representing disorder, this scene opens in King Duncan's camp, a model of order. The stage direction tells the reader that the camp is "near Forres." This phrase was added by an editor in response to a statement made by Banquo in the following scene. Forres would have been significant to Shakespeare's audiences because, in addition to being the Scottish capital at the time, it was the location of a famous coven of witches who allegedly attempted to shipwreck James I, the ruling King of England and Scotland.

Macbeth's valorous deeds

A wounded sergeant reports to Duncan the latest information about a battle against a Scottish nobleman, Macdonwald, who is rebelling against the king. The sergeant, an accomplished warrior who protected Malcolm during an attempt to capture him in battle, relates Macbeth's deeds on the battlefield. Before even introducing the title character, Shakespeare presents Macbeth as valorous and loyal who, "[d]isdaining fortune" (setting aside concern for his own life), found and killed the rebel (17). Here, Macbeth is the agent who restores order to the Scottish kingdom.

Duncan responds by calling Macbeth his "valiant cousin" (24). As the Notes indicate, Macbeth actually was Duncan's cousin. This piece of information will prove important later in the play, because Macbeth has a somewhat legitimate claim to the Scottish throne. But because the throne moves from father to first-born son (succession through *primogeniture*), Macbeth's claim to the throne would be legitimate only if Duncan had no living sons.

The line between good and evil

The sergeant speaks of "[s]hipwracking storms and direful thunders" (26). In the opening scene, Shakespeare created a link between the three witches and stormy weather. He strengthens this link here through the adjective "shipwracking," because in times past people believed that witches used storms to cause shipwrecks. The storms are immediately followed by reinforcements ("furbish'd arms") from the Norwegian king, Sweno (32). The implication is that Macbeth is on the side of good, while Sweno is on the side of evil with the witches; the line between good and evil is very clear. The sergeant explains that despite the renewed attack, Macbeth's good deeds and valorous behavior on the battlefield accumulate. Macbeth and his fellow captain, Banquo, are undeterred by the reinforcements and emerge victorious from the attack.

Ross, a Scottish nobleman or *thane*, relates that the traitorous Thane of Cawdor also joined Norway in the battle against the Scots. Ross uses mythical references, calling Macbeth the bridegroom of Bellona (the Roman goddess of war), to describe Macbeth's valor and loyalty. This scene clearly establishes Macbeth as a hero who is not only able to protect his king but does so repeatedly — defeating all of the king's enemies and traitors.

Macbeth's reward

Duncan ends the scene by ordering the rebellious Thane of Cawdor executed and his title bestowed upon the brave and valiant Macbeth. In addition to rewarding Macbeth's loyalty and reaffirming Macbeth's admirable qualities, this gift indicates the type of warrior society that existed in Scotland at the time. In a warrior society, advancement and promotion comes through valorous deeds on the battlefield and loyalty to the king. As you will see, Macbeth later advances by violating both of these tenets.

Keep in mind that Macbeth does not yet know of his new title. Shakespeare creates dramatic irony by providing more information to the audience than to his protagonist.

Shakespeare's sources

The events described in this scene, the battles in particular, appear in Holinshed's *Chronicles* (see the Introduction to *Macbeth*). The only event not included in the *Chronicles* is the precise amount of the payment ($10,000) by Sweno to Duncan. Shakespearean scholar Sidney Lamb speculates that the payment might be an allusion to a $10,000 gift made to King James's court by his brother-in-law, King Christian IV of Denmark. Thus, this allusion represents another link between the play and the English monarch, James.

Act I, Scene 3

After relating some of their foul deeds, the witches encounter Macbeth and Banquo on their return to Duncan's camp. They prophesize that Macbeth will become Thane of Cawdor as well as the King of Scotland. However, they predict that Banquo, rather than Macbeth, will produce a line of kings. After the weird sisters disappear, Macbeth learns of his obtainment of the thaneship of Cawdor and begins to contemplate the other part of his prophecy.

ACT I, SCENE 3
A heath.

[*Thunder. Enter the three Witches*]

First Witch Where hast thou been, sister?

Second Witch Killing swine.

Third Witch Sister, where thou?

First Witch A sailor's wife had chestnuts in her lap,
And munch'd, and munch'd, and munch'd: 'Give
    me,' quoth I:
'Aroint thee, witch!' the rump-fed ronyon cries.   5
Her husband's to Aleppo gone, master o' the Tiger:
But in a sieve I'll thither sail,
And, like a rat without a tail,
I'll do, I'll do, and I'll do.   10

Second Witch I'll give thee a wind.

First Witch Thou'rt kind.

Third Witch And I another.

First Witch I myself have all the other;
And the very ports they blow,   15
All the quarters that they know
I' the shipman's card.
I'll drain him dry as hay:
Sleep shall neither night nor day

NOTES

6.   *rump-fed:* fed with expensive cuts of meat.

     ronyon: a term of abuse or contempt.

7.   *Aleppo:* in Syria (Asia Minor).

     Tiger: a common name for a ship in Shakespeare's time.

9.   *without a tail:* Witches, according to popular belief, could assume the shape of animals; but because they were creatures of Satan, they weren't transformed perfectly and thus lacked tails.

10.   *I'll do.* She'll work mischief on the ship and extend its journey.

11.   *a wind:* Witches had control of the wind and weather.

14.   *all the other:* By subduing all the other winds and controlling one, she means to keep the Tiger tempest-bound.

15.   *ports they blow:* By controlling the directions of the wind, she'll keep the Tiger out to sea.

17.   *card:* compass face that marks out the directions.

18.   *drain him.* By keeping the Tiger out to sea, the witches will force the ship's crew to use up its supply of water and thus be exhausted from thirst.

Hang upon his pent-house lid;   20
He shall live a man forbid.
Weary se'nnights nine times nine
Shall he dwindle, peak and pine:
Though his bark cannot be lost,
Yet it shall be tempest-tost.   25
Look what I have.

Second Witch Show me, show me.

First Witch Here I have a pilot's thumb,
Wrack'd as homeward he did come. *[Drum within]*

Third Witch A drum! a drum!   30
Macbeth doth come.

All The weird sisters, hand in hand,
Posters of the sea and land,
Thus do go about, about:
Thrice to thine, and thrice to mine,   35
And thrice again, to make up nine.
Peace! the charm's wound up.

[Enter MACBETH and BANQUO]

Macbeth So foul and fair a day I have not seen.

Banquo How far is 't call'd to Forres? What are these,
So wither'd and so wild in their attire,   40
That look not like th' inhabitants o' the earth,
And yet are on 't? Live you? or are you aught
That man may question? You seem to understand me,
By each at once her choppy finger laying
Upon her skinny lips: you should be women,   45
And yet your beards forbid me to interpret
That you are so.

Macbeth   Speak, if you can: what are you?

First Witch All hail, Macbeth! hail to thee, Thane of Glamis!

Second Witch All hail, Macbeth! hail to thee,
Thane of Cawdor!

Third Witch All hail, Macbeth! that shalt be king
hereafter.   50

---

20. *pent-house lid:* the eyelid that resembles a sloped roof.

21. *forbid:* to put under a spell or curse.

22. *se'nnights:* a week.

23. *dwindle, peak, and pine:* literally, to grow thin and waste away.

24. *cannot be lost:* It shall come into harbor anyway.

28. *thumb:* Parts of dead bodies were used to aid the witchcraft.

32. *weird sisters:* Weird meaning fateful. Holinshed's *Chronicles* say that the three women in antique dress who met Macbeth and Banquo in the wood were the three fates of Graeco-Roman mythology. Shakespeare, while changing them from goddesses into witches, has retained the above title for them. The emphasis on their connection with fate has the effect of making them seem more serious and important than ordinary witches. Their precise identity is left vague.

33. *Posters . . . land:* swift travelers. The witches could travel over the land quickly.

35. *thrice to thine . . . to mine:* rotating three times in your direction and three times in mine. This was supposed to complete the charm.

38. *foul and fair:* foul because of the weather; fair because of the victory.

39. *Forres:* the Scottish capital, near Inverness.

42. *are on't:* part of it, belonging to it.

43. *question:* talk to.

44. *choppy:* chopped, cracked.

48. *Glamis:* an Eastern Scottish village.

49. *Cawdor:* a small village near Inverness. Titles are usually attached to some section of the country.

Banquo Good Sir, why do you start, and seem to
   fear
   Things that do sound so fair? I' the name of truth,
   Are ye fantastical, or that indeed
   Which outwardly ye show? My noble partner   55
   You greet with present grace and great prediction
   Of noble having and of royal hope,
   That he seems rapt withal: to me you speak not.
   If you can look into the seeds of time,
   And say which grain will grow and which will not,   60
   Speak then to me, who neither beg nor fear
   Your favours nor your hate.

First Witch Hail!

Second Witch Hail!

Third Witch Hail!   65

First Witch Lesser than Macbeth, and greater.

Second Witch Not so happy, yet much happier.

Third Witch Thou shalt get kings, though thou be none:
   So, all hail, Macbeth and Banquo!

First Witch Banquo and Macbeth, all hail!   70

Macbeth Stay, you imperfect speakers, tell me more:
   By Sinel's death I know I am Thane of Glamis;
   But how of Cawdor? the Thane of Cawdor lives,
   A prosperous gentleman; and to be king
   Stands not within the prospect of belief,   75
   No more than to be Cawdor. Say from whence
   You owe this strange intelligence? or why
   Upon this blasted heath you stop our way
   With such prophetic greeting? Speak, I charge you.
   [*Witches vanish*]

Banquo The earth hath bubbles as the water has,   80
   And these are of them. Whither are they vanish'd?

Macbeth Into the air, and what seem'd corporal melted
   As breath into the wind. Would they had stay'd!

54.	*fantastical:* imaginary creations; of the fancy.
55.	*show:* appear to be.
57.	*noble having:* This refers to the witches' prophecy that Macbeth will become Thane of Cawdor.
58.	*withal:* by it, therewith.
59.	*seeds:* future events that may or may not occur.
68.	*get:* beget, propagate.
71.	*imperfect:* obscure.
72.	*Sinel:* Macbeth's father.
75.	*the prospect of belief:* the greatest distance the mind will venture into the future on what it believes.
76–77.	*from whence . . . intelligence:* Where did you get this information?
77.	*owe:* have, possess.
78.	*blasted:* barren.
81.	*are of them:* belong to that category.
82.	*corporal:* material.

Banquo Were such things here as we do speak about?
   Or have we eaten on the insane root   85
   That takes the reason prisoner?

Macbeth Your children shall be kings.

Banquo   You shall be king.

Macbeth And Thane of Cawdor too; went it not so?

Banquo To the self-same tune and words. Who's here?

[Enter ROSS and ANGUS]

Ross The king hath happily receiv'd, Macbeth,   90
   The news of thy success; and when he reads
   Thy personal venture in the rebels' fight,
   His wonders and his praises do contend
   Which should be thine or his. Silenc'd with that,
   In viewing o'er the rest o' the self-same day,   95
   He finds thee in the stout Norweyan ranks,
   Nothing afeard of what thyself didst make,
   Strange images of death. As thick as hail
   Came post with post, and every one did bear
   Thy praises in his kingdom's great defence,   100
   And pour'd them down before him.

Angus   We are sent
   To give thee from our royal master thanks;
   Only to herald thee into his sight,
   Not pay thee.

Ross And, for an earnest of a greater honour,   105
   He bade me, from him, call thee Thane of Cawdor:
   In which addition, hail, most worthy thane!
   For it is thine.

Banquo   What! can the devil speak true?

Macbeth The Thane of Cawdor lives: why do you dress me
   In borrow'd robes?

Angus   Who was the thane lives yet;   110
   But under heavy judgment bears that life
   Which he deserves to lose. Whether he was combin'd

85. *insane root:* probably either hemlock or henbane.

93-94. *His wonders . . . or his:* He is so struck with wonder that he cannot speak your praises aloud.

94. *with that:* by that mental struggle.

98. *Strange images of death:* death takes on horrible and strange forms.

99. *post with post:* a relay system of messengers.

105. *earnest:* down payment; pledge.

107. *In which addition:* in acquiring another title.

109. *dress me:* Shakespeare is remarkably fond of metaphors related to clothing.

112. *combin'd:* allied secretly.

With those of Norway, or did line the rebel
With hidden help or vantage, or that with both
He labour'd in his country's wrack, I know not;   115
But treasons capital, confess'd and prov'd,
Have overthrown him.

Macbeth   *[Aside]* Glamis, and Thane of Cawdor:
The greatest is behind. *[To ROSS and ANGUS]*
  Thanks for your pains.
[To BANQUO] Do you not hope your children shall
  be kings,
When those that give the Thane of Cawdor to me   120
Promis'd no less to them?

Banquo   That, trusted home,
Might yet enkindle you unto the crown,
Besides the Thane of Cawdor. But 'tis strange:
And oftentimes, to win us to our harm,
The instruments of darkness tell us truths,   125
Win us with honest trifles, to betray's
In deepest consequence.
Cousins, a word, I pray you.

Macbeth *[Aside]*   Two truths are told,
As happy prologues to the swelling act
Of the imperial theme. I thank you, gentlemen.   130
[Aside] This supernatural soliciting
Cannot be ill, cannot be good; if ill,
Why hath it given me earnest of success,
Commencing in a truth? I am Thane of Cawdor:
If good, why do I yield to that suggestion   135
Whose horrid image doth unfix my hair
And make my seated heart knock at my ribs,
Against the use of nature? Present fears
Are less than horrible imaginings;
My thought, whose murder yet is but fantastical,   140
Shakes so my single state of man that function

113.	*line the rebel:* aided Macdonwald.
114.	*hidden help:* Evidently, he was not present in person.
116.	*capital:* meriting the death penalty.
118.	*is behind:* yet to follow.
121.	*home:* to the full.
122.	*enkindle you:* to set afire with aspirations.
126.	*Win us:* gain our confidence.
129.	*prologues:* the introduction to a play (usually a speech).
	swelling: stately.
131.	*supernatural soliciting:* the attempt of the witches to influence him into thinking that he'll be king.
132.	*good:* from a good source.
	ill: from an evil source.
133.	*earnest:* assurance; pledge.
135.	*yield to that suggestion:* refers to the suggestion that he should murder Duncan.
137.	*seated:* not easily stirred up.
138.	*Against the use of nature?:* contrary to my natural thoughts and actions.
138.	*Present fears:* hallucinations of fear
140.	*fantastical:* imaginary.
141.	*my single state of man:* my singleminded state. After this experience, Macbeth is at war with himself. His better nature and his active self don't agree.
	function: the power to perform.

Is smother'd in surmise, and nothing is
But what is not.

Banquo   Look, how our partner's rapt.

Macbeth *[Aside]* If chance will have me king,
     why, chance may crown me,
Without my stir.

Banquo   New honours come upon him,   145
Like our strange garments, cleave not to their mould
But with the aid of use.

Macbeth   *[Aside]* Come what come may,
Time and the hour runs through the roughest day.

Banquo Worthy Macbeth, we stay upon your leisure.

Macbeth Give me your favour: my dull brain was
     wrought   150
With things forgotten. Kind gentlemen, your pains
Are register'd where every day I turn
The leaf to read them. Let us toward the king.
Think upon what hath chanc'd; and, at more time,
The interim having weigh'd it, let us speak   155
Our free hearts each to other.

Banquo   Very gladly.

Macbeth Till then, enough. Come, friends.

[Exeunt]

---

142. *surmise:* conjecture or prophecy as to the future.

142–143. *and nothing is / But what is not:* I am oblivious of the facts and can visualize nothing but the specters of my mind (i.e., the proposed murder of Duncan).

144–145. *If chance will . . . Without my stir:* Macbeth, as a member of the royal family, is eligible for the crown because it's elective. He tries to replace the thoughts of murder with the thought that he'll be elected.

146. *cleave not to their mould:* The honors do not fit themselves comfortably to the wearer.

147. *use:* habit, custom.

148. *Time . . . day:* Hour by hour even the longest day comes to an end. I'll let things go as they will and await the outcome.

149. *stay upon your leisure:* We await your action.

150. *wrought:* disturbed.

152. *regist'red:* kept within my mind.

155. *The interim having weigh'd it:* when we've thought it over in the meantime.

COMMENTARY

Back on the heath, in the middle of another storm, the weird sisters reunite. The opening to this scene firmly establishes the evil nature of the witches through their vengeful behavior. In his *Chronicles,* Holinshed refers to the weird sisters as "goddesses of destiny" (see the Introduction to *Macbeth*). Shakespeare does not use this name to describe them; he does not validate their claims of knowing the future and controlling fate. Therefore, the audience has no reason to trust or believe them. The audience only knows of their evil purposes.

Describing their recent activities, the weird sisters decide to send stormy weather to the seafaring husband of a woman who refused to share her chestnuts with one of the witches. This moment in the play may have historical roots. *News from Scotland* (1591) recounts a trial presided over by James I in which a group of witches was accused of trying to shipwreck James, who was the King of Scotland at that time. In addition to indicating that the witches sailed "in a sieve," this account claims that the king was saved through his faith (8). Shakespeare may be alluding to this trial and account by having the witches torment a ship on the sea. If so, by invoking this historical event in the play, Shakespeare invites the audience to compare James, who was tested by witches, to Banquo and Macbeth who are about to be. Keep this comparison in mind as the play progresses.

The weird sisters' level of evil seems to reach its peak with the display of "a pilot's thumb" (28). Clearly, Shakespeare is establishing these weird sisters as Macbeth's foes, though we have yet to know their purpose.

The meeting on the heath

Macbeth and Banquo arrive, and the meeting that the witches discussed in the opening scene takes place. Macbeth is literally travelling between the battle, which represents disorder, and the capital and court, which represent order. This initial interaction between Macbeth and the weird sisters is crucial for the rest of play. The witches' two-part prophecy drives the action.

Macbeth's first line, describing the day as "foul and fair," strangely echoes the witches' lines from the first scene (38). It also reminds the audience that nature is out of order. Despite the Scottish victory over their enemies, order has not been fully restored.

Before seeing the weird sisters, Banquo asks about the distance to Forres, which not only indicates that he and Macbeth are returning to the capital but also recalls the witch trial in *News from Scotland*; the trial took place in Forres. Upon seeing the sisters, Banquo's response gives the modern reader an idea about their appearance. He describes them as "wither'd" and "wild in their attire" (40). Their appearance is so different that he believes that they are not of this earth. Trying to place them in a category that he can understand, Banquo wants to call them women. However, notice that he is unable to do so because they have facial hair. This ambiguity of gender is significant in placing the sisters outside of nature and out of the proper order. It seems that they do not truly belong in either gender. This ambiguity initiates a question about the definitions of gender that will continue throughout the play.

The sisters' predictions

Upon Macbeth's command, the first sister greets Macbeth by calling him "Thane of Glamis," which is his current title (48). The second sister adds that he is "Thane of Cawdor," and the third tells him that he "shalt be king hereafter" (49–50). Because we already know that Macbeth has been granted the title of Thane of Cawdor (and we assume that he does not yet know of this title), we suspect that the sisters may be trying to manipulate Macbeth. By providing the audience with this information in the previous scene, Shakespeare makes us question the sisters' gift of prophecy. They merely tell Macbeth something that he does not yet know. Thus, the audience remains more skeptical of the prophecy than Macbeth does.

Banquo's response provides us with a textual clue as to Macbeth's on-stage reaction to this prophecy. He informs us that Macbeth appears fearful, which does not make sense to Banquo. In contrast to Macbeth's reaction, Banquo boldly asks for his own prophecy, claiming that he does not fear the sisters' words. The sisters' second prediction indicates that Banquo will not be king himself, but his offspring will be kings.

Succession through death

Macbeth recovers and confronts the sisters. He informs us explicitly that he is already the Thane of Glamis; the play to this point had not established that. His statement also explains that he received the title from "Sinel's death" (72). (According to Holinshed, Sinel was Macbeth's father.)

Note that titles in the play are gained through the death of their holder. Macbeth cannot believe that he is the Thane of Cawdor because Cawdor is alive. But he also states that being king is not "within the prospect of belief" (75). He waivers here between belief and disbelief. If Macbeth is indeed Duncan's cousin, Macbeth's succession to the throne is possible, but not likely. However, his lines later in this scene indicate that he does believe it is possible; he even contemplates regicide, which would facilitate it.

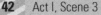

Refusing to answer Macbeth's questions, the witches vanish (by means of a trapdoor in the stage). The dialogue between Macbeth and Banquo after the weird sisters disappear reveals much about their characters. Banquo immediately doubts their appearance, suggesting that maybe they were a hallucination. Macbeth seems much more susceptible to their prediction, turning it into fact by telling Banquo that his (Banquo's) children will be kings. In Holinshed's *Chronicles*, the two men respond to the predictions of the witches with humor by repeating the prophecies to one another. In the play, they repeat the prophecies to each other, but Shakespeare provides no indication that they are joking as they do so.

Thane of Cawdor

Two Scottish noblemen, Ross and Angus, arrive and confirm the first part of Macbeth's prophecy by calling him the Thane of Cawdor. Banquo, upon hearing this, refers to the prophecy as originating from "the devil" (108). Like James I, he connects the witches with evil.

Macbeth indicates his disbelief of the new title and refers to it as "borrow'd robes" (110). Clothing is an important metaphor for identity that will reappear throughout the play. For example, see Banquo's lines 146–147 in this scene.

After being reassured that the traitorous Cawdor will be executed, Macbeth's aside seems to indicate that he fully believes the sisters' words. Banquo, however, is skeptical. In one of his most famous lines, Banquo expresses concern that these "instruments of darkness" may be speaking simple truths — that is, what is already fact — in order to manipulate and "betray" them (125–126).

Imperial ambition

Macbeth, not moved by Banquo's caution, speaks another aside where he sees his current titles as prologues to an "imperial theme," or his kingship (130). This statement is important because it is our first indication of Macbeth's ambition to be king. Also, he refers to a suggestion that is accompanied by a "horrid image" and that will be "[a]gainst the use of nature" (136, 138). It seems clear that Macbeth already is contemplating regicide as a way of attaining the title of king. In the space of three scenes, Macbeth has moved from being an extremely loyal and capable nobleman to someone whose ambition to be king causes him to contemplate murder.

Macbeth begins to resemble the world around him. The prediction, he says, has shaken his "single state of man" to a point that conjecture controls his mind (141). Like the turbulent weather, Macbeth's mind is in a state of disorder. He is at war with himself.

Although he ponders regicide, an important point in this speech is that Macbeth acknowledges that killing the king would be wrong. He concludes by rationally telling himself that the prophecy will come true without his "stir" — without his killing Duncan (145). Macbeth regains control over his evil thoughts. He still wants to be king, but he is content for now to let the crown come to him.

Banquo, noticing the internal struggle that's taking place in Macbeth, echoes Macbeth's earlier line about borrowed robes. He explains Macbeth's turmoil by saying that he needs time in order to become accustomed to the new titles, or "strange garments" (146).

The scene ends with the men returning to the castle. At this point, Macbeth arranges with Banquo to discuss their encounter with the weird sisters at a later time. This indicates that, despite his recent conclusion that he should not act, Macbeth is still not certain about what to do.

Act I, Scene 4

Back at the royal court, Duncan names Malcolm as the heir to the Scottish throne. Significantly, Macbeth sees this recognition of Malcolm as an obstacle that he must overcome in order to become the King of Scotland. The scene ends with Duncan indicating that he will stay at Macbeth's castle that night.

ACT I, SCENE 4
Forres. A room in the palace.

[Flourish. Enter DUNCAN, MALCOLM, DONALBAIN, LENNOX, and Attendants]

Duncan Is execution done on Cawdor? Are not
Those in commission yet return'd?

Malcolm   My liege,
They are not yet come back; but I have spoke
With one that saw him die; who did report
That very frankly he confess'd his treasons,   5
Implor'd your highness' pardon and set forth
A deep repentance. Nothing in his life
Became him like the leaving it; he died
As one that had been studied in his death
To throw away the dearest thing he ow'd,   10
As 'twere a careless trifle.

Duncan   There's no art
To find the mind's construction in the face:
He was a gentleman on whom I built
An absolute trust.
[Enter MACBETH, BANQUO, ROSS, and ANGUS]
                    O worthiest cousin!
The sin of my ingratitude even now   15
Was heavy on me. Thou art so far before
That swiftest wing of recompense is slow
To overtake thee; would thou hadst less deserv'd,
That the proportion both of thanks and payment
Might have been mine! only I have left to say,   20
More is thy due than more than all can pay.

NOTES

2.   *Those in commission:* the royal commissioners appointed to attend to Cawdor's trial and execution.

6.   *Implor'd:* begged; *set forth:* showed; revealed.

9–11. *had been . . . trifle:* had learned how, at death, to part easily with his dearest possession — life.

9.   *studied:* i.e., as one who had rehearsed the act of meeting death.

10.   *ow'd:* owned, possessed.

11.   *As:* as if.

      careless: uncared for. Worthless, insignificant.

11–12. *There's . . . face:* It's impossible to tell the character of a man's thoughts from the expression on his face.

12.   *construction:* meaning.

16.   *Thou:* Duncan uses the familiar and affectionate "thou" instead of the more formal "you" when speaking to his nearest kinsman.

18–20. *would thou . . . mine:* I wish that you had deserved less, so the reward I give you might be more instead of less than your deserts.

19.   *the proportion:* the larger proportion (which would be the right proportion).

20.   *mine:* on my side of the account: so that the balance might stand in my favor (as having paid more than I owed).

21.   *More is . . . pay:* We owe you more than all of us together could pay.

Macbeth The service and the loyalty I owe,
In doing it, pays itself. Your highness, part
Is to receive our duties; and our duties
Are to your throne and state, children and servants;   25
Which do but what they should, by doing everything
Safe toward your love and honour.

Duncan   Welcome hither:
I have begun to plant thee, and will labour
To make thee full of growing. Noble Banquo,
That hast no less deserv'd, nor must be known   30
No less to have done so, let me infold thee
And hold thee to my heart.

Banquo   There if I grow,
The harvest is your own.

Duncan   My plenteous joys
Wanton in fulness, seek to hide themselves
In drops of sorrow. Sons, kinsmen, thanes,   35
And you whose places are the nearest, know
We will establish our estate upon
Our eldest, Malcolm, whom we name hereafter
The Prince of Cumberland; which honour must
Not unaccompanied invest him only,   40
But signs of nobleness, like stars, shall shine
On all deservers. From hence to Inverness,
And bind us further to you.

Macbeth The rest is labour, which is not us'd for you:
I'll be myself the harbinger, and make joyful   45
The hearing of my wife with your approach;
So, humbly take my leave.

Duncan   My worthy Cawdor!

Macbeth *[Aside]* The Prince of Cumberland! that is a step
On which I must fall down, or else o'er-leap,
For in my way it lies. Stars, hide your fires!   50
Let not light see my black and deep desires;
The eye wink at the hand; yet let that be
Which the eye fears, when it is done, to see. *[Exit]*

---

23.   *pays itself:* is its own reward.

24–25.   *our duties . . . servants:* It's our duty to serve you.

26–27.   *everything . . . honour:* everything that tends to safeguard and fulfill our obligation to love and honor you.

27.   *Safe toward:* so as not to fail in the love and honor that is due to you.

28.   *to plant thee:* i.e., by making thee Thane of Cawdor.

32–33.   *There if . . . your own:* If I take root when you press me to your heart, and grow there like a tree, whatever fruit I bear shall be yours.

34.   *Wanton:* unrestrained, perverse, contrary.

35.   *drops of sorrow:* tears.

37.   *We will:* it's our royal purpose.

    establish our estate upon: settle the succession of the throne; name as our successor.

41–42.   *But signs . . . deservers:* There's a general distribution of honors when the Prince is formally invested with his new title.

42.   *From hence:* let us go from here.

    Inverness: The location of Macbeth's castle.

43.   *bind us further:* oblige us to you further by serving as our host.

44.   *The rest . . . for you:* Our leisure time is wearisome if it's not spent in your service.

45.   *harbinger:* an officer sent ahead (when a king intends to visit a place) to arrange for proper lodgings for the king and his suite.

48.   *a step:* an advance in honor (for Malcolm).

52.   *The eye wink at the hand:* Let my eyes not see the deed that my hand commits; be blind to my hand's deeds.

Duncan True, worthy Banquo; he is full so valiant,
And in his commendations I am fed;
It is a banquet to me. Let's after him,
Whose care is gone before to bid us welcome:
It is a peerless kinsman. *[Flourish. Exeunt]*

55

54–55. *True, worthy . . . I am fed:* Banquo has every reason to be jealous of Macbeth; but he is generous enough to add his commendations to Duncan's praise of his rival.

COMMENTARY

This scene opens at court with the rebellion having been put down successfully. The scene is important because it deals directly with the questions of royal succession that the weird sisters raised.

Before Macbeth and the other noblemen arrive, Shakespeare includes a description of Cawdor's death, noting that he confessed his treason and repented for it. Malcolm makes the famous comment that "[n]othing in his life / Became him like the leaving it" (7–8). Cawdor's best attribute was the nobility with which he faced his own death, acknowledging his previous actions as wrong. This description of Cawdor's noble death does not appear in Holinshed, Shakespeare's primary source. It is possible that Shakespeare may be foreshadowing Macbeth's own treason and death in this scene. The fact that both men hold the title of Thane of Cawdor certainly invites this comparison. (Take note of how Macbeth dies in Act V, Scene 8. Consider what the differences in their deaths say about Macbeth.)

Hidden thoughts and schemes

Duncan's response that it is impossible to discern the "mind's construction" (a person's inner thoughts) from the face invokes the disjunction between appearance and reality that will appear throughout the play (12). Immediately prior to Macbeth's arrival, Duncan describes Cawdor as someone on whom he had built "absolute trust" (14). In giving the title to Macbeth, Duncan indicates his "absolute trust" in him as well. The bitter irony is, of course, that both Cawdors betray Duncan.

The irony of this scene deepens as Macbeth describes to Duncan the duties of a noble thane, which should be directed at the throne and country. This statement is spoken by someone who already has contemplated killing Duncan in order to take his place.

In Holinshed's account, Duncan and Macbeth seem to be quite close to the same age, being the offspring of two sisters. In Shakespeare's play, Duncan is more fatherly to Macbeth. The king metaphorically describes their relationship as a gardener (Duncan) tending and growing a young plant (Macbeth). Shakespeare presents the king as a mature and benevolent ruler rather than a younger contemporary of Macbeth.

Heir to the throne

Duncan names Malcolm, his oldest son, as his heir. The act of officially naming an heir was usually done in the interest of maintaining order through the smooth succession of kings. The practice of succession through the first-born male was a relatively new one at the time of Duncan's reign. Just a few generations before, a council of thanes elected the Scottish king. Under the old system, Macbeth, as Duncan's cousin, would have had a better chance to become king. Though the weird sisters did not specify how he would succeed to the throne, notice that Macbeth perceives the naming of Malcolm as heir as an event that could prevent the prediction from coming true.

The disjunction between reality and illusion reappears as Macbeth asks that the stars not shine on his "black and deep desires" (51). While Macbeth still realizes the difference between right and wrong, he finds himself unable to control his ambition. It is ironic that the scene begins with Duncan's comment that it is impossible to know someone's inner thoughts and plans, and it ends with Macbeth asking that his inner thoughts and desires be disguised.

Act I, Scene 5

Upon hearing the news of the prophecy and Macbeth's new title through a letter, Lady Macbeth reveals her imperial ambitions through her famous "unsex me here" speech. Before Macbeth's arrival, she predicts that he won't have the will to actively pursue the throne, so she feels that she will have to convince him. When Macbeth arrives, she presumes that they will kill Duncan, but Macbeth refuses to discuss it at that time.

ACT I, SCENE 5
Inverness. Macbeth's castle.

[Enter LADY MACBETH, reading a letter]
They met me in the day of success; and I have learned by
the perfectest report, they have more in them than
mortal knowledge. When I burned in desire to question
them further, they made themselves air, into which
they vanished. Whiles I stood rapt in the wonder   5
of it, came missives from the king, who all-hailed
me, 'Thane of Cawdor;' by which title, before, these
weird sisters saluted me, and referred me to the
coming on of time, with, 'Hail, king that shalt be!'
This have I thought good to deliver thee, my dearest   10
partner of greatness, that thou mightest not lose the
dues of rejoicing, but being ignorant of what greatness
is promised thee. Lay it to thy heart, and farewell.
Glamis thou art, and Cawdor; and shalt be
What thou art promis'd. Yet do I fear thy nature;   15
It is too full o' the milk of human kindness
To catch the nearest way; thou wouldst be great,
Art not without ambition, but without
The illness should attend it; what thou wouldst highly,
That thou wouldst holily; wouldst not play false,   20
And yet wouldst wrongly win; thou'dst have, great Glamis,
That which cries, 'Thus thou must do, if thou have it;'
And that which rather thou dost fear to do
Than wishest should be undone. Hie thee hither,
That I may pour my spirits in thine ear,   25

NOTES

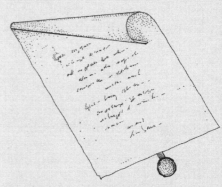

The letter from Macbeth inspires thoughts of regicide in Lady Macbeth.

2.   *report:* intelligence, information.

3.   *mortal:* human.

6.   *missives:* usually letters; here, messengers.

9.   *the coming on of time:* future.

11.   *partner of greatness:* Macbeth and his wife are so deeply attached to each other that neither can think of any division or individuality in their interest.

12.   *the dues of rejoicing:* the opportunity to rejoice that is due to you.

15.   *fear:* fear for, i.e., fear the weakness of.

17.   *the nearest way:* meaning murder.

19.   *illness:* evil, ill qualities.

24.   *Hie:* hasten.

25.   *my spirits:* my resolutions and energy of will.

And chastise with the valour of my tongue
All that impedes thee from the golden round,
Which fate and metaphysical aid doth seem
To have thee crown'd withal.
[Enter a Messenger]
                                        What is your tidings?

Messenger The king comes here to-night.

Lady Macbeth   Thou'rt mad to say it.   30
Is not thy master with him? who, were't so,
Would have inform'd for preparation.

Messenger So please you, it is true: our thane is coming;
One of my fellows had the speed of him,
Who, almost dead for breath, had scarcely more
Than would make up his message.

Lady Macbeth   Give him tending;   35
He brings great news. — *[Exit Messenger]* The raven
    himself is hoarse
That croaks the fatal entrance of Duncan
Under my battlements. Come, you spirits
That tend on mortal thoughts! unsex me here,
And fill me from the crown to the toe top full   40
Of direst cruelty; make thick my blood,
Stop up the access and passage to remorse,
That no compunctious visitings of nature
Shake my fell purpose, nor keep peace between
The effect and it! Come to my woman's breasts,   45
And take my milk for gall, you murdering ministers,
Wherever in your sightless substances
You wait on nature's mischief! Come, thick night,
And pall thee in the dunnest smoke of hell,
That my keen knife see not the wound it makes,   50
Nor heaven peep through the blanket of the dark,
To cry, 'Hold, hold!'
[Enter MACBETH]
                              Great Glamis! worthy Cawdor!
Greater than both, by the all-hail hereafter!
Thy letters have transported me beyond
This ignorant present, and I feel now   55
The future in the instant.

26. *chastise:* drive away all the scruples and fears that may keep you from gaining the crown; rebuke, suppress.

27. *All that impedes thee.* i.e., your fear, gentleness of nature, and scruples of conscience.

     the golden round. sovereignty, the crown.

28. *metaphysical:* supernatural.

28–29. *seem . . . withal:* seem to intend you to be crowned.

33. *had the speed of him:* made better speed than he.

36. *The raven:* The croaking of the raven was supposed to forbode death. Perhaps Lady Macbeth refers to the hoarse voice of the messenger.

39. *mortal:* murderous, deadly.

41. *make thick my blood:* Blood thickened by melancholy was thought to cause a gloomy and ferocious disposition.

42. *the access . . . remorse:* every way of approach by which regret can reach my heart.

43. *compunctious . . . nature:* natural instincts of compassion.

44. *fell:* cruel, savage.

46. *murdering ministers:* the spirits that tend on mortal thoughts.

47. *sightless:* invisible.

48. *nature's mischief:* the evil things in our nature.

49. *dunnest:* darkest.

50. *my keen knife:* Lady Macbeth thinks of the deed as her own.

53. *the all-hail hereafter:* She speaks as if she actually heard the witches.

54. *transported me:* carried me forward as a vision.

55. *ignorant:* ignorant because unaware of what the future brings.

56. *instant:* the present moment.

Macbeth   My dearest love,
Duncan comes here to-night.

Lady Macbeth   And when goes hence?

Macbeth To-morrow, as he purposes.

Lady Macbeth   O! never
Shall sun that morrow see.
Your face, my thane, is as a book where men   60
May read strange matters. To beguile the time,
Look like the time; bear welcome in your eye,
Your hand, your tongue: look like the innocent flower,
But be the serpent under 't. He that's coming
Must be provided for; and you shall put   65
This night's great business into my dispatch;
Which shall to all our nights and days to come
Give solely sovereign sway and masterdom.

Macbeth We will speak further.

Lady Macbeth   Only look up clear;
To alter favour ever is to fear.   70
Leave all the rest to me. *[Exeunt]*

61. *To beguile the time:* to deceive the people of the time, or the world.

65. *provided for:* attended to. In other words, murdered.

66. *This night's great business:* the great thing that she is going to do — murder Duncan.

dispatch: management.

69–70. *Only look . . . fear:* Appear to be innocent; if the expression on your face changes, we will have reason to fear.

Lady Macbeth claims the raven "croaks the fatal entrance of Duncan."

COMMENTARY

This scene marks the introduction of Lady Macbeth, one of Shakespeare's most famous female characters. Scene 5 is also important because it provides the audience with an extended view of her character. When the scene opens, she is reading a letter from Macbeth that informs her of the predictions of the weird sisters, but claims to do so only in an effort to allow her to begin rejoicing their happy fates. The letter reaffirms for the audience Macbeth's decision to take no action.

Lady Macbeth's resolution

Having read the letter, Lady Macbeth's immediate response to herself is that Macbeth's nature is not suited to the task of regicide. Whereas Holinshed's Macbeth has a cruel nature, Lady Macbeth informs the audience that Shakespeare's Macbeth is "full o' the milk of human kindness" and possesses the ambition but not the cruelty to "catch the nearest way" to the throne (16–17). She reminds us of Macbeth's internal conflict, which we witnessed in earlier scenes.

In her soliloquy, Lady Macbeth also details her plans to "pour" her spirits into her husband's ear so that he can overcome his nature and take the crown (25). Interestingly, in *Hamlet,* Claudius kills his brother King Hamlet by pouring poison into his ear. This connection between plays suggests a link between Lady Macbeth and regicide.

When Lady Macbeth learns that Duncan is staying at their castle that night, she becomes the first character to actually voice the regicidal act that is required. She indicates that the raven, a traditional metaphor for a messenger,

will "croak the *fatal* entrance" of the king under *her* battlements (37–38). Here, she assumes a dominant role over the castle defense — its battlements — a role that is typically held by the lord of the castle.

"Unsex me"

This assumption of masculinity continues in one of her most famous speeches, which comes in the form of a prayer. Interestingly, this prayer is directed toward "spirits," which means that her religious attitudes are pagan (38). The prayer indicates that these spirits are malignant. Gender becomes a key issue as Lady Macbeth asks the spirits to "unsex" her. She wants the spirits to remove from her any feminine attributes that will interfere with her plan to murder Duncan. The request implies that men are more capable of cruelty than women. Lady Macbeth's words are ironic because Macbeth, who has excelled in military prowess, is conflicted about committing murder. Even before her prayer, Lady Macbeth seems more suited to committing regicide than her husband.

Jon Finch and Francesca Annis star in the 1971 film directed by Roman Polanski.
Everett Collection

Like Macbeth earlier, she also asks that darkness and the "smoke of hell" disguise her actions (49). It is significant that she asks for a cover for her actions, and he asks that his desires be disguised. At this point in the play, she is clearly the more active agent of the two.

Macbeth's homecoming

When Macbeth arrives, he shows no indication that he plans to commit a crime toward Duncan. He tells Lady Macbeth that the king will depart from their household the next morning. In keeping with her more active role, Lady Macbeth warns her husband not to let his face betray his thoughts, once again invoking a separation between illusion and reality.

Lady Macbeth also describes her husband as the serpent under the bush. Interestingly, he later appropriates the same metaphor when referring to Banquo and Fleance.

Macbeth refuses to commit to any course of action regarding the sisters' prophecy. He puts off any decisions, as he did with Banquo in the third scene, until a later discussion. However, he also does nothing to stop his wife's preparations for the demise of Duncan.

Lady Macbeth's active and dominant role in this situation enables the audience to feel more sympathy with Macbeth, who is obviously tormented by being caught between his ambition and his knowledge of right and wrong.

Act I, Scene 6

Duncan and his party arrive at the gates of Macbeth's castle. Lady Macbeth greets them and leads them into the castle.

ACT I, SCENE 6
The same. Before the castle.

[Hautboys and torches. Enter DUNCAN, MALCOLM, DON-ALBAIN, BANQUO, LENNOX, MACDUFF, ROSS, ANGUS and Attendants]

Duncan This castle hath a pleasant seat; the air
Nimbly and sweetly recommends itself
Unto our gentle senses.

Banquo   This guest of summer,
The temple-haunting martlet, does approve
By his lov'd mansionry that the heaven's breath   5
Smells wooingly here: no jutty, frieze,
Buttress, nor coign of vantage, but this bird
Hath made his pendent bed and procreant cradle:
Where they most breed and haunt, I have observ'd
The air is delicate.

[Enter LADY MACBETH]

Duncan   See, see, our honour'd hostess!   10
The love that follows us sometime is our trouble,
Which still we thank as love. Herein I teach you
How you shall bid God 'eyld us for your pains,
And thank us for your trouble.

Lady Macbeth   All our service,
In every point twice done, and then done double,   15
Were poor and single business, to contend
Against those honours deep and broad wherewith
Your majesty loads our house: for those of old,
And the late dignities heap'd up to them,
We rest your hermits.

Duncan   Where's the Thane of Cawdor?   20
We cours'd him at the heels, and had a purpose

NOTES

1.   *seat:* setting, site, situation.

4.   *The temple-haunting martlet:* The martin (a bird) makes its home in the steeples of churches.

     approve: prove, show.

5.   *mansionry:* house-building.

     heaven's breath: inviting air.

6.   *jutty:* projecting part.

     frieze: projection at the top of the columns in the building.

7.   *coign of vantage:* suitable corner for nesting.

8.   *pendent bed:* hanging nest.

     procreant cradle: the nest where the young are bred.

11–14   *The love . . . your trouble.* A visit from the ones we love gives us trouble, but we're thankful for the trouble because we know that they love us.

16.   *single:* weak.

16–17.   *to contend / Against:* offset, vie with.

19.   *late dignities:* the thaneship of Cawdor.

20.   *We rest your hermits:* We're your debtors and are bound to pray for you.

21.   *cours'd:* followed closely behind him, rode quickly behind him.

To be his purveyor; but he rides well,
And his great love, sharp as his spur, hath holp him
To his home before us. Fair and noble hostess,
We are your guest to-night.

Lady Macbeth   Your servants ever   25
Have theirs, themselves, and what is theirs, in compt,
To make their audit at your highness' pleasure,
Still to return your own.

Duncan   Give me your hand;
Conduct me to mine host: we love him highly,
And shall continue our graces towards him.   30
By your leave, hostess. *[Exeunt]*

22. *purveyor:* officer who prepares the king's receptions on trips.

23. *holp:* helped.

26. *in compt:* on deposit, on account (something they don't own but which is entrusted to them).

27. *make their audit:* render an account.

28. *Still:* always.

30. *graces:* royal favors.

31. *By your leave:* permit me (he offers his arm to Lady Macbeth).

COMMENTARY

Duncan's arrival at Macbeth's castle transpires in this short scene. It opens with Duncan and his party in front of the castle. Shakespeare contrasts the dark and powerful discussion in the previous scene with Duncan's trust and ignorance. Duncan comments on the castle's "pleasant seat" and the air that is appropriate for their "gentle senses" (1–3). Ironically, there is a disjunction in appearances and reality even in nature. Whereas storms indicated a disorder in nature in earlier scenes, there is no sense of impending danger here.

Banquo's reference in line 4 to the "temple-haunting martlet," a bird that lives in church steeples, stands in stark contrast to Lady Macbeth's raven in the previous scene, who was supposed to "croak" Duncan's entrance.

In the previous scene, Lady Macbeth sent her husband to greet the king and cautioned him to disguise his thoughts. But Macbeth does not appear in this scene. Lady Macbeth greets the visitors by herself, and she seems to have no problem hiding her intentions. Like Macbeth in Act I, Scene 4, Lady Macbeth details her duties and their relationship to the king. She claims that as subjects of the king, their belongings are at his disposal, and she says that any service they provide to the king does not measure up to the honors he has bestowed on them.

Hand in hand, she conducts the king under the battlements and into her castle. Despite the frequent references to love and the pleasantness of the castle, the final image of Lady Macbeth leading Duncan into the castle is a sinister one.

Act I, Scene 7

In his first true soliloquy, Macbeth contemplates the consequences of killing Duncan from a variety of perspectives, revealing his inner struggle with the question. Also, Lady Macbeth executes her plans to convince her husband to commit regicide through a combination of insulting her husband's masculinity and demonstrating her own fierce support of this course of action. This scene ends the first act with Macbeth resolved to kill Duncan and obtain the Scottish throne.

ACT I, SCENE 7
The same. A room in the castle.

[Hautboys and torches. Enter, and pass over the stage, a Sewer, and divers Servants with dishes and service. Then, enter MACBETH]

Macbeth If it were done when 'tis done, then 'twere well
It were done quickly; if the assassination
Could trammel up the consequence, and catch
With his surcease success: that but this blow
Might be the be-all and the end-all. Here,   5
But here, upon this bank and shoal of time,
We'd jump the life to come. But in these cases
We still have judgment here; that we but teach
Bloody instructions, which, being taught, return
To plague the inventor; this even-handed justice   10
Commends the ingredients of our poison'd chalice
To our own lips. He's here in double trust:
First, as I am his kinsman and his subject,
Strong both against the deed; then, as his host,
Who should against his murderer shut the door,   15
Not bear the knife myself. Besides, this Duncan
Hath borne his faculties so meek, hath been
So clear in his great office, that his virtues
Will plead like angels trumpet-tongu'd against
The deep damnation of his taking-off;   20
And pity, like a naked new-born babe,
Striding the blast, or heaven's cherubin, hors'd

NOTES

1–7.   *If it were done . . . life to come:* If the murder could be committed without any after effects or results, then I would be glad to have it over with. If I could be sure of success and of the end of everything, then it would be good if the murder were done.

3.   *trammel up:* catch as in a net.

4.   *his surcease:* Duncan's death.

5.   *the be-all:* everything, the whole thing.

6.   *this bank and shoal of time:* A man's lifetime is a mere sandbank or bar, soon to be covered by the sea of eternity.

7.   *jump:* disregard, jump over, risk eternity.

7–12. *But in these . . . own lips:* We always have punishment in this life. If I were to murder Duncan, someone would plan to murder me. If I gave Duncan poison, someone would try to poison me.

8.   *still:* always.

       here: in this world.

10.   *even-handed:* giving each one exactly what he deserves.

11.   *Commends:* offers.

       chalice: cup.

17.   *borne his faculties so meek:* performed his duties so humbly.

18.   *clear:* free from blame.

21.   *And pity . . . babe.* Pity is like a baby because it touches our tenderness.

22.   *Striding the blast:* riding upon the storm or the wind.

Upon the sightless couriers of the air,
Shall blow the horrid deed in every eye,
That tears shall drown the wind. I have no spur   25
To prick the sides of my intent, but only
Vaulting ambition, which o'er-leaps itself
And falls on the other.—
[Enter LADY MACBETH]
                              How now! what news?

Lady Macbeth He has almost supp'd: why have
    you left the chamber?

Macbeth Hath he ask'd for me?

Lady Macbeth   Know you not he has?   30

Macbeth We will proceed no further in this business:
He hath honour'd me of late; and I have bought
Golden opinions from all sorts of people,
Which would be worn now in their newest gloss,
Not cast aside so soon.

Lady Macbeth   Was the hope drunk,   35
Wherein you dress'd yourself? hath it slept since,
And wakes it now, to look so green and pale
At what it did so freely? From this time
Such I account thy love. Art thou afeard
To be the same in thine own act and valour   40
As thou art in desire? Wouldst thou have that
Which thou esteem'st the ornament of life,
And live a coward in thine own esteem,
Letting 'I dare not' wait upon 'I would,'
Like the poor cat i' the adage?

Macbeth   Prithee, peace   45
I dare do all that may become a man;
Who dares do more is none.

Lady Macbeth   What beast was't, then,
That made you break this enterprise to me?
When you durst do it, then you were a man;
And, to be more than what you were, you would   50
Be so much more the man. Nor time nor place
Did then adhere, and yet you would make both:

23.	*sightless:* invisible.
	couriers of the air: winds.
25.	*drown the wind:* tears shall be as plentiful as raindrops that cause the winds to die down.
	no spur: comparing himself to a rider.
27.	*Vaulting ambition:* He's comparing himself to a rider who leaps too quickly when mounting and then lands on the other side.
29.	*chamber:* the dining room, hall.
32.	*bought:* won.
34.	*would:* should.
35–38.	*Was the hope . . . freely?:* Was your hope like a reveler who wakes the next morning green-faced and nauseated by the mere thought of what it did last night?
39.	*Such:* just as fickle as your resolution has proved.
42.	*the ornament of life:* the crown; the highest possession.
43.	*And live a coward:* do without it now and ever-after accuse yourself of cowardice.
	esteem: opinion.
44.	*wait upon:* always follow, wait upon constantly.
48.	*break:* disclose.
50–51.	*And, to be . . . man:* You'd be more of a man if you were more daring than you appeared.
52.	*adhere:* agree with the plan.

They have made themselves, and that their fitness now
Does unmake you. I have given suck, and know
How tender 'tis to love the babe that milks me: 55
I would, while it was smiling in my face,
Have pluck'd my nipple from his boneless gums,
And dash'd the brains out, had I so sworn as you
Have done to this.

Macbeth   If we should fail, —

Lady Macbeth   We fail?
But screw your courage to the sticking-place,   60
And we'll not fail. When Duncan is asleep,
Whereto the rather shall his day's hard journey
Soundly invite him, his two chamberlains
Will I with wine and wassail so convince,
That memory, the warder of the brain,   65
Shall be a fume, and the receipt of reason
A limbeck only; when in swinish sleep
Their drenched natures lie, as in a death,
What cannot you and I perform upon
The unguarded Duncan? what not put upon   70
His spongy officers, who shall bear the guilt
Of our great quell?

Macbeth   Bring forth men-children only;
For thy undaunted mettle should compose
Nothing but males. Will it not be receiv'd,
When we have mark'd with blood those sleepy two   75
Of his own chamber and us'd their very daggers,
That they have done't?

Lady Macbeth   Who dares receive it other,
As we shall make our griefs and clamour roar
Upon his death?

Macbeth   I am settled, and bend up
Each corporal agent to this terrible feat.   80
Away, and mock the time with fairest show:
False face must hide what the false heart doth know.

[Exeunt]

53.	*have made themselves:* Duncan is now in our power.
54.	*unmake:* unnerve.
59.	*If we should fail, —:* Here Macbeth drops the defense of scruples and tries to oppose the act on another ground — risk of failure.
60.	*But:* only.
62.	*the rather:* all the more.
62-63.	*Whereto . . . him:* His long journey will make him sleep soundly.
63.	*chamberlains:* grooms or body guards who slept by his bed.
64.	*convince:* overpower, overcome.
66.	*receipt:* receptacle.
68.	*drenched:* drowned.
71.	*spongy:* drunk, saturated with liquor.
72.	*quell:* murder, killing.
73.	*mettle:* quality.
74.	*receiv'd:* believed and accepted as true.
77.	*receive it other:* take it otherwise.
79.	*settled:* resolute, determined.
79-80.	*bend up . . . agent:* strain all the powers of my body.
81.	*mock the time:* beguile or deceive the world.
	show: looks and bearings, appearance.

COMMENTARY

This final scene of Act I is important in a number of ways. Primarily, it focuses on the Macbeths, providing an in-depth look at each character as Lady Macbeth leads the discussion of which course of action to take.

Weighing the consequences

Although Macbeth had extended asides earlier in the act, he opens this scene with his first true soliloquy. In this speech, he examines regicide rationally from a variety of perspectives. He realizes that the impact of a decision to kill the king will not end with the murder itself. The consequences of regicide would be extensive.

For instance, from a religious perspective, Duncan's death would "jump" or risk the afterlife because murder is a mortal sin (7). Furthermore, from a more earthbound standpoint, Macbeth understands that as king he would be as vulnerable to regicide as Duncan. And finally, the act of regicide would violate not only his bond to Duncan as a subject but also his bond as a blood relative. Thus, Macbeth demonstrates that he is acutely aware of the implications of his proposed action.

Macbeth also knows that there is no good reason for him to commit such an act, because Duncan is a virtuous and good king. With horror, he also ponders the enormous grief that would grip the country if Duncan were killed. Notice that he makes this argument in terms of natural disorder, indicating that "tears shall drown the wind" if Duncan dies (25). Ultimately, his personal ambition is the only reason to commit regicide.

Rationalizing regicide

Lady Macbeth interrupts the soliloquy by asking why he is not with the king's party. At this point, Macbeth has decided once again to turn away from the evil deed of regicide. He strongly informs Lady Macbeth that they will not proceed with their plans. Notice the reappearance of clothing metaphors as she responds by asking, "Was the hope drunk / Wherein you dress'd yourself?" (35-36).

For the remainder of the scene, Lady Macbeth works to alter her husband's resolve. She begins by returning to the issue of gender, questioning his masculinity by calling him a coward.

The "poor cat i' the adage" that Lady Macbeth refers to here is the Latin phrase *catus amat pisces sed non vult tingere plantas* (45). The phrase means that the cat loves fish but does not wish to wet his feet. This saying accurately describes Macbeth; he possesses the ambition to be king but not the resolve to take the action necessary to achieve it.

Macbeth defends himself by claiming that not killing the king actually makes him more of a man. His reason tells him that killing a king, especially one who trusts him as much as Duncan does, diminishes his manhood.

Lady Macbeth's response may shed light on Macbeth's initial reaction to the prediction by the weird sisters. By referring to a previous moment where neither the time nor the place were convenient for this act — Macbeth "would make both" (52) — she seems to indicate that the plan to kill Duncan may not be a recent one. In fact, she gives us, for the first time, an indication that Macbeth may have broached the subject even before the prophecy. Possibly, Macbeth was already susceptible to the idea of regicide when he was on the battlefield defending Duncan.

Lady Macbeth next attacks her husband's honor. She claims that had she sworn to kill her own child, she would. Lady Macbeth's evil disposition seems to reach its peak in this statement as she demonstrates her monstrous determination. Through inverted logic, she indicates that honoring a commitment to regicide is more important than honoring a commitment to one's king.

Emotion versus reason

Notice that Lady Macbeth argues on emotion. Her passionate arguments contrast sharply with Macbeth's more rational exploration of the consequences of murder, which opened the scene. Pay attention to the behavior of the Macbeths after the crime. Consider whether they still act with the same respective focus on reason and emotion.

In this speech, Lady Macbeth mentions that she has been a mother. This line may be confusing because the Macbeths are childless. However, Sidney Lamb points out that Lady Macbeth had a child with her first husband; Macbeth is her second husband. Regardless, it is important to keep in mind that because Lady Macbeth is childless, she runs no risk of having to act on her horrific statement.

Lady Macbeth describes to her husband how they will commit the crime and subsequently frame Duncan's servants for the murder. After she assures him that they will not be blamed for the crime, a shift occurs in Macbeth. Although he still realizes that regicide is wrong, he commits to that course of action.

Macbeth's final line of the scene — "False face must hide what the false heart doth know" — illustrates the disparity between his face, which is false because it is not an accurate representation, and his heart, which is false because he is being traitorous (82).

The full title indicates that this play is a tragedy, and the choice that ends this first act begins Macbeth's tragic fall. Under the notion of divine right kingship (see the Introduction to Early Modern England), regicide is the highest crime. After Shakespeare's protagonist pledges himself to that course of action, we should consider whether we are still sympathetic with the play's central character, and if so, why.

Notes

Notes

Notes

CLIFFSCOMPLETE

MACBETH
ACT II

Lennox *The night has been unruly: where we lay,*
Our chimneys were blown down; and, as they say,
Lamentings heard i' the air; strange screams of death,
And prophesying with accents terrible
Of dire combustion and confus'd events
New hatch'd to the woeful time. . . .

Macbeth *'Twas a rough night.*

Act II, Scene 1

Although Banquo admits that he has been having dreams of pursuing the prophecy, he maintains his resolve to passively await the predictions when Macbeth broaches the possibility of taking action. Left alone, Macbeth hallucinates a dagger that leads him toward Duncan's chamber, where Lady Macbeth has drugged his servants.

ACT II, SCENE 1
Inverness. Court within the castle.

*[Enter BANQUO and FLEANCE, with a Servant bearing
a torch before him]*

Banquo How goes the night, boy?

Fleance The moon is down; I have not heard the clock.

Banquo And she goes down at twelve.

Fleance 　　　　　　　　　　I take 't, 'tis later, sir.

Banquo Hold, take my sword. There's husbandry in heaven;
Their candles are all out. Take thee that too.　　　　　　5
A heavy summons lies like lead upon me,
And yet I would not sleep: merciful powers!
Restrain in me the cursed thoughts that nature
Gives way to in repose.
[Enter MACBETH, and a Servant with a torch]
Give me my sword.—　　　　　　　　　　　　　　10
Who's there?

Macbeth A friend.

Banquo What, sir! not yet at rest? The king's a-bed·
He hath been in unusual pleasure, and
Sent forth great largess to your offices.
This diamond he greets your wife withal,　　　　　15
By the name of most kind hostess; and shut up
In measureless content.

Macbeth 　　　　　　　　　Being unprepar'd,
Our will became the servant to defect,
Which else should free have wrought.

Banquo 　　　　　　　　　　　　All's well.
I dreamt last night of the three weird sisters:　　　20
To you they have show'd some truth.

NOTES

3.　*at twelve:* Evidently, it's past midnight and very dark.

4.　*husbandry:* thrift, economy.

5.　*that:* his dagger, probably.

6.　*A heavy summons:* a feeling of heavy drowsiness.

8–9.　*cursed . . . repose:* dreams which we're unable to control.

14.　*largess:* gratuities, gifts.

　　offices: servant's quarters.

15.　*withal:* with.

16.　*shut up:* retired to rest.

18–19.　*Our will . . . wrought:* We weren't prepared; if we were, we would have done more for him.

Macbeth   I think not of them:
Yet, when we can entreat an hour to serve,
We would spend it in some words upon that business,
If you would grant the time.

Banquo   At your kind'st leisure.

Macbeth If you shall cleave to my consent, when'tis,   25
It shall make honour for you.

Banquo   So I lose none
In seeking to augment it, but still keep
My bosom franchis'd and allegiance clear,
I shall be counsell'd.

Macbeth   Good repose the while!

Banquo Thanks, sir: the like to you.   30

[Exeunt BANQUO and FLEANCE]

Macbeth Go bid thy mistress, when my drink is ready
She strike upon the bell. Get thee to bed.
[Exit Servant]
Is this a dagger which I see before me,
The handle toward my hand? Come, let me clutch thee:
I have thee not, and yet I see thee still.   35
Art thou not, fatal vision, sensible
To feeling as to sight? or art thou but
A dagger of the mind, a false creation,
Proceeding from the heat-oppressed brain?
I see thee yet, in form as palpable   40
As this which now I draw.
Thou marshall'st me the way that I was going;
And such an instrument I was to use.

22.   *entreat . . . serve:* find an hour for the purpose.

24.   *At your kind'st leisure:* any time that's convenient for you will suit me.

25.   *cleave to my consent:* Join my party; give me your support when the time comes.

26.   *So:* provided that.

27.   *still:* always.

27–28.   *keep / My bosom franchis'd:* remain free from blame or reproach.

28.   *clear:* stainless, unmarked.

29.   *I shall be counsell'd:* You shall advise me.

31.   *drink:* the customary drink taken before retiring.

32.   *the bell:* The bell is obviously the prearranged signal that everything is ready for the murder.

36.   *fatal:* fateful, ominous.

  sensible: perceptible.

39.   *heat-oppressed:* capable of being handled.

42.   *marshall'st me:* urge me on.

Mine eyes are made the fools o' the other senses,
Or else worth all the rest: I see thee still;   45
And on thy blade and dudgeon gouts of blood
Which was not so before. There's no such thing:
It is the bloody business which informs
Thus to mine eyes. Now o'er the one half-world
Nature seems dead, and wicked dreams abuse   50
The curtain'd sleep; witchcraft celebrates
Pale Hecate's offerings; and wither'd murder,
Alarum'd by his sentinel, the wolf,
Whose howl's his watch, thus with his stealthy pace,
With Tarquin's ravishing strides, toward his design   55
Moves like a ghost. Thou sure and firm-set earth,
Hear not my steps, which way they walk, for fear
Thy very stones prate of my whereabout,
And take the present horror from the time,
Which now suits with it. Whiles I threat, he lives: 60
Words to the heat of deeds too cold breath gives.
[A bell rings]
I go, and it is done; the bell invites me.
Hear it not, Duncan; for it is a knell
That summons thee to heaven or to hell.

Macbeth questions the dagger's existence.

44–45. *Mine eyes . . . rest:* Macbeth is aware of the dagger's existence only by the use of his eyes. If the sight is mere fancy, his eyes have become fools to be mocked at by his other senses. But if the dagger is real, his eyes are more trustworthy than all of his other senses together.

46. *dudgeon:* handle.

     gouts: drops.

48. *informs:* gives (false) information, i.e. "My murderous purpose presents this vision to my eyes."

51. *The curtain'd sleep:* referring to a curtained bed or one curtained off from the room.

52. *Pale:* Hecate was associated with the moon (Goddess of the moon).

     Hecate: queen of the witches, the classical goddess of the underworld and witchcraft.

     wither'd murder: murder pictured as an old man or possibly a ghost.

53. *Alarum'd:* summoned to action.

54. *Whose howl's his watch:* For him, the wolf's howl is like the cry of the night-watchman calling the hour.

57. *Hear not my steps . . . walk:* do not hear the direction in which my steps are going.

58. *prate:* chatter, gossip.

60. *threat:* talk about murder.

61. *Words to the heat . . . gives:* Talking destroys the passion necessary to act.

COMMENTARY

This scene opens with a conversation between Banquo and his son, Fleance, in the courtyard of Macbeth's castle late at night. Fleance represents the second part of the weird sisters' prophecy, which foretold that although Banquo will never become king himself, he will have a line of kings.

Banquo refers to the stars as "candles" and notes that they "are all out" (5). The darkness of this night resonates with the requests we heard from Macbeth and his wife in earlier scenes for darkness to hide their evil thoughts and plans.

Banquo's inner battle

Despite being fatigued, Banquo is avoiding sleep because of "cursed thoughts" that invade his unconscious (8). Unlike Macbeth, Banquo is able to resist traitorous ideas when he is awake, but he cannot erase such thoughts from his dreams. The fact that Banquo is also plagued by these thoughts, albeit in his sleep, allows us to have some sympathy for Macbeth. If Banquo were able to dismiss altogether any thoughts of his family assuming control of the throne, we may condemn Macbeth further for his inability to reign in his ambitions.

When Macbeth enters the scene, he and Banquo discuss their encounter with the weird sisters. Banquo explicitly states that he does not wish to take an active role in helping Macbeth become king. He tells Macbeth, "So I lose none / In seeking to augment it, but still keep / My bosom franchis'd and allegiance clear, I shall be counsell'd" (26–28). He does, however, agree to discuss the matter further as long as he will not lose honor or stain his allegiance to Duncan. Banquo resolves to honor his commitment to Duncan, placing him in opposition to Lady Macbeth, who has convinced Macbeth that commitment to regicide is more honorable than commitment to the king.

Shakespeare deviates significantly from his historical source by not having Banquo serve as Macbeth's accomplice in Duncan's murder. This deviation ennobles Banquo, who keeps his loyalty intact. It also may have served the practical political purpose of flattering James I, Banquo's alleged descendant. At the same time, this plot change removes a potential point of sympathy for Macbeth because Banquo, who harbors the same ambitious thoughts as Macbeth, does not take action against the king.

Preparing for murder

Macbeth orders his servant to "bid thy mistress, when my drink is ready / She strike upon the bell" (31–32). Some critics argue that the line does not refer to an actual drink being prepared for Macbeth. Instead, this line may provide the servant with an explanation of the ringing bell in advance. Furthermore, Macbeth's reference to the drink may metaphorically link back to the "poisoned chalice" of betrayal that he mentioned in his previous soliloquy (I.7.11). Clearly, Lady Macbeth is to ring the bell when all is ready for Macbeth to commit the murder.

Following the servant's departure, Macbeth speaks his second crucial soliloquy. Once again, there is a

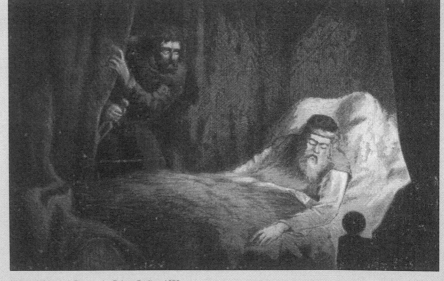

Macbeth Murders Duncan *by Robert Dudley, 1856.*
AKG, Berlin/SuperStock

fissure between illusion and reality as Macbeth imagines that he sees a dagger hovering in the air in front of him. Previously, Macbeth was responsible for creating the disparity between illusion and reality; he put on a "false face" to hide his ambitions. Now, a shift has occurred, and Macbeth is the victim of the disparity between illusion and reality; he cannot distinguish between the two. Notice that the evil and disorder in which he is participating horrifies Macbeth but does not dissuade him from his course of action.

In the midst of his soliloquy, Macbeth refers to Hecate. Hecate was originally the name of the Roman goddess of the night; however, she is traditionally associated with the devil and specifically believed to be the guardian of witches. Scholars speculate that this reference may have inspired dramatist Thomas Middleton to add the appearance of Hecate in Act III, Scene 5. (See the "Introduction to *Macbeth*" for an explanation of Middleton's role in creating the text of the play.)

When the bell calls Macbeth to his deed, his response reveals a slight shift in thinking. When he was pondering the murder earlier, he was assured of the king's salvation because of Duncan's many virtues (I.7.16–28). Now, he hopes that Duncan cannot hear the bell that either summons the king "to heaven or to hell" (64). Macbeth is no longer certain that the king is bound for heaven, which makes the cruelty of his crime even greater.

Act II, Scene 2

Macbeth joins Lady Macbeth after killing Duncan. Macbeth is extremely distraught over his actions and claims to have heard voices saying that he had murdered sleep. Lady Macbeth is much more calm and composed, however. She returns the daggers to Duncan's bedchambers and smears blood on Duncan's servants.

ACT II, SCENE 2
The same.

[Enter LADY MACBETH]

Lady Macbeth That which hath made them drunk
    hath made me bold,
What hath quench'd them hath given me fire. Hark!
    Peace!
It was the owl that shriek'd, the fatal bellman,
Which gives the stern'st good-night. He is about it:
The doors are open, and the surfeited grooms   5
Do mock their charge with snores: I have drugg'd
    their possets,
That death and nature do contend about them,
Whether they live or die.

Macbeth *[Within]* Who's there? what, ho!

Lady Macbeth Alack! I am afraid they have awak'd.   10
And 'tis not done; the attempt and not the deed
Confounds us. Hark! I laid their daggers ready;
He could not miss them. Had he not resembled
My father as he slept, I had done 't. My husband!

[Enter MACBETH]

Macbeth I have done the deed. Didst thou not hear   15
    a noise?

Lady Macbeth I heard the owl scream and the crickets cry.
    Did not you speak?

Macbeth   When?

Lady Macbeth   Now.

Macbeth   As I descended?

Lady Macbeth Ay.

NOTES

1.   *That:* the wine.

2.   *quench'd:* stupefied.

3.   *the owl:* considered a bird of ill-omen.

Lady Macbeth hears an owl screech while waiting for Macbeth's return.

  fatal bellman: refers to the person who rang bells for St. Sepulchre's Church during the night before prisoners were to be executed.

5.   *surfeited:* overstuffed with food and drink.

6.   *Do mock . . . snores:* Obviously they're asleep — a ridiculous way to keep watch.

  possets: a drink made from hot curdled milk, ale, wine, and so on, taken usually when retiring for the night.

7.   *nature:* life vital forces.

11–12.   *the attempt . . . Confounds us:* If he has failed in the attempt, we're ruined.

16.   *crickets cry:* thought of as an omen of death.

Macbeth Hark!
Who lies i' the second chamber?

Lady Macbeth   Donalbain.   20

Macbeth [*Looking on his hands*] This is a sorry sight.

Lady Macbeth A foolish thought to say a sorry sight.

Macbeth There's one did laugh in 's sleep, and one
    cried 'Murder!'
That they did wake each other: I stood and heard them;
But they did say their prayers, and address'd them   25
Again to sleep.

Lady Macbeth   There are two lodg'd together.

Macbeth One cried 'God bless us!' and 'Amen' the other:
As they had seen me with these hangman's hands.
Listening their fear, I could not say 'Amen,'
When they did say 'God bless us!'

Lady Macbeth   Consider it not so deeply. 30

Macbeth But wherefore could not I pronounce 'Amen'?
I had most need of blessing, and 'Amen'
Stuck in my throat.

Lady Macbeth   These deeds must not be thought
After these ways; so, it will make us mad.

Macbeth Methought I heard a voice cry 'Sleep no more!   35
Macbeth does murder sleep,' the innocent sleep,
Sleep that knits up the ravell'd sleave of care,
The death of each day's life, sore labour's bath,
Balm of hurt minds, great nature's second course,
Chief nourisher in life's feast, —

Lady Macbeth   What do you mean?   40

Macbeth Still it cried, 'Sleep no more!' to all the house:
'Glamis hath murder'd sleep, and therefore Cawdor
Shall sleep no more, Macbeth shall sleep no more!'

Macbeth is horrified by the deed he has done.

21.   *sorry:* miserable.

23.   *There's one, . . . 'Murder!':* Macbeth tells what he heard as he passed a bedroom on the way back from Duncan's room.

25.   *address'd them ;* applied themselves.

27.   *'God bless us!' and 'Amen':* mark the conclusion of the prayers mentioned in line 25.

29.   *Listening their fear:* listening to their expressions of alarm.

30.   *it:* not the murder, but his inability to say amen. To say amen when you heard someone utter a blessing was habitual in those days.

33.   *thought:* regarded.

37.   *knits up:* straightens out.

     sleave: skein (of silk).

38.   *sore labour's bath:* as refreshing as a bath to a laborer after work.

40.   *life's feast:* Life nourishes us in two ways, through food and sleep. Macbeth is saying that sleep is more important.

42.   *Glamis . . . Cawdor:* The titles indicate that this cry is in part an echo of the weird sisters' greeting.

Lady Macbeth Who was it that thus cried? Why,
     worthy thane
   You do unbend your noble strength to think   45
   So brainsickly of things. Go get some water,
   And wash this filthy witness from your hand.
   Why did you bring these daggers from the place?
   They must lie there: go carry them, and smear
   The sleepy grooms with blood.

Macbeth   I'll go no more: 50
   I am afraid to think what I have done;
   Look on 't again I dare not.

Lady Macbeth   Infirm of purpose!
   Give me the daggers. The sleeping and the dead
   Are but as pictures; 'tis the eye of childhood
   That fears a painted devil. If he do bleed,   55
   I'll gild the faces of the grooms withal;
   For it must seem their guilt.

[Exit. Knocking within]

Macbeth   Whence is that knocking?
   How is 't with me, when every noise appals me?
   What hands are here! Ha! they pluck out mine eyes.
   Will all great Neptune's ocean wash this blood   60
   Clean from my hand? No, this my hand will rather
   The multitudinous seas incarnadine,
   Making the green one red.

[Re-enter LADY MACBETH]

Lady Macbeth My hands are of your colour, but I shame
   To wear a heart so white.— *[Knocking within]* I hear
     a knocking   65
   At the south entry; retire we to our chamber;
   A little water clears us of this deed;
   How easy is it, then! Your constancy
   Hath left you unattended. *[Knocking within]* Hark!
     more knocking.
   Get on your night-gown, lest occasion call us,   70
   And show us to be watchers. Be not lost
   So poorly in your thoughts.

45.   *unbend:* relax.

46.   *brainsickly:* foolishly.

47.   *witness:* evidence.

54.   *as pictures:* just as harmless as pictures.

56.   *gild:* stain or smear.

s.d.   *within:* behind the scenes.

62.   *multitudinous:* referring to many big waves.

        incarnadine: turn blood-red.

63.   *Making the green one red:* turning the green color
        of the sea into one universal red.

66.   *entry:* entrance.

68–69. *Your . . . unattended:* Your usual resolution is
        gone.

70.   *night-gown:* dressing gown.

        lest occasion call us: lest we're called on.

72.   *So poorly:* in such a poor-spirited way.

Macbeth To know my deed 'twere best not know myself.
  [Knocking within]
  Wake Duncan with thy knocking! I would thou couldst!

[Exeunt]

73. *To know my deed:* if I must know what I have done.

COMMENTARY

The action of this scene immediately follows the action of Act II, Scene 1. Minimal time has passed as the play's perspective switches from Macbeth to his accomplice, Lady Macbeth.

Lady Macbeth says that she has heard an owl, which "shriek'd . . . the stern'st good-night" (3–4). The owl, with its nocturnal behavior and night-piercing call, was thought to be the form in which the devil appeared to witches. Its cries in the night were generally considered bad omens.

Lady Macbeth's role

Lady Macbeth's lines convey her active role in the regicide. She has drugged Duncan's servants so that Macbeth can enter and leave Duncan's chamber unnoticed. (As we will see, the Macbeths also consider the servants the natural choices for men to frame with the king's murder.)

Lady Macbeth's participation in the events surrounding the murder differs from the role she plays in Shakespeare's source, the Holinshed *Chronicles*. Holinshed does show Lady Macbeth convincing her husband to take action against Duncan. But the act of drugging the king's guards and later placing the daggers in their possession seems to be based on a different story related by Holinshed — the story of the murder of King Duffe by Donwald and his wife.

Continuing the bold statements she has used in earlier scenes, Lady Macbeth claims that she would have committed the crime herself if Duncan did not resemble her father. This line is significant in a number of ways. First, it illustrates that there is a disjunction between Lady Macbeth's words and deeds. Recall that in Act I, Scene 7 she told her husband that she would kill her own child if needed, but she is not at any risk for having to perform this heinous act. Second, the link to Duncan as a father figure holds significance for Macbeth as well. As seen in Act I, Scene 4, Duncan behaves in a fatherly manner toward his seemingly loyal subject.

The deed is done

When Macbeth enters the scene, his wife says that she "heard the owl scream and the crickets cry" (16). While the owl's scream is a bad omen, crickets traditionally were thought to make noise when a murder was committed.

Macbeth has, indeed, committed the crime. Having done so, he is unable to even utter an "Amen," which indicates his separation from God (29). The separation he experiences supports the *divine right* theory of kingship where God appoints kings. Not only has Macbeth violated political, ethical, and moral tenets by killing his king and cousin, he also has usurped God's power by trying to appoint himself king.

Lady Macbeth is very practical in this critical moment. Seeing that Macbeth has carried the murder weapons with him, and determining that he is incapable of returning to Duncan's chamber, she takes over. She returns the daggers to the location of the crime and spreads Duncan's blood on the drugged servants guarding the king's door. She returns and chides Macbeth for becoming "lost" in his thoughts about the king's death (71). Her behavior reveals her cruel strength, but it also reveals her shortsightedness. Lady Macbeth believes that after the murder is accomplished, its consequences will be only good. This, of course, contradicts Macbeth's earlier sentiment that violence begets violence (I.7.7–10).

A scene from a Royal Shakespeare Company Barbican production, 1993.
Clive Barda/PAL

Images of remorse

Sleep has a great deal of significance in this scene and in the entire play. Macbeth introduces the theme of sleep in lines 35–36 when he claims to have heard a voice that banishes him from its comforts. Duncan and his servants were asleep when the crimes against them were committed. In contrast, Macbeth's paranoia and his guilt over his behavior — evidenced by his inability to return to Duncan's chamber — will prevent him from sleeping. The inability to sleep also indicates the disorder and unnaturalness of this play and, in particular, the crime of regicide. Watch for other references to sleep in the play. Try to determine how they are significant in their context and in the play as a whole.

The issue of cleanliness also arises at the end of the scene. Macbeth feels such deep guilt that he realizes all the water in the ocean will not clean him of the deed. Conversely, Lady Macbeth claims that a "little water" clears them of the deed (67). The issue of cleanliness also suggests a comparison to Banquo who, in the previous scene, agrees to discuss Macbeth's ambitions as long as doing so does not "stain" his allegiance.

This scene ends with Macbeth expressing his remorse over his crime, both by not wanting to know himself and also by wishing that Duncan was able to awake. Macbeth, incapable of sleeping, stands in direct contrast to Duncan, who is incapable of waking. Pay special attention to Macbeth's line in the next scene after he greets Lennox.

Act II, Scene 3

The comedic porter opens the gate and allows Macduff and Lennox to enter. Shortly after a humorous exchange between the porter and Macduff, the thane discovers Duncan's murder. Chaos ensues. In the conversation between the thanes, we learn that Macbeth, in a "fury," killed the two servants, thereby removing from the servants the possibility of defending themselves. Malcolm and Donalbain, Duncan's sons, flee to England and Ireland for their own safety.

ACT II, SCENE 3
The same.

[Knocking within. Enter a Porter]

Porter Here's a knocking indeed! If a man were
porter of hell-gate, he should have old turning the key.
[Knocking within] Knock, knock, knock! Who's
there, i' the name of Beelzebub? Here's a farmer that
hanged himself on the expectation of plenty; come in   5
time; have napkins enough about you; here you'll
sweat for 't. *[Knocking within]* Knock, knock! Who's
there, i' the other devil's name! Faith, here's an equivocator, that could swear in both the scales against either
scale; who committed treason enough for God's sake,   10
yet could not equivocate to heaven: O! come in, equivocator. *[Knocking within]* Knock, knock, knock! Who's
there? Faith, here's an English tailor come hither for
stealing out of a French hose: come in, tailor; here you
may roast your goose. *[Knocking within]* Knock,   15
knock; never at quiet! What are you? But this place
is too cold for hell. I'll devil-porter it no further: I had
thought to have let in some of all professions, that go
the primrose way to the everlasting bonfire. *[Knocking
within]* Anon, anon! I pray you,   20
remember the porter.

[Opens the gate. Enter MACDUFF and LENNOX]

Macduff Was it so late, friend, ere you went to bed,
That you do lie so late?

Porter Faith, sir, we were carousing till the second cock:
and drink, sir, is a great provoker of three things.   25

NOTES

2.   *should:* certainly would.

       have old: have a great deal of trouble (a slang term).

4.   *Beelzebub:* a name for Satan.

5–6. *come in time:* your arrival is opportune.

6.   *napkins:* handkerchiefs.

8–9. *equivocator:* one who purposely makes misleading statements.

11.   *equivocate to heaven:* get himself into heaven by equivocation.

13–14. *tailor . . . hose:* French hose (i.e., breeches) were tight fitting and would make it difficult to embezzle any cloth from them.

15.   *goose:* tailor's iron.

17.   *devil-porter it:* act the part of a demon porter at the gate of hell.

20.   *Anon, anon:* In a moment!

21.   *remember the porter:* The porter expects a tip.

23.   *so late:* It's early in the morning, but it's late for the porter to be on duty.

24.   *the second cock:* about two in the morning.

Macduff What three things does drink especially provoke?

Porter Marry, sir, nose-painting, sleep, and urine.
Lechery, sir, it provokes, and unprovokes; it provokes the desire, but it takes away the performance:
therefore, much drink may be said to be an equivo-   30
cator with lechery: it makes him, and it mars him;
it sets him on, and it takes him off; it persuades
him, and disheartens him; makes him stand to, and
not stand to; in conclusion, equivocates him in a
sleep, and, giving him the lie,   35
leaves him.

Macduff I believe drink gave thee the lie last night.

Porter That it did, sir, i' the very throat on me:
but I requited him for his lie; and, I think, being
too strong for him, though he took up my legs some-   40
time, yet I made a shift to cast him.

Macduff Is thy master stirring?
[Enter MACBETH]
Our knocking has awak'd him; here he comes.

Lennox Good morrow, noble sir.

Macbeth   Good morrow, both.

Macduff Is the king stirring, worthy thane?

Macbeth   Not yet.   45

Macduff He did command me to call timely on him:
I have almost slipp'd the hour.

Macbeth   I'll bring you to him.

Macduff I know this is a joyful trouble to you;
But yet 'tis one.

Macbeth The labour we delight in physics pain.   50
This is the door.

Macduff   I'll make so bold to call,
For 'tis my limited service. *[Exit]*

Lennox Goes the king hence to-day?

Macbeth   He does: he did appoint so.

---

46.   *timely:* early.

47.   *slipp'd the hour:* passed the appointed time.

       bring: escort, conduct.

50.   *physics:* cures.

52.   *limited:* appointed.

53.   *appoint:* arrange, plan.

Lennox The night has been unruly: where we lay,
Our chimneys were blown down; and, as they say,   55
Lamentings heard i' the air; strange screams of death,
And prophesying with accents terrible
Of dire combustion and confus'd events
New hatch'd to the woeful time. The obscure bird
Clamour'd the livelong night; some say the earth   60
Was feverous and did shake.

Macbeth   'Twas a rough night.

Lennox My young remembrance cannot parallel
A fellow to it.

[Re-enter MACDUFF]

Macduff O horror! horror! horror! Tongue nor heart
Cannot conceive nor name thee!

Macbeth and Lennox   What's the matter?   65

Macduff Confusion now hath made his masterpiece!
Most sacrilegious murder hath broke ope
The Lord's anointed temple, and stole thence
The life o' the building!

Macbeth What is 't you say? the life?   70

Lennox Mean you his majesty?

Macduff Approach the chamber, and destroy your sight
With a new Gorgon: do not bid me speak;
See, and then speak yourselves.
[Exeunt MACBETH and LENNOX]
                              Awake! awake!
Ring the alarum-bell. Murder and treason!   75
Banquo and Donalbain! Malcolm! awake!
Shake off this downy sleep, death's counterfeit,
And look on death itself! up, up, and see
The great doom's image! Malcolm! Banquo!
As from your graves rise up, and walk like sprites,   80
To countenance this horror! Ring the bell.

[Bell rings. Enter LADY MACBETH]

---

56. *Lamentings . . . air:* This is a sign that a great man has died.

58. *combustion:* commotion and disorder in the state.

59. *New hatch'd to the woeful time:* born especially for this terrible time.

The obscure bird: the owl.

66. *Confusion:* destruction.

68. *The Lord's anointed temple:* the body of Duncan, who, as king, was appointed by God.

73. *Gorgon:* in Greek mythology the Gorgons were three sisters that turned anyone who looked at them to stone.

77. *death's counterfeit:* the image or picture of death.

79. *great doom's image:* a sight as terrible as the day of judgment.

80. *As . . . graves:* Macduff dwells upon the thought of the day of judgment.

sprites: spirits, ghosts.

81. *countenance:* mirror.

Lady Macbeth What's the business,
That such a hideous trumpet calls to parley
The sleepers of the house? speak, speak!

Macduff   O gentle lady!
'Tis not for you to hear what I can speak;   85
The repetition in a woman's ear
Would murder as it fell.
[Enter BANQUO]
                 O Banquo! Banquo!
Our royal master's murder'd!

Lady Macbeth   Woe, alas!
What! in our house?

Banquo   Too cruel any where.
Dear Duff, I prithee, contradict thyself,   90
And say it is not so.

[Re-enter MACBETH and LENNOX]

Macbeth Had I but died an hour before this chance
I had liv'd a blessed time; for, from this instant,
There's nothing serious in mortality.
All is but toys; renown and grace is dead,   95
The wine of life is drawn, and the mere lees
Is left this vault to brag of.

[Enter MALCOLM and DONALBAIN]

Donalbain What is amiss?

Macbeth   You are, and do not know 't:
The spring, the head, the fountain of your blood
Is stopp'd; the very source of it is stopp'd.   100

Macduff Your royal father's murder'd.

Malcolm   O! by whom?

Lennox Those of his chamber, as it seem'd, had done 't:
Their hands and faces were all badg'd with blood;
So were their daggers, which unwip'd we found
Upon their pillows: they star'd, and were distracted;   105
no man's life was to be trusted with them.

---

83. *parley:* conference.

86. *repetition:* recital, report.

92. *chance:* event.

94. *nothing . . . mortality:* nothing worthwhile in human life.

95. *toys:* trifles.

grace: goodness, virtue.

96. *vault:* may mean both the heavens and a wine cellar.

98. *You are:* You are amiss, i.e., you're missing a father — a word play on *amiss.*

103. *badg'd:* marked (as with a badge).

105. *they star'd . . . distracted:* When roused from their drugged sleep, Macbeth killed them before they could say a word.

Macbeth O! yet I do repent me of my fury.
  That I did kill them.

Macduff   Wherefore did you so?

Macbeth Who can be wise, amaz'd, temperate and furious,
  Loyal and neutral, in a moment? No man: 110
  The expedition of my violent love
  Outran the pauser, reason. Here lay Duncan,
  His silver skin lac'd with his golden blood;
  And his gash'd stabs look'd like a breach in nature
  For ruin's wasteful entrance: there, the murderers,   115
  Steep'd in the colours of their trade, their daggers
  Unmannerly breech'd with gore: who could refrain,
  That had a heart to love, and in that heart
  Courage to make's love known?

Lady Macbeth   Help me hence, ho!

Macduff Look to the lady.

Malcolm   [*Aside to DONALBAIN*] Why do we hold
    our tongues,   120
  That most may claim this argument for ours?

Donalbain [*Aside to MALCOLM*] What should be spoken
  Here where our fate, hid in an auger-hole,
  May rush and seize us? Let's away: our tears
  Are not yet brew'd.

Malcolm [*Aside to DONALBAIN*] Nor our strong sorrow   125
  Upon the foot of motion.

Banquo   Look to the lady:
  [*LADY MACBETH is carried out*]
  And when we have our naked frailties hid,
  That suffer in exposure, let us meet,
  And question this most bloody piece of work,
  To know it further. Fears and scruples shake us: 130
  In the great hand of God I stand, and thence
  Against the undivulg'd pretence I fight
  Of treasonous malice.

---

107. *yet:* even so.

111–112. *The expedition . . . reason:* The strength of my love made me act hastily instead of using reason. Reason would've made me pause.

113. *silver skin:* a vivid picture of deathly pallor.

  lac'd: streaked as with lace.

117. *breech'd:* clothed.

120. *Look to the lady:* Malcolm and Donalbain take advantage of the confusion that follows to exchange a few words.

122. *That . . . ours:* We have the right to talk about this subject.

123. *hid in an auger-hole:* coming from a source so small that we may not suspect its presence.

124–125. *tears . . . brew'd:* We're not yet ready to shed tears. This is sarcastic. They suspect Macbeth's feigned grief.

126. *Upon . . . motion:* ready to express itself.

127. *naked frailties:* shivering, scantily clad bodies.

129. *question:* investigate.

130. *scruples:* doubts, vague suspicions.

132–133. *undivulg'd pretence . . . malice:* the as yet undiscovered purpose of malicious traitors.

Macduff   And so do I.

All   So all.

Macbeth Let's briefly put on manly readiness,
  And meet i' the hall together.

All   Well contented.   135

[*Exeunt all but MALCOLM and DONALBAIN*]

Malcolm What will you do? Let's not consort with them:
  To show an unfelt sorrow is an office
  Which the false man does easy. I'll to England.

Donalbain To Ireland, I; our separated fortune
  Shall keep us both the safer: where we are,   140
  There's daggers in men's smiles: the near in blood,
  The nearer bloody.

Malcolm   This murderous shaft that's shot
  Hath not yet lighted, and our safest way
  Is to avoid the aim: therefore, to horse;
  And let us not be dainty of leave-taking,   145
  But shift away: there's warrant in that theft
  Which steals itself when there's no mercy left.

[*Exeunt*]

134. *manly readiness:* our clothes — this contrasts with "naked frailties."

138. *the false man:* i.e., any false man. They suspect everybody.

141–142. *the near . . . bloody:* The closer one of these nobles is to us in kinship, the more likely he is to murder us.

146. *shift away:* steal away unperceived.

146–147. *there's warrant . . . left:* A man has a right to steal himself away from a place of danger.

COMMENTARY

In most of Shakespeare's plays, we see a variety of subplots and comic moments and characters. These dramatic devices help not only to diversify the play but, especially in the case of tragedies, also provide important and often needed moments of comic relief. Usually, comic relief occurs right after a particularly tense and dramatic scene. Having entrapped the audience in the drama and tension of the play, the dramatist will give his audience a short break with which to relax before continuing. *Macbeth* only has one moment of comic relief that breaks the steady and continual action of the play. It occurs at the beginning of this scene with the entrance and dialogue of the porter.

The guardian of the gate

Even in the porter's humorous dialogue, however, Shakespeare embeds serious threads and allusions. Notice how disorderly the porter is; he is drunk, unkempt, and surly. In addition, his first line refers to the "porter of hell-gate" (2). In his 20-line opening speech, he mentions the devil or hell a total of five times. Though he is being humorous, there is a sinister parallel between his activity — opening the gates of Macbeth's castle — and opening the gates of hell.

The porter's statement about the "farmer that hanged himself on the expectation of plenty" refers to the farming practice of hoarding crops in times of abundance and low prices in order to make a great profit in time of famine (4–5). According to Sidney Lamb, for this reason some farmers would hang themselves when wonderful harvests were predicted.

The porter also describes the knocker as an equivocator. This line has been used to place the composition of *Macbeth* in 1606, because the porter is most likely referring to a Jesuit thinker named Henry Garnet who wrote *A Treatise of Equivocation*. This work claimed that a statement was not a lie if it could be viewed as truth from another perspective. The porter indicates this notion by saying that his equivocator "could swear in both the scales against either scale" — meaning the person could take any side of an argument and it would be true (9–10). Garnet, in addition to being a Catholic (which was illegal in England at this time), was convicted and executed for his role in the Gunpowder Plot, the 1605 assassination attempt of James I.

The porter opens the gate to let in Macduff and Lennox, who have come to summon Duncan. The theme of sleep makes a reappearance in this scene in the humorous exchange between Macduff and the porter. The porter says that drink "is a great provoker of three things . . . nose-painting, sleep, and urine" (25–27). (Nose-painting refers to the red color of the nose that often occurs when a person is inebriated.) The porter clarifies that drink's relationship to lechery is a complicated one: "[I]t provokes the desire, but it takes away the performance" (28–29). This comical statement hauntingly echoes Macbeth's initial indecision after hearing the sisters' prophecy. He had the desire to become king but not the will to act on that desire.

Unnatural night

Macbeth enters and greets Macduff and Lennox. Macbeth's brief exchange with them, through line 65, exemplifies the theory of equivocation that the porter alluded to. If we can view his responses from the right perspective, they are actually truthful.

As Macduff goes to the king's chamber, Lennox reveals that nature has been "unruly" the entire night (54). He claims to have heard "strange screams of death" in the air (56). The "obscure bird" that "[c]lamour'd the livelong night" is, again, the owl (60). Compare his report to Macbeth's predictions of the effect of Duncan's death on Scotland in Act I, Scene 7, Line 16–27. (Note that in Shakespeare's tragedy *Julius Caesar*, Caesar's "unnatural" death is also followed by extreme disruptions in nature.)

Macduff returns and reports the king's death. His reference to Duncan's body as the "Lord's anointed temple" is another statement of the divine right theory of kingship, because the king is God's appointed deputy (69). Macduff shouts to wake the household, telling its inhabitants to "[s]hake off this downy sleep, death's counterfeit, / And look on death itself!" (77–78). Consider how this description of sleep relates to other sleep references in the play.

The question of gender also reappears in this scene as Macduff tells Lady Macbeth that merely hearing about the terrible deed would murder her. The irony in this line is twofold. First, of course, Lady Macbeth has been an active participant in the deed. Second, Macduff's statement will eventually prove true. Duncan's murder will haunt Lady Macbeth until she takes her own life. Ultimately, the crime does kill her.

Feigning innocence

Macbeth tries to hide his crime by killing the king's servants, claiming that he does so out of rage over their murder of Duncan. Notice that Macduff, however, is immediately suspicious of Macbeth's action. Macduff asks Macbeth directly why he killed them. Macbeth claims that his actions originate from his devotion and loyalty to the king. He tries to cover his traitorous deeds by demonstrating an intense loyalty to the crown, which he displays with his murderous rage against the servants.

Notice that in his defense, Macbeth describes the wounds on Duncan as "a breach" in nature (114). Nature has been disrupted by this act of regicide.

Duncan's sons, Malcolm and Donalbain, also suspect that the servants were not the murderers. They decide to flee for their own safety. That the sons are not yet to the grieving stage (their "tears / Are not yet brew'd") seems to be a comment on Macbeth's grief, which is already great (124–125). They may suspect that his grief is insincere; however, we, knowing Macbeth's inner thoughts, realize that he seems to have remorse for his actions.

In reading the play, many of the visual and audible aspects are lost. It is important to imagine this scene and its great chaos. People shout and cry, bells ring, a large number of exits and entrances occur, characters are only half-clothed, and Lady Macbeth even faints. The stage is very busy and noisy.

Calm in the chaos

In the midst of this chaos stands Banquo. He solidly attempts to restore order to the scene. It is also likely that he already suspects Macbeth for the crime. Therefore, his resolve to fight "treasonous malice" is significant (133). Banquo is still unwilling to compromise his honor and loyalty in order to fulfill the prophecy. Many scholars and critics have attributed this admirable portrayal of Banquo as a tribute to James I, because James is supposed to have been a direct descendent in Banquo's line of kings.

The disordered scene ends with Duncan's sons fleeing to Ireland and England. Malcolm suspects that a kinsman did the murder, because someone related to them would have the most cause to kill Duncan. This statement begins to pose the question of motive. The servants had no reason to kill their king, although Macbeth and his wife want everyone to believe that their drunken stupor is to blame. With Malcolm already named as Duncan's heir, anyone who wanted the Scottish throne would have to kill him, too. A kinsman would have a good chance to be crowned if Malcolm died.

It is interesting that rather than assume control of the country, Malcolm flees. What might Shakespeare be saying about Malcolm in this scene?

Act II, Scene 4

This conversation between Ross and an old man recounts recent events for the audience. In addition to describing the natural disturbances that have followed the king's murder, their conversation reveals that Malcolm and Donalbain are being accused of planning the crime because they fled into exile. Ross also informs the old man that Macbeth has been named King of Scotland.

ACT II, SCENE 4
The same. Without the castle.

[Enter Ross and an OLD MAN]

Old Man Threescore and ten I can remember well;
Within the volume of which time I have seen
Hours dreadful and things strange, but this sore night
Hath trifled former knowings.

Ross   Ah! good father,
Thou seest, the heavens, as troubled with man's act,   5
Threaten his bloody stage: by the clock 'tis day,
And yet dark night strangles the travelling lamp.
Is 't night's predominance, or the day's shame,
That darkness does the face of earth entomb,
When living light should kiss it?

Old Man   'Tis unnatural,   10
Even like the deed that's done. On Tuesday last,
A falcon, towering in her pride of place,
Was by a mousing owl hawk'd at and kill'd.

Ross And Duncan's horses, — a thing most strange
          and certain, —
Beauteous and swift, the minions of their race,   15
Turn'd wild in nature, broke their stalls, flung out,
Contending 'gainst obedience, as they would
Make war with mankind.

NOTES

1.   *Old Man:* The benign and dignified figure of the old man serves a function similar to that of a chorus in a Greek tragedy.

2.   *volume:* time is compared to a book.

3.   *sore:* dreadful.

4.   *trifled . . . knowings:* made all my previous experience trivial.

6.   *his bloody stage:* earth, on which man performs murder.

7.   *travelling lamp:* the sun.

8–10.   *Is't . . . kiss it:* Is it dark because night has become more powerful than day or because day is hiding its face in shame?

12.   *towering . . . place:* soaring proudly at the very highest position of flight.

15.   *minions:* darlings.

16.   *flung out:* kicked and plunged wildly.

The horses' behavior symbolizes the discord after Duncan's death.

Old Man   'Tis said they eat each other.

Ross They did so, to the amazement of mine eyes,
That look'd upon 't. Here comes the good Macduff.   20
[Enter MACDUFF]
How goes the world, sir, now?

Macduff   Why, see you not?

Ross Is 't known who did this more than bloody deed?

Macduff Those that Macbeth hath slain.

Ross   Alas, the day!
What good could they pretend?

Macduff   They were suborn'd.
Malcolm and Donalbain, the king's two sons,   25
Are stol'n away and fled, which put upon them
Suspicion of the deed.

Ross   'Gainst nature still!
Thriftless ambition, that wilt ravin up
Thine own life's means! Then 'tis most like
The sovereignty will fall upon Macbeth.   30

Macduff He is already nam'd, and gone to Scone
To be invested.

Ross   Where is Duncan's body?

Macduff Carried to Colmekill,
The sacred storehouse of his predecessors
And guardian of their bones.

Ross   Will you to Scone?   35

Macduff No cousin, I'll to Fife.

Ross   Well, I will thither.

Macduff Well, may you see things well done there: adieu!
Lest our old robes sit easier than our new!

Ross Farewell, father.

Old Man God's benison go with you: and with those   40
That would make good of bad, and friends of foes!

[Exeunt]

18.   *eat:* past tense of eat; pronounced et.

19.   *amazement:* astonishment.

21.   *Why, see you not?:* Macduff's vague feelings of uneasiness and suspicion are shown in his short, dry answers.

24.   *pretend:* intend to gain for themselves.

24.   *suborn'd:* secretly induced or hired.

27.   *'Gainst nature still:* continuing the old man's thoughts in line 10.

28–29.   *Thriftless . . . means!:* Ambition that will plunder its own means of livelihood is unwise.

31.   *nam'd:* elected (by the council of nobles).

           Scone: where Scottish kings were crowned.

32.   *invested:* crowned.

33.   *Colmekill:* St. Columba's Call on the island of Iona, one of the Western Isles that's among the most ancient Christian communities in Britain. This was a traditional burial place for the Scottish kings.

34.   *storehouse:* burial place.

36.   *Fife:* Macduff's own home.

           thither: to Scone (where Scottish kings were crowned).

38.   *Lest . . . new:* We may not, I fear, be as happy under the new ruler as under the old.

40.   *benison:* blessing.

40–41.   *and with . . . foes:* and with all other unsuspecting persons who, like you, insist upon regarding bad men as good and friends as foes.

COMMENTARY

This short scene, which ends the second act, extends the disorder of the previous scene to the entire country of Scotland and relates some of the other major disturbances in nature.

Ross, a Scottish nobleman, discusses the recent events with an old man and then with Macduff. Dramatically, scenes like this are used to keep the audience aware of events through discussion rather than stage presentation. In effect, it allows the play to speed up by glossing over events that are essential but would have lengthened the play.

Disordered nature

The old man and Ross discuss the disorders in nature that are still occurring as a result of the regicide. Many of these events occur in Holinshed's account of King Duffe's death, but Shakespeare integrates them into the Duncan story in order to emphasize the theme of disorder and chaos. (See the "Introduction to *Macbeth*" for details about Holinshed's accounts.)

Interestingly, Ross notes that darkness grips both night and day. This darkness is significant, because both Macbeth (in Act I, Scene 4) and Lady Macbeth (in Act I, Scene 5) request darkness to hide their deeds. Ironically, the darkness does not hide their actions; rather, it occurs in response to their deeds. Why might this be the case?

Also note that the owl reappears. Sidney Lamb notes that the use of the owl is an alteration from Holinshed, who mentions a hawk. In light of the frequent appearance of the owl in relation to Macbeth's deed, this deviation illustrates Shakespeare's close integration of his source material into his own themes. The murder of a falcon by a lower bird, in this case the owl, parallels Macbeth's crime of regicide and associates him with the owl.

Shifting suspicions

Macduff's entry and discussion with Ross helps to accelerate the plot to the point where Duncan's sons, having fled, are suspected of the crime. Again, the motivation of the servants is called into question. Because the servants had nothing to gain from the murder, Macduff concludes that they were hired or induced to do it. As we know, he is not quite correct but close.

In addition, we learn that Macbeth has been named king. It is interesting that in being *named* as king, Macbeth's claim to the throne derives from a system other than that of divine right. As we saw in the "Introduction to *Macbeth*," the system of accession transformed from an election by thanes to the process of primogeniture and divine right only a few generations before the historical Macbeth became King of Scotland.

Macduff's final lines in the scene mark the reemergence of the clothing metaphor. Macduff is concerned that "our old robes sit easier than our new," meaning that he suspects things will not go as well under Macbeth's reign as they did under Duncan's (30).

Notes

Notes

Notes

CLIFFSCOMPLETE

MACBETH

ACT III

Lady Macbeth *O proper stuff!*
This is the very painting of your fear;
This is the air-drawn dagger which, you said,
Led you to Duncan. O! these flaws and starts —
Impostors to true fear — would well become
A woman's story at a winter's fire,
Authoriz'd by her grandam. Shame itself!

Act III, Scene 1

In this scene, Banquo contemplates Macbeth's role in the murder of Duncan. Macbeth enters and encourages Banquo to attend the banquet, during which Macbeth will try to secure the support of the other thanes. However, the friendship present in their previous interaction has been replaced with a mutual suspicion. After Banquo's departure, Macbeth arranges his murder and the murder of his son, Fleance.

ACT III, SCENE 1
Forres. A room in the palace.

[Enter BANQUO]

Banquo Thou hast it now: King, Cawdor, Glamis, all,
As the weird women promis'd; and, I fear,
Thou play'dst most foully for 't; yet it was said
It should not stand in thy posterity,
But that myself should be the root and father　　　5
Of many kings. If there come truth from them, —
As upon thee, Macbeth, their speeches shine, —
Why, by the verities on thee made good,
May they not be my oracles as well,
And set me up in hope? But, hush! no more.　　　10

[Sennet sounded. Enter MACBETH, as king; LADY MACBETH, as queen; LENNOX, ROSS, Lords, Ladies, and Attendants]

Macbeth Here's our chief guest.

Lady Macbeth　　　　　　　　If he had been forgotten,
It had been as a gap in our great feast,
And all-thing unbecoming.

Macbeth To-night we hold a solemn supper, sir,
And I'll request your presence.

Banquo　　　　　　　　　　　Let your highness　　　15
Command upon me; to the which my duties
Are with a most indissoluble tie
For ever knit.

Macbeth Ride you this afternoon?

Banquo　　　　　　　　　　　　　Ay, my good lord.

NOTES

4.　　*stand . . . posterity:* remain with your descendants.

7.　　*their . . . shine:* their prophecies were brilliantly fulfilled.

8.　　*verities:* prophecies come true.

9.　　*oracles:* people through whom deities were believed to speak. Oracles were commonly consulted in Graeco-Roman times and were famous for the ambiguity of their messages.

s.d.　*Sennet:* a fanfare.

13.　*all-thing:* altogether, quite.

14.　*solemn supper:* a supper of ceremony, a state supper.

16.　*Command:* in emphatic contrast with Macbeth's word "request."

19.　In the dialogue that follows, Macbeth camouflages his three questions, starting with "Ride you this afternoon?," with compliments.

Macbeth We should have else desir'd your good   20
    advice —
Which still hath been both grave and prosperous —
In this day's council; but we'll take to-morrow.
Is 't far you ride?

Banquo As far, my lord, as will fill up the time
'Twixt this and supper; go not my horse the better,   25
I must become a borrower of the night
For a dark hour or twain.

Macbeth   Fail not our feast.

Banquo My lord, I will not.

Macbeth We hear our bloody cousins are bestow'd
In England and in Ireland, not confessing   30
Their cruel parricide, filling their hearers
With strange invention; but of that to-morrow,
When therewithal we shall have cause of state
Craving us jointly. Hie you to horse; adieu
Till you return at night. Goes Fleance with you?   35

Banquo Ay, my good lord; our time does call upon 's.

Macbeth I wish your horses swift and sure of foot;
And so I do commend you to their backs.
Farewell. *[Exit BANQUO]*
Let every man be master of his time   40
Till seven at night; to make society
The sweeter welcome, we will keep ourself
Till supper-time alone; while then, God be with you!
[Exeunt all but MACBETH and an Attendant]
Sirrah, a word with you. Attend those men our pleasure?

Attendant They are, my lord, without the palace gate.   45

Macbeth Bring them before us. *[Exit Attendant]*
To be thus is nothing;
But to be safely thus. Our fears in Banquo
Stick deep, and in his royalty of nature
Reigns that which would be fear'd: 'tis much he dares,   50
And, to that dauntless temper of his mind,

21.   *still:* always.

    grave and prosperous: weighty and successful.

25–27.   *go . . . twain:* Unless my horse goes too fast to make it necessary, I shall have to continue my ride an hour or two after dark.

29.   *cousins:* Malcolm and Donalbain.

    bestow'd: taken refuge.

31.   *parricide:* father-murder.

32.   *strange invention:* fictitious stories of the murder.

33.   *therewithal:* besides that.

    cause of state: public business.

34.   *Craving us jointly:* requiring both your attention and mine.

36.   *our time . . . upon's:* Time summons us to depart.

38.   *commend you:* entrust you with my best wishes.

41–43.   *to make . . . alone:* In order that your society may be all the more agreeable to me, I'll deprive myself of it for a time.

44.   *Sirrah:* often used in addressing a servant, inferior, or child.

47.   *To be thus:* to be King.

50.   *would be:* requires to be.

51.   *to that:* in addition to.

He hath a wisdom that doth guide his valour
To act in safety. There is none but he
Whose being I do fear; and under him
My genius is rebuk'd, as it is said   55
Mark Antony's was by Caesar. He chid the sisters
When first they put the name of king upon me,
And bade them speak to him; then, prophet-like,
They hail'd him father to a line of kings.
Upon my head they plac'd a fruitless crown,   60
And put a barren sceptre in my gripe,
Thence to be wrench'd with an unlineal hand,
No son of mine succeeding. If 't be so,
For Banquo's issue have I fil'd my mind;
For them the gracious Duncan have I murder'd;   65
Put rancours in the vessel of my peace
Only for them; and mine eternal jewel
Given to the common enemy of man,
To make them kings, the seed of Banquo kings!
Rather than so, come fate into the list,   70
And champion me to the utterance! Who's there?
[Re-enter Attendant, with two Murderers]
Now go to the door, and stay there till we call.
[Exit Attendant]
Was it not yesterday we spoke together?

First Murderer It was, so please your highness.

Macbeth   Well then, now
Have you consider'd of my speeches? Know   75
That it was he in the times past which held you
So under fortune, which you thought had been
Our innocent self. This I made good to you
In our last conference, pass'd in probation with you,
How you were borne in hand, how cross'd, the   80
    instruments,
Who wrought with them, and all things else that might
To half a soul and to a notion craz'd
Say, 'Thus did Banquo.'

First Murderer   You made it known to us.

Macbeth I did so; and went further, which is now
Our point of second meeting. Do you find   85

55.   *genius:* It was believed that each person possessed a controlling genius (spirit) that directed his actions.

       rebuk'd: put to shame, abashed

55–56.   *as it is said . . . Caesar:* According to Plutarch's *Life of Antony*, a soothsayer told Antony that his good angel and spirit was courageous when alone but fearful when near Caesar's guiding spirit.

62.   *with:* by.

64.   *fil'd:* defiled.

66.   *rancours:* the deepest hostility or spite. The figure is of a vessel of wholesome liquid into which poison has been poured.

67.   *mine eternal jewel:* my soul.

68.   *common enemy of man:* enemy common to all men, i.e., the devil.

70.   *list:* the enclosed ground where tournaments were fought.

71.   *champion me to the utterance!:* Fight on my side to the death. (This is a tricky passage to pin down. This interpretation is based on the traditional meaning of "champion." Another interpretation is possible. The witches represent fate, and they have declared that Banquo's descendants will reign. In this line, Macbeth may be denying the necessity of their prophecy or that they have power over the future. Chance did not crown him king — he performed the murder himself, and the thanes elected him king because he was the natural successor in Malcolm's disgrace. Some scholars accept the reading that Macbeth is defying fate here.)

76–77.   *held . . . fortune:* thwarted your careers.

78.   *made good:* proved.

79.   *pass'd . . . you:* I reviewed the facts with you and gave you proofs.

80.   *borne in hand:* to be dealt with hypocritically.

       instruments: documents.

82.   *notion:* mind.

83.   *Banquo:* With this word, we learn for the first time whom Macbeth has been accusing.

85.   *Our . . . meeting:* the purpose of this second meeting.

Your patience so predominant in your nature
That you can let this go? Are you so gospell'd
To pray for this good man and for his issue,
Whose heavy hand hath bow'd you to the grave
And beggar'd yours for ever?

First Murderer   We are men, my liege.   90

Macbeth Ay, in the catalogue ye go for men;
As hounds and greyhounds, mongrels, spaniels, curs,
Shoughs, water-rugs, and demi-wolves, are clept
All by the name of dogs; the valu'd file
Distinguishes the swift, the slow the subtle,   95
The housekeeper, the hunter, every one
According to the gift which bounteous nature
Hath in him clos'd; whereby he does receive
Particular addition, from the bill
That writes them all alike: and so of men.   100
Now, if you have a station in the file,
Not i' the worst rank of manhood, say it;
And I will put that business in your bosoms,
Whose execution takes your enemy off,
Grapples you to the heart and love of us,   105
Who wear our health but sickly in his life,
Which in his death were perfect.

Second Murderer   I am one, my liege,
Whom the vile blows and buffets of the world
Have so incens'd that I am reckless what
I do to spite the world.

First Murderer   And I another,   110
So weary with disasters, tugg'd with fortune,
That I would set my life on any chance,
To mend it or be rid on 't.

Macbeth   Both of you
Know Banquo was your enemy.

Second Murderer   True, my lord.

Macbeth So is he mine; and in such bloody distance   115
That every minute of his being thrusts
Against my near'st of life: and though I could

87.   *so gospell'd:* so permeated with the spirit of the gospel, i.e., love your enemies, etc.

90.   *yours:* your families and descendants.

91.   *in the catalogue:* in a list, census.

93.   *Shoughs:* shaggy-haired dogs.

   water-rugs: rough water dogs.

   demi-wolves: dogs bred from wolves.

   clept: called.

94.   *valu'd file:* a list with the worth of each.

96.   *housekeeper:* watchdog.

99.   *Particular addition:* particular title (such as hunter, etc.)

   from the bill: apart from the list.

104.   *Whose . . . off:* the carrying out of which gets rid of your enemy.

105.   *Grapples:* binds.

109.   *incens'd:* irritated.

111.   *tugg'd with:* pulled about by.

112.   *set:* stake.

   chance: cast of the dice, hazard.

115-117.   *such bloody . . . of life:* The figure is that of two men dueling at close quarters (bloody distance).

117.   *my near'st of life:* my most vital spot.

With bare-fac'd power sweep him from my sight
And bid my will avouch it, yet I must not,
For certain friends that are both his and mine,   120
Whose loves I may not drop, but wail his fall
Whom I myself struck down; and thence it is
That I to your assistance do make love,
Masking the business from the common eye
For sundry weighty reasons.

Second Murderer   We shall, my lord,   125
Perform what you command us.

First Murderer   Though our lives —

Macbeth Your spirits shine through you. Within
    this hour at most
I will advise you where to plant yourselves,
Acquaint you with the perfect spy o' the time,
The moment on 't; for 't must be done to-night,   130
And something from the palace; always thought
That I require a clearness: and with him —
To leave no rubs nor botches in the work —
Fleance his son, that keeps him company,
Whose absence is no less material to me   135
Than is his father's, must embrace the fate
Of that dark hour. Resolve yourselves apart;
I'll come to you anon.

Second Murderer   We are resolv'd, my lord.

Macbeth I'll call upon you straight: abide within.
    [Exeunt Murderers]
It is concluded: Banquo, thy soul's flight,   140
If it find heaven, must find it out to-night. *[Exit]*

119. *And bid . . . it:* justify myself on the sole ground that it was my wish.

121. *but wail:* but I must lament.

123. *That I . . . love:* that I appeal to you for help.

126. *Though our lives —:* Macbeth, now sure of his men, cuts them short.

129. *the perfect . . . time:* the exact time when the deed should be done.

131. *something:* somewhat, i.e., some distance.

      always thought: being always understood.

132. *clearness:* clearness from suspicion.

133. *rubs:* roughness.

      botches: imperfections caused by clumsiness.

137. *Resolve . . . apart:* Make up your minds in private.

170. *straight:* straightway, immediately.

COMMENTARY

The third act of this play marks the beginning of Macbeth's reign as King of Scotland. The principal event of this act will be a banquet, described in Act III, Scene 4, at which Macbeth hopes to acquire the support of the thanes. As early as Act I, Macbeth realized that he will be as vulnerable to traitors as Duncan was. Therefore, his actions are driven by his desire to safeguard his position.

Macbeth changes in this act; his thoughts and deeds take on a more sinister character. Note these differences as you read and consider why this change has occurred.

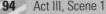

Banquo's suspicions

In the opening soliloquy of this first scene, Banquo voices the first explicit suggestion that Macbeth murdered Duncan. (The fact that Banquo is the first to suspect Macbeth of the crime could be another way that Shakespeare flatters King James I.) In doing so, Banquo also considers that because the witches' predictions for Macbeth have come true (regardless of the hand Macbeth played in making them happen), their prediction for him might come true as well. Although Banquo may be flirting with temptation here, he never mentions his intention to commit any nefarious deeds. His words merely indicate that he might hope to be the father of a line of kings. Macbeth interrupts Banquo's musings, so we never actually learn the full extent of his thoughts.

The discussion between Macbeth and Banquo is tense. A chasm now lies between them — a coldness is evident in their speech. In particular, note Banquo's line to Macbeth in which he calls him "your highness" and speaks of the "indissoluble" tie between them (15–17). How might an actor deliver this line? Earlier in the play, there was discussion concerning the disjunction between a person's face and his heart. Does Banquo's face represent his heart here?

Banquo seems to suspect that Macbeth plans further wrongdoing. His answers to Macbeth's questions are vague and, though seemingly accurate, do not provide any substantial information.

Violence leads to violence

After Banquo leaves, Macbeth delivers his third soliloquy. Here, he demonstrates his realization that violence spawns violence and his evil actions must continue. He notes that being king is worthless if he is not safely king — that is, if he becomes a victim of regicide. After the first crime has been committed, other crimes must follow in order for him to retain his position.

Interestingly, Macbeth fears Banquo, not Duncan's sons. In particular, he seems disturbed by Banquo's careful answers to his questions. He asserts that Banquo "hath a wisdom that doth guide his valour / To act in safety" (52–53). Banquo's previous interaction with Macbeth could be described as safe if Banquo was considering killing Macbeth.

Macbeth also notes in Banquo a "royalty of nature" (49). This line is significant because it continues the flattering portrait of Banquo and places him on the side of nature in opposition to Macbeth, whose deeds and ascension to the throne are unnatural. Banquo's previous resolve to remain honorable casts doubt on any treacherous intentions. It further suggests that Macbeth's fears of Banquo may be unfounded.

Macbeth seems particularly distraught that, according to the prophecies, the murder of Duncan will benefit Banquo's line rather than his own. (Macbeth, of course, has no son to assume the throne.) Macbeth laments that he has defiled his own mind for Banquo's descendants.

Macbeth's soliloquy again shows his acute awareness of the consequences of his actions. "[R]ancours," or spite, has filled his "vessel of . . . peace" (66). His ambition again controls him. He is not satisfied with being king but wants to produce a line of kings as well, despite the fact that he does not have any children.

Though much of this play seems to be in praise of King James, Macbeth's assertion that his actions enable Banquo's descendents to become kings may implicate James. As we saw in the Introduction to *Macbeth*, James I tied his ancestry back to Banquo. If Macbeth's assertion here is correct, then James held his royal position as a direct result of Macbeth's act of regicide.

The soliloquy reaches its climax as Macbeth invites fate into his "list" or enclosed ground (70). Macbeth determines to battle fate, to try to change the second prediction of the weird sisters. This implies that Macbeth believes he achieved the crown not through the witches' prophecy but through his own actions. Interestingly, this assertion of free will makes Macbeth fully responsible for Duncan's death by removing the explanation of fate as the cause of his crime. Macbeth's final statement in the soliloquy — "champion me to the utterance" — also seems to indicate his decision to kill Banquo (71).

Defying prophecy

The soliloquy ends with the arrival of two murderers. Though the preceding speech seemed to indicate that Macbeth just now decided on a course of action (to get rid of Banquo), his first line to the murderers illustrates that he has been considering Banquo's death for a longer time. He has even previously spoken to these men, planting in them seeds of hatred for Banquo.

Throughout their exchange, Macbeth persuades the two men to murder Banquo by accusing him of being the cause of their troubles. Macbeth tells them that Banquo's "heavy hand hath bow'd you to the grave / And beggar'd yours for ever" (88–89). Interestingly, in telling the men that Banquo is responsible for their station in life, he also claims that they previously believed that Macbeth's "innocent self" was responsible (78). These lines imply that Macbeth, before he succumbed to his ambition, helped thwart their questionable behavior.

Macbeth asks the men if they believe in the Christian principle of loving their enemy. Their response is quite interesting; they assert that they are men. This exchange seems to place men in opposition to Christianity and may serve as a criticism of the masculine warrior society, where promotion is gained through violence.

Macbeth next discusses the hierarchical structure of men, referring to ranks and file. (See the Introduction to Early Modern England for a discussion of the universal hierarchy.) By killing Duncan, Macbeth clearly violated that hierarchy. Here, he offers the same opportunity to transgress that hierarchy to the murderers.

Distorted logic

Interestingly, Macbeth's strategy with the murderers is very similar to the one his wife used to convince him to kill Duncan. To spur the murderers into action, Macbeth questions their manhood and position in society.

He insightfully plays to their own ambitions of increasing their station as well as proving their manhood. According to Macbeth's disordered logic, killing Banquo, an innocent man, will prove that they are not "the worst rank of manhood" (102). The audience, of course, realizes that killing an innocent man will prove exactly the opposite. Macbeth adds to the murderers' incentive the promise of favor through his "love" (105).

Macbeth also resembles his wife in this deed by planning the murder and arranging the time and place for it, though not directly committing it.

The plan to kill Banquo is Macbeth's first onstage act as king. Compare him to Duncan, who commanded a large army of valiant soldiers in his defense. Macbeth, in contrast, commands two murderers in order to protect himself from someone who has yet to perform an aggressive act against him. Furthermore, he includes Banquo's son Fleance in the crime. He plans to kill two innocent men in order to feed his ambition.

Macbeth accuses Banquo of plotting against his life (115–116), but the audience knows that this is not necessarily true. In light of Banquo's previous resolve to retain his honor, it seems even more unlikely.

Macbeth's last line, about Banquo's soul finding heaven, echoes the line about Duncan's soul immediately prior to his murder (I.1.64). Despite his descent into tyranny and the knowledge that he is sacrificing his own salvation, Macbeth remains concerned with the afterlife.

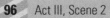

Act III, Scene 2

Macbeth and his wife discuss their course of action. Lady Macbeth is not as content as she was in previous scenes. She indicates her desire to place their evil actions in the past. Although he tells his wife to watch Banquo closely, Macbeth no longer includes her in his plans to maintain the throne.

ACT III, SCENE 2
The same. Another room in the palace.

[Enter LADY MACBETH and a Servant]

Lady Macbeth Is Banquo gone from court?

Servant Ay, madam, but returns again to-night.

Lady Macbeth Say to the king, I would attend his leisure
For a few words.

Servant　　　　　　Madam, I will. *[Exit]*

Lady Macbeth　　　　　　　Nought's had, all's spent,
Where our desire is got without content:　　　　　5
'Tis safer to be that which we destroy
Than by destruction dwell in doubtful joy.
[Enter MACBETH]
How now, my lord! why do you keep alone,
Of sorriest fancies your companions making,
Using those thoughts which should indeed have died　10
With them they think on? Things without all remedy
Should be without regard: what's done is done.

Macbeth We have scotch'd the snake, not kill'd it:
She'll close and be herself, whilst our poor malice
Remains in danger of her former tooth.　　　　　15
But let the frame of things disjoint, both the worlds
　suffer,
Ere we will eat our meal in fear, and sleep
In the affliction of these terrible dreams
That shake us nightly. Better be with the dead,
Whom we, to gain our peace, have sent to peace,　20
Than on the torture of the mind to lie
In restless ecstasy. Duncan is in his grave;
After life's fitful fever he sleeps well;

NOTES

3–4.　*I would . . . few words:* I'd like to speak to him when he's at his leisure.

4.　*Nought's had:* We've gained nothing.

5.　*content:* happiness.

9.　*sorriest fancies:* most gloomy and despicable thoughts.

10.　*Using:* keeping in your mind.

11.　*without all:* beyond all.

13.　*scotch'd:* slashed, gashed.

14.　*close:* come together.

14–15.　*whilst our . . . tooth:* while we, with our feeble hostility revealed, will remain in as much danger as ever from its still venomous fangs.

16.　*let the ... disjoint:* let the whole structure of the universe fall apart.

20.　*our peace:* our peace of mind.

21–22.　*Than on . . . ecstasy:* The mind is compared to a rack on which a prisoner is tortured.

22.　*ecstasy:* frenzy.

23.　*life's fitful fever:* Life seems like a tormenting malarial fever to Macbeth.

Treason has done his worst: nor steel, nor poison,
Malice domestic, foreign levy, nothing   25
Can touch him further.

Lady Macbeth   Come on;
Gentle my lord, sleek o'er your rugged looks;
Be bright and jovial among your guests to-night.

Macbeth So shall I, love; and so, I pray, be you.
Let your remembrance apply to Banquo;   30
Present him eminence, both with eye and tongue:
Unsafe the while, that we
Must lave our honours in these flattering streams,
And make our faces vizards to our hearts,
Disguising what they are.

Lady Macbeth   You must leave this.   35

Macbeth O! full of scorpions is my mind, dear wife;
Thou know'st that Banquo and his Fleance lives.

Lady Macbeth But in them nature's copy's not eterne.

Macbeth There's comfort yet; they are assailable;
Then be thou jocund. Ere the bat hath flown   40
His cloister'd flight, ere to black Hecate's summons
The shard-born beetle with his drowsy hums
Hath rung night's yawning peal, there shall be done
A deed of dreadful note.

Lady Macbeth   What's to be done?

Macbeth Be innocent of the knowledge, dearest chuck   45
Till thou applaud the deed. Come, seeling night,
Scarf up the tender eye of pitiful day,
And with thy bloody and invisible hand
Cancel and tear to pieces that great bond
Which keeps me pale! Light thickens, and the crow   50
Makes wing to the rooky wood;
Good things of day begin to droop and drowse,
Whiles night's black agents to their preys do rouse.
Thou marvell'st at my words: but hold thee still;
Things bad begun make strong themselves by ill: 55
So, prithee, go with me. *[Exeunt]*

24.	*his:* its.
25.	*foreign levy:* invasion.
27.	*Gentle my lord:* my gentle lord.
30.	*Let . . . Banquo:* Remember to show particular attention to Banquo.
31.	*Present him eminence:* Do him special honors.
32–33.	*Unsafe . . . streams:* Although they wash ("lave") away suspicions of their honor with flattery, they themselves are unsafe.
34.	*vizards:* masks.
35.	*this:* such wild remarks.
38.	*But . . . not eterne:* Nature has granted them a temporary lease of life. Lady Macbeth is merely reminding him that they must someday die a natural death.
40.	*jocund:* joyful.
41.	*cloister'd:* in belfries and cloisters — in darkness and solitude.
42.	*shard:* a fragment of pottery. The covering of a beetle's wings are crisp and hard.
44.	*of dreadful note:* dreadful to be known.
45.	*chuck:* chicken, a term of endearment.
46.	*seeling:* To seel is to sew up a falcon's eyelids with silk in order to tame it.
47.	*Scarf up:* blindfold, as with a scarf.
49.	*bond:* the prophecy by which Fate has bound itself to give the throne to Banquo's descendants.
51.	*rooky:* a resort of rooks or crows.
53.	*agents:* all evil beings that act by night, e.g., wild beasts, murderers, witches, etc.
56.	*go with me:* come with me. Macbeth gives her his hand to lead her off the stage.

COMMENTARY

This scene again focuses on the Macbeths and their relationship. It becomes immediately clear that Macbeth's indecision is gone. He no longer needs Lady Macbeth in order to act, although now they both psychologically suffer for their actions.

"Doubtful joy"

In the opening lines, Lady Macbeth acknowledges that she and her husband have not gained any happiness even though their desires to be king and queen have been met. She also begins to see more fully the consequences of their actions. She laments their "doubtful joy" — their fear that they themselves will be the victims of usurpers (7).

Upon Macbeth's arrival, she tries to reassert her pragmatism. She argues that brooding over their acts will not bring them any peace. Although she voices a resolute conviction that "what's done is done," we know from her previous lines that she realizes that this is not the case (12). Also, notice that she misinterprets her husband's behavior. He is no longer brooding over their past crimes but plotting future ones. This lack of insight stands in contrast to Lady Macbeth's first appearance, when she accurately predicted his thoughts and apprehensions. This scene indicates the gulf that is widening between them.

Responding to his wife's assertion with his rational knowledge that he must continue the violence in order to maintain the throne, Macbeth invokes the metaphor of the snake. The traditional metaphor associates the snake with the devil, so the image is an interesting one for Macbeth to choose. This choice seems to be an attempt to place himself on the side of good, even though his later lines in this scene acknowledge his relationship to evil.

During this response, Macbeth also echoes his wife's lines with his envy for the dead who are safe and free from torment. He notes that treason has done all it can to Duncan. The bitter irony is that the same treason is not finished torturing Macbeth.

The disparity between illusion and reality reappears when Macbeth recommends that they use their faces to mask their hearts; they cannot let Banquo know their

Cynthia Makris and Jorma Hynninen star in this 1997 Savonlinna Opera Festival production.
Clive Barda/PAL

murderous plans. The roles of Macbeth and his wife have now reversed; he serves as the driving force in their continued course of evil.

Comfort in darkness

Note the way in which Macbeth's speech becomes blacker, containing more references to evil such as Hecate and the bat. That process began with the simple request for darkness to hide his desires (I.4.50). At this point in the play, Macbeth has moved from attempting to hide in the dark to finding his comfort there (39). Furthermore, Macbeth's speech has acquired the darkness and invocation of supernatural evil that Lady Macbeth's speech previously contained. Evil seems to be consuming Macbeth. He thrives and grows from it — making himself strong through ill deeds.

Lady Macbeth moves from determining what action to take and how to accomplish it to not even knowing Macbeth's plans. She is forced to ask him, "What's to be done?" (44). Macbeth does not tell her of his plans, urging her to remain "innocent of the knowledge . . . Till thou applaud the deed" (45-46).

The scene ends with Macbeth inviting his wife to accompany him. Literally, this invitation is to leave the scene, but because of the darkness in his last speech, Macbeth may be inviting her to join him in his evil. Notice the parallel between Macbeth leading his wife offstage in this scene and Lady Macbeth leading Duncan offstage (into the castle) in Act I, Scene 6.

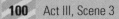

Act III, Scene 3

The two murderers are joined by a third. Together, they attack Banquo and Fleance as they return to the castle. Banquo is killed but Fleance manages to escape.

ACT III, SCENE 3
The same. A park with a road leading to the palace.

[Enter three Murderers]

First Murderer But who did bid thee join with us?

Third Murderer   Macbeth.

Second Murderer He needs not our mistrust, since
        he delivers
    Our offices and what we have to do
    To the direction just.

First Murderer   Then stand with us.
    The west yet glimmers with some streaks of day: 5
    Now spurs the lated traveller apace
    To gain the timely inn; and near approaches
    The subject of our watch.

Third Murderer   Hark! I hear horses.

Banquo *[Within]* Give us a light there, ho!

Second Murderer   Then 'tis he: the rest
    That are within the note of expectation   10
    Already are i' the court.

First Murderer   His horses go about.

Third Murderer Almost a mile; but he does usually,
    So all men do, from hence to the palace gate
    Make it their walk.

[Enter BANQUO and FLEANCE, with a torch]

Second Murderer   A light, a light!

Third Murderer   'Tis he.

First Murderer Stand to 't.   15

Banquo It will be rain to-night.

First Murderer   Let it come down.

NOTES

1.   The reader hears only the end of this dialogue.

2.   *delivers:* reports.

3.   *offices:* duties.

4.   *To the direction just:* exactly according to our instructions.

6.   *lated:* belated.

7.   *To gain the timely inn:* to reach the inn in good time (before it's quite dark).

9.   *Give . . . ho!:* a call to a servant of the palace to light their way with a torch.

10.   *within . . . expectation:* in the list of expected guests.

11.   *His horses go about:* Fleance has taken the torch and the servant has taken the horses around to the rear of the castle. Macbeth has arranged that the murder take place after Banquo and Fleance dismount. This allows the use of fewer assailants. It also avoids bringing horses on stage.

16.   *It will rain to-night:* This casual remark shows that Banquo is off his guard and informs the audience of the cloudy sky — in harmony with murder.

[They set upon BANQUO]

Banquo O, treachery! Fly, good Fleance, fly, fly, fly!
  Thou mayst revenge. O slave!

[Dies. FLEANCE escapes]

Third Murderer Who did strike out the light?

First Murderer   Was 't not the way?

Third Murderer There's but one down; the son is fled.

Second Murderer   We have lost   20
  Best half of our affair.

First Murderer Well, let's away, and say how
  much is done. *[Exeunt]*

COMMENTARY

Despite its brevity, this scene is very important to the play because it reminds the reader of the theatrical nature of the text. With its emphasis on lightness and darkness as well as its action, the scene is much richer visually than textually. Similar to the special effects of modern movies, the assassination of Banquo is a spectacle designed to thrill the audience. This is also the first time that the violence in this play occurs onstage. All of the other deaths transpire out of the audience's view. Why might Shakespeare have chosen this scene to be dramatized? What is the effect of having this scene as the first onstage violence?

The presence of the third murderer is an excellent indicator of Macbeth's increasing paranoia. He sends a third murderer to ensure that the first two carry out the

Fleance and Banquo are attacked as they return to the castle.

murders. He does not seem to trust anyone. Keep in mind that he refused to inform Lady Macbeth of his plans in the previous scene.

Many readers and critics question the identity of the third murderer, speculating that he (or she) may have been one of the major characters in disguise. No textual evidence exists to support this conjecture.

Notice that although Banquo is killed, Fleance escapes; thus, Macbeth's plan to defy the witches' prophecy fails. Literally carrying the torch when he flees, Fleance allows darkness to consume the scene. Moreover, the connection between Fleance and light symbolically opposes the connection between Macbeth and darkness.

Act III, Scene 4

The banquet begins with the seating of the noblemen and Macbeth's insistence to sit among the thanes rather than in his royal position. Banquo's ghost enters and sits in Macbeth's chair — literally and figuratively taking his place. The appearance of the ghost seriously disturbs Macbeth. Despite Lady Macbeth's attempts to retain order, Macbeth's disturbances and direct addresses to a ghost that only he can see cause the banquet to end in disorder. After the thanes depart, Macbeth notes Macduff's absence and decides to consult the witches.

ACT III, SCENE 4
The same. A room of state in the palace.

[A Banquet prepared. Enter MACBETH, LADY MACBETH, ROSS, LENNOX, Lords, and Attendants]

Macbeth You know your own degrees; sit down: at
    first and last,
The hearty welcome.

Lords   Thanks to your majesty.

Macbeth Ourself will mingle with society
And play the humble host.
Our hostess keeps her state, but in best time   5
We will require her welcome.

Lady Macbeth Pronounce it for me, sir, to all our friends;
For my heart speaks they are welcome.

[Enter First Murderer, to the door]

Macbeth See, they encounter thee with their hearts' thanks;
Both sides are even: here I'll sit i' the midst: 10
Be large in mirth; anon, we'll drink a measure
The table round. *[Approaching the door]* There's
    blood upon thy face.

Murderer 'Tis Banquo's, then.

Macbeth 'Tis better thee without than he within.
Is he dispatch'd?   15

NOTES

1.   *degrees:* ranks.

     at first and last: once and for all.

3.   *Ourself:* Royalty customarily uses the plural pronoun to represent the whole country.

5–6.   *Our hostess . . . her welcome:* Our hostess will keep her chair of state, but when the proper moment comes ("in best time") we'll call on her to make us welcome.

8.   The first three speeches of the king and queen each end with "welcome," which is thus strongly emphasized.

9.   *encounter:* respond to.

11.   *large:* lavish, abundant.

     measure: a large goblet.

14.   *'Tis . . . within:* It's better that the blood is on the outside of your face than inside Banquo's body.

Murderer My lord, his throat is cut; that I did for him.

Macbeth Thou art the best o' the cut-throats; yet he's good
That did the like for Fleance: if thou didst it,
Thou art the nonpareil.

Murderer　　　　　　　　　Most royal sir,
Fleance is 'scap'd.　　　　　　　　　　　　　　　　　　　20

Macbeth Then comes my fit again: I had else been
　　　perfect;
Whole as the marble, founded as the rock,
As broad and general as the casing air:
But now I am cabin'd, cribb'd, confined, bound in
To saucy doubts and fears. But Banquo's safe?　　25

Murderer Ay, my good lord; safe in a ditch he bides,
With twenty trenched gashes on his head,
The least a death to nature.

Macbeth　　　　　　　　　Thanks for that.
There the grown serpent lies: the worm that's fled
Hath nature that in time will venom breed,　　　30
No teeth for the present. Get thee gone; to-morrow
We'll hear ourselves again. *[Exit Murderer]*

Lady Macbeth　　　　　　　My royal lord,
You do not give the cheer: the feast is sold
That is not often vouch'd, while 'tis a-making,
'Tis given with welcome: to feed were best at home;　35
From thence, the sauce to meat is ceremony;
Meeting were bare without it.

Macbeth　　　　　　　　　Sweet remembrancer!
Now good digestion wait on appetite,
And health on both!

Lennox　　　　　　　May it please your highness sit?

*[The Ghost Of BANQUO enters, and
sits in MACBETH'S place]*

Macbeth Here had we now our country's honour roof'd,　40
Were the grac'd person of our Banquo present;

19.	*nonpareil:* without equal.
21.	*my fit:* my fit of feverous anxiety.
	perfect: completely secure.
22.	*founded:* firmly established.
23.	*broad and general:* free and unconfined.
	casing: all-embracing.
24.	*cabin'd, cribb'd:* shut up in a cabin, a stall.
25.	*To saucy:* with insolent.
27.	*trenched:* deep-cut.
29.	*worm:* serpent.
32.	*hear ourselves:* talk by ourselves.
33.	*give the cheer:* make your guests feel welcome.
33–35.	*the feast . . . welcome:* Unless guests are made welcome, the meal is like a feast for which they're paying.
03.	*to feed . . . home:* As for mere eating, one could do it better at home.
37.	*remembrancer:* one who reminds one of his duty.
38.	*wait on :* attend, accompany.
40.	*had we ... roof'd:* We should now have all the noblest men of Scotland under one roof.

Who may I rather challenge for unkindness
Than pity for mischance!

Ross   His absence, sir,
Lays blame upon his promise. Please 't your highness
To grace us with your royal company.   45

Macbeth The table's full.

Lennox   Here is a place reserv'd, sir.

Macbeth Where?

Lennox Here, my good lord. What is 't that moves
      your highness?

Macbeth Which of you have done this?

Lords   What, my good lord?

Macbeth Thou canst not say I did it: never shake   50
Thy gory locks at me.

Ross Gentlemen, rise; his highness is not well.

Lady Macbeth Sit, worthy friends: my lord is often thus,
And hath been from his youth: pray you, keep seat;
The fit is momentary; upon a thought   55
He will again be well. If much you note him,
You shall offend him and extend his passion:
Feed, and regard him not. Are you a man?

Macbeth Ay, and a bold one, that dare look on that
Which might appal the devil.

Lady Macbeth   O proper stuff!   60
This is the very painting of your fear;
This is the air-drawn dagger which, you said,
Led you to Duncan. O! these flaws and starts —
Impostors to true fear — would well become
A woman's story at a winter's fire,   65
Authoriz'd by her grandam. Shame itself!
Why do you make such faces? When all's done,
You look but on a stool.

42–43.   *Who may . . . mischance:* Macbeth intends to compliment Banquo by saying that the pain of being without him outweighs the anxiety concerning what might've delayed him.

45.   *grace:* honor.

48.   *moves:* disturbs.

51.   *gory locks:* The hair of the apparition is matted with blood from the "twenty trenched gashes."

55.   *upon a thought:* in a moment.

58.   *Feed.:* The guests apply themselves to the banquet and don't hear what follows.

60.   *O proper stuff:* A fine thing this!

61.   *painting of your fear:* an imaginary vision prompted by fear.

63.   *flaws:* outbursts.

64.   *to:* in comparison with.

66.   *Authoriz'd:* vouched for.

Macbeth Prithee, see there! behold! look! lo!
　　how say you?
　Why, what care I? If thou canst nod, speak too.　　70
　If charnel-houses and our graves must send
　Those that we bury back, our monuments
　Shall be the maws of kites. *[Ghost disappears]*

Lady Macbeth　　　　　　　What! quite unmann'd in folly?

Macbeth If I stand here, I saw him.

Lady Macbeth　　　　　　　Fie, for shame!

Macbeth Blood hath been shed ere now, i' the olden　　75
　　time,
　Ere human statute purg'd the gentle weal;
　Ay, and since too, murders have been perform'd
　Too terrible for the ear: the times have been,
　That, when the brains were out, the man would die,
　And there an end; but now they rise again,　　80
　With twenty mortal murders on their crowns,
　And push us from our stools: this is more strange
　Than such a murder is.

Lady Macbeth　　　My worthy lord,
　Your noble friends do lack you.

Macbeth　　　　　　　I do forget,
　Do not muse at me, my most worthy friends;　　85
　I have a strange infirmity, which is nothing
　To those that know me. Come, love and health to all;
　Then, I'll sit down. Give me some wine; fill full.
　I drink to the general joy of the whole table.
　And to our dear friend Banquo, whom we miss;　　90
　Would he were here! to All, and him, we thirst,
　And all to all.

Lords　　　Our duties, and the pledge.

[Re-enter Ghost]

Macbeth Avaunt! and quit my sight! Let the earth hide thee!
　Thy bones are marrowless, thy blood is cold;
　Thou hast no speculation in those eyes　　95
　Which thou dost glare with.

69–73. During the utterance of these lines, the ghost rises, glares fixedly at Macbeth, nods its head, and moves toward the back of the stage.

71. *charnel-houses:* houses or vaults used as storehouses for bones found while digging new graves.

72–73. *our monuments . . . kites:* If the dead are thrown out to be devoured by birds of prey such as kites, their only monuments will be kites' bellies.

76. *Ere . . . weal:* before civilizing laws cleansed society of savagery and made it gentle.

77. *since too:* since then too.

81. *twenty . . . crowns:* an echo of the murderer's words in lines 27–28.

mortal murders: murderous wounds.

83. *My worthy lord:* The guests hear Macbeth's speeches that follow this line.

84. *lack you:* miss your company.

85. *muse:* wonder, be astonished.

90–91. *And to our . . . here!:* Macbeth has persuaded himself that the ghost was an illusion. With superb self-assurance, he repeats his wish that Banquo were present. Instantly the ghost accepts the challenge.

92. *And all to all:* let everyone drink to everyone else.

Our duties . . . pledge: Our toast is homage to your king and health to all and to Banquo.

95. *speculation:* intelligent sight. The ghost's eyes are fixed in a glassy stare.

Lady Macbeth Think of this, good peers,
But as a thing of custom: 'tis no other;
Only it spoils the pleasure of the time.

Macbeth What man dare, I dare:
Approach thou like the rugged Russian bear,   100
The arm'd rhinoceros, or the Hyrcan tiger;
Take any shape but that, and my firm nerves
Shall never tremble: or be alive again,
And dare me to the desert with thy sword;
If trembling I inhabit then, protest me   105
The baby of a girl. Hence, horrible shadow!
Unreal mockery, hence! *[Ghost vanishes]*
                    Why, so; being gone,
I am a man again. Pray you, sit still.

Lady Macbeth You have displac'd the mirth, broke
          the good meeting,
With most admir'd disorder.

Macbeth   Can such things be   110
And overcome us like a summer's cloud,
Without our special wonder? You make me strange
Even to the disposition that I owe,
When now I think you can behold such sights,
And keep the natural ruby of your cheeks,   115
When mine are blanch'd with fear.

Ross   What sights, my lord?

Lady Macbeth I pray you, speak not; he grows
          worse and worse;
Question enrages him. At once, good-night;
Stand not upon the order of your going,
But go at once.

Lennox   Good-night; and better health   120
Attend his majesty!

Lady Macbeth   A kind good-night to all!

[Exeunt Lords and Attendants]

Macbeth It will have blood, they say; blood will have blood:
Stones have been known to move and trees to speak;

---

97. *no other:* nothing else.

101. *arm'd:* referring either to the thick hide or to the tusks.

Hyrcan: Hyrcania was a district south of the Caspian Sea. Their tigers were represented in classical literature as being particularly fierce.

104. *to the desert:* to some solitary place for a duel without witnesses.

105. *inhabit:* give lodging to.

105–106. *protest . . . a girl:* declare me the child of a very young mother, i.e., timid weakling.

107. *being gone:* now that it's gone.

108. *Pray . . . still:* The guests are rising in horrified amazement.

110. *With . . . disorder:* by an amazing fit of distraction.

111–112. *overcome . . . wonder:* come over us as suddenly as a cloud in summer, yet excite no more surprise than such a cloud.

112–113. *You . . . owe:* You make me feel that I do not know my own nature ("disposition"), which I thought was that of a brave man.

113. *owe:* own.

118. *At . . . night:* I bid you all, as a group, a hasty goodnight.

119. *Stand . . . going:* Under ordinary circumstances, the guests would depart ceremoniously, in the order of their rank, as they leave the hall.

123. *Stones . . . move:* so as to reveal the body that the murderer had hidden.

Augures and understand relations have
By maggot-pies and choughs and rooks brought forth   125
The secret'st man of blood. What is the night?

Lady Macbeth Almost at odds with morning, which
    is which.

Macbeth How sayst thou, that Macduff denies his person
    At our great bidding?

Lady Macbeth   Did you send to him, sir?

Macbeth I hear it by the way; but I will send.   130
    There's not a one of them but in his house
    I keep a servant fee'd. I will to-morrow —
    And betimes I will — to the weird sisters:
    More shall they speak; for now I am bent to know,
    By the worst means, the worst. For mine own good   135
    All causes shall give way: I am in blood
    Stepp'd in so far, that, should I wade no more,
    Returning were as tedious as go o'er.
    Strange things I have in head that will to hand.
    Which must be acted ere they may be scann'd.   140

Lady Macbeth You lack the season of all natures, sleep.

Macbeth Come, we'll to sleep. My strange and self-abuse
    Is the initiate fear that wants hard use:
    We are yet but young in deed. *[Exeunt]*

124.	*Augures:* auguries, signs from the flight of birds.
125.	*By:* by means of.
	maggot pies: magpies.
	choughs: a kind of crow.
128.	*How . . . that:* what do you say to the fact that.
130.	*by the way:* in the ordinary course of affairs.
131-132.	*There's not . . . fee'd:* Macbeth explains that the report has come from one of his spies in Macduff's household.
133.	*betimes:* soon, without delay.
134.	*bent:* determined
135.	*By:* even by. Macbeth no longer doubts that the weird sisters are powers of evil.
136.	*All causes:* all considerations, including scruples about seeking help from evil powers.
139.	*will to hand:* are bound to be executed.
140.	*ere . . . scann'd:* before I pause to consider them.
141.	*the season:* the preservative.
142.	*My . . . self-abuse:* my strange self-deception. He persuades himself that the ghost was an illusion.
143.	*the initiate fear:* fear felt by a beginner.
	wants: lacks.
	hard use: practice that hardens one.

COMMENTARY

This scene portrays the banquet that Macbeth and Banquo discussed in Scene 1 of this act. Pay close attention to the ways in which Macbeth attempts to curry the favor of the other thanes and to impose order on the disorder that his crimes cause.

In Holinshed's *Chronicles*, Banquo is murdered on his way home from the banquet rather than upon his arrival back at Macbeth's castle. By altering the course of events, Shakespeare can have Banquo's ghost appear at the feast.

External and internal order

With the first lines, Macbeth attempts to impose order by commanding the thanes to sit according to their rank. Ironically, in his attempts to ingratiate himself to these thanes, he disrupts the order by being the "humble host" and sitting "i' the midst" of them (4, 10).

Macbeth's own mental order is disturbed a few lines later when he learns of Fleance's escape. He descends back into disorder as he begins to sense his inability to contradict the prediction of the weird sisters. Fleance's escape preempts the security that he felt Banquo's death would bring him.

Notice the reference to the "casing," or, encompassing, air of the castle, which echoes Duncan's arrival to Macbeth's castle in the first act (23).

After hearing the murderer's report, Macbeth asks, "But Banquo's safe?" (25). Macbeth is not asking whether Banquo escaped the attack with his life; he asks whether Banquo is now incapable of causing him any further problems. Interestingly, he again refers to Banquo and Fleance by using snake metaphors, which are traditionally associated with the devil.

Banquo's ghost joins the feast

The ghost of Banquo enters the scene and sits in Macbeth's seat. Literally, the ghost may have chosen his seat according to Banquo's rank. (Remember that Macbeth was not sitting in the king's accustomed position.) The ghost's choice of seats is symbolic, as well. Despite being dead, Banquo fills Macbeth's place — that is, his offspring, not Macbeth's, will be future kings.

Macbeth's question — "Which of you have done this?" — implies that he may believe he is seeing Banquo's corpse rather than his ghost (49). Macbeth thinks that what he sees is reality. But no one else sees the ghost, suggesting that it may be an illusion. Most likely, in an Early Modern production, the ghost would have been visible to the audience whereas Macbeth's earlier hallucination of the dagger would not have been.

At this point, the relationship between appearance and reality falls apart, even for the audience. Sidney Lamb asserts that this confusion could be an allusion to King James's work on witches, called *Daemonologie*, which contends that ghosts were punishment for the guilty or faithless. That would explain why Macbeth can see the ghost but none of his guests can. It does not explain, however, why Lady Macbeth cannot see the ghost. Though she is not specifically guilty of Banquo's death, she does seem faithless.

Traditional belief at the time assumed that a ghost would bleed profusely in the presence of its killer. Thus, this scene may have been quite gory on the stage.

Unlike modern plays, the printed texts of Shakespeare's play contain very few stage directions. Some aspects of performance can be located in internal stage directions. A good example of this type of direction occurs when Macbeth addresses the ghost. He tells him not to "shake [his] gory locks" (51). This indicates that the ghost shook his head in response to Macbeth's initial question. These clues are invaluable for helping to determine what transpired onstage during an Early Modern production of one of Shakespeare's plays.

Questioning Macbeth's manhood

From Lady Macbeth's question to her husband, "Are you a man?" (58) to Macbeth's lines that end with "Than such a murder is" (82), Macbeth and his wife are having a private conversation that the thanes cannot hear. Note that she facilitates this conversation by telling the thanes to ignore Macbeth. This would have been accomplished onstage by having the couple move to a remote portion of the stage, probably toward the front. This position would allow the audience members to hear their dialogue while creating the illusion that the dinner guests cannot.

During this private conversation, Lady Macbeth again raises the question of masculinity by associating her husband's reaction to the ghost with a "woman's story at a winter's fire" (65). She equates the ghost to the "air-drawn dagger" Macbeth saw earlier, but Early Modern audiences may not have agreed with her criticism (62). To many of Shakespeare's contemporaries, the ghost would be viewed not as an hallucination but as a "real" spirit.

Though Macbeth attempts to recover from the fit that the ghost creates in him, each return of the ghost upsets him anew. Interestingly, Macbeth seems to be most concerned that the ghost is interrupting his attempts to secure the support of the thanes. The ghost's numerous entrances and exits disrupt Macbeth and send the banquet into disorder. Macbeth manages to force the ghost to disappear, but disorder has already ruined his feast.

In line 99, Macbeth's challenge to the ghost — "[w]hat man dare, I dare" — echoes an earlier line in the play, "I dare do all that may become a man" (I.7.46). Both of these lines come in response to threats to his masculinity, indicating Macbeth's sensitivity to threats and implications that he is not a "man."

Like the weird sisters earlier in the play, the ghost of Banquo vanishes by means of a trapdoor in the floor of the stage. Note that the ghost's final departure returns Macbeth's masculinity to him.

The feast disbands

The feast is so disorderly that Lady Macbeth dismisses the custom of leaving according to rank and asks the thanes to depart at once.

Remember that Macduff is the only living thane who does not attend the required feast. This absence, as we shall see, will be very costly to Macduff's family. Macbeth's paranoia causes him (rightly in this case) to suspect that Macduff's absence is an act of defiance. This paranoia has led Macbeth to establish an extensive spy system, through paid servants, in every nobleman's household.

Macbeth's lines end with an extremely important revelation that he has already committed too many crimes to turn back. His only choice, he claims, is to continue his violence and his tyranny. Keep in mind that in Holinshed's account, Scotland enjoyed ten years of peaceful rule under Macbeth. Here, it seems to have only taken a matter of days for that peace to disintegrate.

The scene ends on the question of reality versus illusion as Macbeth tries to convince himself that Banquo's ghost was just an illusion. (These lines echo Banquo's lines in Act I, Scene 3, where he suggests that the weird sisters may have been illusions.) Macbeth consoles himself with the notion that because he is a beginner in evil, it will get easier as he continues.

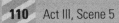

Act III, Scene 5

Hecate appears and confronts the witches with their entrapment of Macbeth. Hecate informs the witches of a plan to use illusions to fool Macbeth into a false sense of security that will eventually cause his downfall.

ACT III, SCENE 5
A heath.

[Thunder. Enter the three witches, meeting HECATE]

First Witch Why, how now, Hecate! you look angerly.

Hecate Have I not reason, beldams as you are,
  Saucy and overbold? How did you dare
  To trade and traffic with Macbeth
  In riddles and affairs of death;   5
  And I, the mistress of your charms,
  The close contriver of all harms,
  Was never call'd to bear my part,
  Or show the glory of our art?
  And, which is worse, All you have done   10
  Hath been but for a wayward son,
  Spiteful and wrathful; who, as others do,
  Loves for his own ends, not for you.
  But make amends now: get you gone,
  And at the pit of Acheron   15
  Meet me i' the morning: thither he
  Will come to know his destiny:
  Your vessels and your spells provide,
  Your charms and every thing beside.
  I am for the air; this night I'll spend   20
  Unto a dismal and a fatal end:
  Great business must be wrought ere noon:
  Upon the corner of the moon
  There hangs a vaporous drop profound;
  I'll catch it ere it come to ground: 25
  And that distill'd by magic sleights
  Shall raise such artificial sprites
  As by the strength of their illusion
  Shall draw him on to his confusion:
  He shall spurn fate, scorn death, and bear   30
  His hopes 'bove wisdom, grace, and fear;

NOTES

1.   *angerly:* angrily.

2.   *beldams:* hags.

7.   *close:* secret.

    of all harms: of the evil deeds

11.   *a wayward son:* indicating that Macbeth is unfaithful to the evil spirits whose lead he followed.

13.   *Loves:* Macbeth has never professed to love the sisters or to be a devotee of magic. The distinction here is between a lover of evil and one who merely makes use of an evil means. Macbeth is not yet a lover of evil.

15.   *the pit of Acheron:* Macbeth goes to find the witches in a Scottish cavern, not to Acheron (a mythical river of the infernal regions).

21.   *dismal:* disastrous.

24.   *a . . . profund:* a drop of condensed vapor, deep-hanging, pearshaped, and ready to fall. This moon-vapor is nowhere mentioned in the later scene that takes place around the witches's cauldron.

26.   *sleights:* sacred arts.

27.   *artificial sprites:* spirits produced by magic.

29.   *confusion:* destruction, ruin.

And you all know, security
Is mortals' chiefest enemy.

[Song within, 'Come away, come away,'etc.]
Hark! I am call'd; my little spirit, see,
Sits in a foggy cloud, and stays for me. *[Exit]*

First Witch Come, let's make haste; she'll soon
be back again. *[Exeunt]*

35.

31. *grace:* goodness, virtue.

32. *security:* a sense of security that makes mortals overbold.

s.d. *Come away:* This song appears in full in a play by Thomas Middleton called *The Witch*. It was probably written by Middleton and used in productions of *Macbeth* after Shakespeare left the theatre.

COMMENTARY

Many critics argue that this scene is out of line with the progression of the play and was most likely added at a later date (around 1609) by playwright Thomas Middleton. The additions likely were made to capitalize as much as possible on the interest in witches and to take advantage of mechanical devices available in the private, indoor theaters.

Although Shakespeare may not have been its author, do not dismiss this scene as unimportant. Its addition may reflect Early Modern dramatic tastes, and it draws attention to the highly collaborative nature of the theatre that many scholars and critics have glossed over in the past.

This scene does include some of the themes that Shakespeare would have engaged. Specifically, Hecate's disapproval of the weird sisters' meddling with Macbeth highlights an important aspect of Macbeth's character. Hecate asserts that Macbeth "[l]oves for his

Hecate is the ruler of the weird sisters.

own ends" (13). Macbeth's self-centered ambitions and desires prevent him from being loyal to anyone but himself; he is not even loyal to those who aided in the fulfillment of those ambitions. Hecate is right, of course. Macbeth has already attempted to defy the sisters' prophecy by trying to destroy Banquo's line.

Hecate informs the audience of a plan to fool Macbeth with a false sense of security that will eventually cause his downfall. Though some scholars argue that this scene is pointless, it explains Hecate's motivation. Evil forsakes Macbeth because of his selfish ambition.

Act III, Scene 6

Lennox and another lord discuss recent events in this scene. Lennox mocks the implication that Duncan's sons were responsible for his death by applying the same logic to Fleance and Banquo. The lord informs Lennox of Malcolm's activity in England and Macduff's recent trip to join Malcolm in preparation for a rebellion against Macbeth. Through the lord, we also learn that Macbeth is preparing for war.

ACT III, SCENE 6
Forres. A room in the palace.

[Enter LENNOX and another LORD]

Lennox My former speeches have but hit your thoughts,
  Which can interpret further: only, I say,
  Things have been strangely borne. The gracious Duncan
  Was pitied of Macbeth: marry, he was dead:
  And the right-valiant Banquo walk'd too late;   5
  Whom, you may say, if 't please you, Fleance kill'd
  For Fleance fled: men must not walk too late.
  Who cannot want the thought how monstrous
  It was for Malcolm and for Donalbain
  To kill their gracious father? damned fact!   10
  How it did grieve Macbeth! did he not straight
  In pious rage the two delinquents tear,
  That were the slaves of drink and thralls of sleep?
  Was not that nobly done? Ay, and wisely too;
  For 'twould have anger'd any heart alive   15
  To hear the men deny 't. So that, I say,
  He has borne All things well; and I do think
  That, had he Duncan's sons under his key, —
  As an 't please heaven, he shall not, — they should find
  What 'twere to kill a father; so should Fleance.   20
  But, peace! for from broad words, and 'cause he fail'd
  His presence at the tyrant's feast, I hear
  Macduff lives in disgrace. Sir, can you tell
  Where he bestows himself?

NOTES

1.   *My former speeches:* Lennox has been talking to this man before.

2.   *Which . . . further:* Your mind can easily draw its own conclusions from my hints about who murdered Duncan.

3.   *strangely borne:* oddly managed by Macbeth.

4.   *marry:* an exclamation.

6–7.   *Whom . . . fled:* ironic argument. Macbeth's sole proof of Duncan's sons' guilt is their flight.

10.   *fact:* evil deed, crime.

11–13.   *did he . . . sleep?:* Lennox uses irony here. Macbeth's real motive for killing the king's chamberlains (to keep them from talking) is plainly hinted at in line 16.

13.   *the slaves of drink:* Lennox insinuates that the grooms couldn't have killed Duncan because they slept in a drunken stupor all night.

16–17.   *So that . . . well:* The upshot of the whole matter is that Macbeth has managed everything wisely.

19.   *should find:* would be sure to find; ironic.

21.   *from broad words:* because of too free or unguarded expressions.

24.   *bestows himself:* has taken refuge.

Lord   The son of Duncan,
From whom this tyrant holds the due of birth,   25
Lives in the English court, and is receiv'd
Of the most pious Edward with such grace
That the malevolence of fortune nothing
Takes from his high respect. Thither Macduff
Is gone to pray the holy king, upon his aid   30
To wake Northumberland and war-like Siward:
That, by the help of these — with him above
To ratify the work — we may again
Give to our tables meat, sleep to our nights,
Free from our feasts and banquets bloody knives,   35
Do faithful homage and receive free honours;
All which we pine for now. And this report
Hath so exasperate the king that he
Prepares for some attempt of war.

Lennox   Sent he to Macduff?

Lord He did: and with an absolute, 'Sir, not I,'   40
The cloudy messenger turns me his back,
And hums, as who should say, 'You'll rue the time
That clogs me with this answer.'

Lennox   And that well might
Advise him to a caution to hold what distance
His wisdom can provide. Some holy angel   45
Fly to the court of England and unfold
His message ere he come, that a swift blessing
May soon return to this our suffering country
Under a hand accurs'd!

Lord   I'll send my prayers with him!
    [Exeunt]

25.	*holds:* withholds.
	due of birth: birthright.
27.	*Of:* by.
	grace: favor.
	Edward: Edward the Confessor.
29.	*his high respect:* the high regard in which he's held.
30.	*upon his aid:* for his assistance.
31.	*wake:* call to arms.
	Northumberland: the people of that region.
	Siward: Earl of Northumberland.
34.	*meat:* food.
36.	*faithful:* sincere.
37.	*this report:* the favor in which Malcolm is treated.
38.	*exasperate:* exasperated.
41.	*cloudy:* frowning, gloomy.
42.	*hums:* a surly murmuring sound.
43.	*clogs:* stuffs.
46.	*unfold:* disclose, reveal.

COMMENTARY

Like Act II, Scene 4, this scene contains only discussion that informs the audience of events without having to stage them. Again, this discussion takes place between a minor character and an unnamed one (the lord).

The thanes lose faith

Lennox's speech reveals a great deal about the thanes' sentiment concerning Macbeth. Macbeth has lost their support as they have begun to suspect and even become aware of his crimes. Certainly, as we have already seen, the country has been in a state of disorder since the murder.

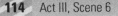

Lennox prefaces his lines by signaling that he has already determined the other lords' beliefs. This wariness seems to suggest that opposition against Macbeth is not yet widespread or that, maybe, the thanes are aware of Macbeth's spies (III.4.131–132). The thanes are also still within the king's palace and therefore would have to be careful with their speech.

Lennox mocks the theory that Malcolm and Donalbain killed their father and implicated themselves by fleeing. He argues that according to the same logic, Fleance killed Banquo because he fled the murder scene.

An underlying sarcasm seems to punctuate his lines as he summarizes much of the political action up to this point in the play. He asks if Macbeth's murder of the chamberlains "[w]as not . . . nobly done?" (14). This summary serves the double purpose of reminding the audience of these events and casting them in the light shared by the other noblemen. Despite this sarcasm, Lennox's position is clear when he refers to Macbeth's banquet as "the tyrant's feast" (22).

Organizing rebellion

Note that the lord's lines do more than recount previous events. He indicates Malcolm's and Macduff's separate activities in England as well as their plans to enlist the English to aid in the removal of Macbeth from the throne. This information is significant, and the scene parallels the first act where we learned of Macbeth's new title before he met the weird sisters. The audience now knows of the impending rebellion, and we know that it is spearheaded not by Malcolm but by Macduff. This information will be crucial when Macbeth visits the witches.

The lord also refers to Macbeth as a tyrant and refers to Malcolm's "due of birth," which is, of course, another statement supporting patrilineal succession (25).

The lord follows with a description of the English king, Edward. Notice the words surrounding the English king. They include "pious," "grace," "pray," and "holy" (27, 30). Edward stands on the opposite side of the good versus evil dichotomy from Macbeth, who lost the ability to pray as soon as he committed regicide.

The lord also provides more information about the conditions in Scotland since Macbeth's reign began, and he expresses his hope for a restoration of order. Note the additional reference to sleep in line 34.

This scene also has a discontinuity that editors have not been able to resolve. The lord's lines indicate that Macbeth is aware of Macduff's flight and is making preparations. But, in the next act, Macbeth learns onstage that Macduff has fled. This nonlinearity suggests that this scene originally may have been placed later in the play.

Notes

Notes

CLIFFSCOMPLETE

MACBETH
ACT IV

Lady Macduff *Whither should I fly?*
I have done no harm. But I remember now
I am in this earthly world, where to do harm
Is often laudable, to do good sometime
Accounted dangerous folly; why then, alas!
Do I put up that womanly defence,
To say I have done no harm?

Act IV, Scene 1

Macbeth revisits the witches, and they show him four apparitions that predict the future. The first apparition, an armed head, tells Macbeth to beware of Macduff. The second, a bloody child, informs the king that no man born of a woman will be able to kill Macbeth. The third, a crowned child holding a tree, indicates that until Birnam Wood comes to Dunsinane Hill, he will not be conquered. A fourth apparition depicts the initial prophecy of Banquo's royal descendants. Macbeth learns of Macduff's departure and orders the execution of Macduff's family.

ACT IV, SCENE 1
A cavern. In the middle, a boiling cauldron.

[Thunder. Enter the three Witches]

First Witch Thrice the brinded cat hath mew'd.

Second Witch Thrice and once the hedge-pig whin'd,

Third Witch Harpier cries: 'Tis time, 'tis time.

First Witch Round about the cauldron go;
In the poison'd entrails throw.
Toad, that under cold stone   5
Days and nights hast thirty-one
Swelter'd venom sleeping got,
Boil thou first i' the charmed pot.

All Double, double toil and trouble;   10
Fire burn and cauldron bubble.

Second Witch Fillet of a fenny snake,
In the cauldron boil and bake;
Eye of newt, and toe of frog,
Wool of bat, and tongue of dog,   15
Adder's fork, and blind-worm's sting,
Lizard's leg, and howlet's wing
For a charm of powerful trouble,
Like a hell-broth boil and bubble.

All Double, double toil and trouble;   20
Fire burn and cauldron bubble.

NOTES

The witches gather around their cauldron to conjure spirits.

1.   *brinded:* striped, streaked, brindled

2.   *hedge-pig:* hedgehog

3.   *Harpier:* an attendant demon.

6.   *cold:* the "o" is prolonged with a change of pitch to give the effect of two syllables.

8.   *Swelter'd:* coming out in drops (like sweat).

12.   *Fillet:* strip or slice

     fenny: living in a bog, marsh.

16.   *Adder's fork:* meaning forked tongue.

     blind-worm: small, snake-like lizard erroneously supposed to be sightless and venomous.

17.   *howlet:* owlet.

Third Witch Scale of dragon, tooth of wolf,
Witches' mummy, maw and gulf
Of the ravin'd salt-sea shark,
Root of hemlock digg'd i' the dark,   25
Liver of blaspheming Jew,
Gall of goat, and slips of yew
Sliver'd in the moon's eclipse,
Nose of Turk, and Tartar's lips,
Finger of birth-strangled babe   30
Ditch-deliver'd by a drab,
Make the gruel thick and slab:
Add there to a tiger's chaudron,
For the ingredients of our cauldron.

All Double, double toil and trouble;   35
Fire burn and cauldron bubble.

Second Witch Cool it with a baboon's blood,
Then the charm is firm and good.

[Enter HECATE]

Hecate O! well done! I commend your pains,
And every one shall share i' the gains.   40
And now about the cauldron sing,
Like elves and fairies in a ring,
Enchanting all that you put in.

[Music and a song, 'Black Spirits,' etc.]

Second Witch By the pricking of my thumbs,
Something wicked this way comes.   45
Open, locks,
Whoever knocks.

[Enter MACBETH]

Macbeth How now, you secret, black, and midnight hags!
What is 't you do?

All   A deed without a name.

Macbeth I conjure you, by that which you profess, —   50
Howe'er you come to know it, — answer me:

23.	*Witches' mummy:* Bits of Egyptian mummy, or what passed for it (often a powdered substance), were traditional parts of these spells.
	maw and gulf: stomach and gullet.
24.	*ravin'd:* ravenous.
25.	*hemlock:* a poisonous herb.
27.	*yew:* evergreen found in church yards (poisonous).
30.	*birth-strangled:* hence unbaptized.
32.	*slab:* slimy.
33.	*chaudron:* insides, entrails.
39–43.	Hecate's speech is written by the same person who wrote Act III, Scene 5, probably Thomas Middleton. The comparison with elves and fairies is quite out of order.
s.d.	*Black Spirits:* This song also occurs in Middleton's *The Witch.*
46.	*Open, locks:* This doesn't imply that the sisters are in a locked room instead of a cave. It's a formula that releases any spells that prevent the entrance of intruders.
50.	*conjure:* call upon solemnly, by oath.

Though you untie the winds and let them fight
Against the churches; though the yesty waves
Confound and swallow navigation up;
Though bladed corn be lodg'd and trees blown down;   55
Though castles topple on their warders' heads;
Though palaces and pyramids do slope
Their heads to their foundations; though the treasure
Of Nature's germens tumble all together,
Even till destruction sicken; answer me   60
To what I ask you.

First Witch   Speak.

Second Witch   Demand.

Third Witch   We'll answer.

First Witch Say if thou'dst rather hear it from our mouths,
Or from our masters'?

Macbeth   Call 'em: let me see 'em.

First Witch Pour in sow's blood, that hath eaten
Her nine farrow; grease that's sweaten   65
From the murderer's gibbet throw
Into the flame.

All   Come, high or low;
Thyself and office deftly show.

[Thunder. First Apparition of an armed Head]

Macbeth Tell me, thou unknown power, —

First Witch   He knows thy thought:
Hear his speech, but say thou nought.   70

First Apparition Macbeth! Macbeth! Macbeth!
   beware Macduff;
Beware the Thane of Fife. Dismiss me. Enough.

[Descends]

Macbeth Whate'er thou art, for thy good caution thanks;
Thou hast harp'd my fear aright. But one word more, —

53.	*yesty:* foaming.
54.	*Confound:* destroy, ruin.
55.	*lodg'd:* laid flat.
57.	*pyramids:* steeple (a common usage of the time).
	slope: let fall.
59.	*Nature's germens:* the seeds of all life in nature.
60.	*sicken:* grow weary of destroying.
61.	*Demand:* ask.
62–63.	*Say . . . masters'?:* The sisters give Macbeth his choice between visions and mere prophecy.
65.	*nine farrow:* litter of pigs.
67.	*high or low:* in the upper or lower air.
68.	*office:* function.
	deftly: skillfully, smartly.
70.	*Hear . . . nought:* Notice how the witches' attitude towards Macbeth has changed since Act I, Scene 3.
74.	*harp'd . . . aright:* expressed it truly.

First Witch He will not be commanded: here's another,   75
More potent than the first.

[Thunder. Second Apparition, a bloody Child]

Second Apparition Macbeth! Macbeth! Macbeth! —

Macbeth Had I three ears, I'd hear thee.

Second Apparition Be bloody, bold, and resolute;
        laugh to scorn
The power of man, for none of woman born   80
Shall harm Macbeth. *[Descends]*

Macbeth Then live, Macduff: what need I fear of thee?
But yet I'll make assurance double sure,
And take a bond of fate: thou shalt not live;
That I may tell pale hearted fear it lies,   85
And sleep in spite of thunder.
*[Thunder. Third Apparition, a Child crowned, with
a tree in his hand]*
                        What is this,
That rises like the issue of a king,
And wears upon his baby brow the round
And top of sovereignty?

All   Listen but speak not to 't.

Third Apparition Be lion-mettled, proud, and take
        no care   90
Who chafes, who frets, or where conspirers are:
Macbeth shall never vanquish'd be until
Great Birnam Wood to high Dunsinane Hill
Shall come against him. *[Descends]*

Macbeth   That will never be:
Who can impress the forest, bid the tree   95
Unfix his earth-bound root? Sweet bodements! good!
Rebellion's head, rise never till the wood
Of Birnam rise, and our high-plae'd Macbeth
Shall live the lease of nature, pay his breath

84. *take . . . fate:* bind fate, as securely as with a legal bond, to fulfill this prediction of safety (by killing Macduff himself).

s.d.: *a Child crowned:* refers to Malcolm, who became king.

87. *like:* in the shape of

89. *top:* a crown.

91. *chafes:* is resentful.

95. *impress:* forcibly enlist.

96. *bodements:* prophecies.

99. *lease:* appointed time. The whole clause takes its metaphor from the laws governing renting property.

To time and mortal custom. Yet my heart   100
Throbs to know one thing: tell me — if your art
Can tell so much, — shall Banquo's issue ever
Reign in this kingdom?

All   Seek to know no more.

Macbeth I will be satisfied: deny me this,
And an eternal curse fall on you! Let me know.   105
Why sinks that cauldron? and what noise is this?

[Hautboys]

First Witch Show!

Second Witch Show!

Third Witch Show!

All Show his eyes, and grieve his heart;   110
Come like shadows, so depart.

[A show of Eight Kings; the last with a glass
in his hand: BANQUO'S GHOST following]

Macbeth Thou art too like the spirit of Banquo; down!
Thy crown does sear mine eyeballs: and thy hair,
Thou other gold-bound brow, is like the first:
A third is like the former. Filthy hags!   115
Why do you show me this? A fourth! Start, eyes!
What! will the line stretch out to the crack of doom?
Another yet? A seventh! I'll see no more:
And yet the eighth appears, who bears a glass
Which shows me many more; and some I see   120
That two fold balls and treble sceptres carry
Horrible sight! Now, I see, 'tis true;
For the blood-bolter'd Banquo smiles upon me,
And points at them for his. *[Apparitions vanish]*
                    What! is this so?

First Witch Ay, sir, all this is so: but why   125
Stands Macbeth thus amazedly?
Come sisters, cheer we up his sprites,
And show the best of our delights.
I'll charm the air to give a sound,
While you perform your antick round,   130
That this great king may kindly say
Our duties did his welcome pay.

100. *mortal custom:* dying, which is common to all men.

104. *I will be satisfied:* I want full information.

106. *noise:* music.

112. *Thou . . . Banquo:* said to the first of the eight kings.

119. *glass:* mirror

121. *balls:* an emblem of sovereignty.

123. *blood-bolter'd:* having his hair matted with blood.

127. *sprites:* spirits.

130. *round:* dance in a circle.

132. *Our duties . . . pay:* Macbeth has not welcomed the sisters. Their words are teasing and ironical.

[Music. The Witches dance, and then
vanish with HECATE]

Macbeth Where are they? Gone? Let this pernicious hour
Stand aye accursed in the calendar!
Come in, without there!

[Enter LENNOX]

Lennox   What's your Grace's will?   135

Macbeth Saw you the weird sisters?

Lennox   No, my Lord.

Macbeth Came they not by you?

Lennox   No indeed, my Lord.

Macbeth Infected be the air whereon they ride,
And damn'd all those that trust them! I did hear
The galloping of horse: who was 't came by?   140

Lennox 'Tis two or three, my Lord, that bring you word
Macduff is fled to England.

Macbeth   Fled to England!

Lennox Ay, my good Lord.

Macbeth Time, thou anticipat'st my dread exploits;
The flighty purpose never is o'ertook   145
Unless the deed go with it; from this moment
The very firstlings of my heart shall be
The firstlings of my hand. And even now,
To crown my thoughts with acts, be it thought and done;
The castle of Macduff I will surprise;   150
Seize upon Fife; give to the edge of the sword
His wife, his babes, and all unfortunate souls
That trace him in his line. No boasting like a fool;
This deed I'll do before this purpose cool:
But no more sights! Where are these gentlemen?   155
Come, bring me where they are. *[Exeunt]*

s.d.: *with Hecate:* Hecate has been standing at the back of the stage throughout.

s.d. *Enter Lennox:* Lennox is one of Macbeth's most trusted advisors, but the audience knows that he's ringleader of a conspiracy against Macbeth.

139. *damn'd:* Macbeth unknowingly curses himself.

144. *anticipat'st:* forestall, prevent.

147. *firstlings:* first born.

153. *trace:* follow.

155. *these gentlemen:* these who brought the news.

COMMENTARY

The fourth act is one of the longest in *Macbeth* and contains one of the most visually rich scenes (Scene 1) and one of the most static scenes (Scene 3). It prepares us for the final act where Macbeth and his enemies will meet in battle, resolving the extended action of the play.

In this first scene, the weird sisters and Hecate reappear, continuing the strong supernatural presence in the play. As in Act I, Scene 3, the witches give prophetic information to Macbeth that shapes his course of action throughout the rest of the play. Keep in mind the differences between the prophesies delivered in the first act and this scene, the ways they are delivered, and the interaction between the witches and Macbeth in these two scenes. Consider what these differences say about Macbeth and the witches' role in his behavior. Notice how these changes affect our perception of Macbeth and our level of sympathy for him.

Calling on the spirits

In the first three lines of this scene, the witches are listening to their spirits (sometimes called *familiars*), who often inform them when it is time to commit evil. The unnaturalness of the witches is visibly represented through their appearance, textually represented through their speech, and dramatically represented through the colorful contents of their cauldron. Shakespeare used many sources, including *News from Scotland* and King James's *Daemonologie,* to create the list of ingredients that the witches put into their brew.

Interestingly, dramatic portrayals of witches have not changed much in the centuries since Shakespeare wrote *Macbeth*. Today's witches may use more disturbing ingredients in their brews, such as human body parts, but it is not uncommon to see modern portrayals of witches using "eye of newt and toe of frog" — many times copying Shakespeare's exact language (14).

Many scholars think that Hecate's reappearance at this point is again the work of playwright Thomas Middleton. (See the "Introduction to *Macbeth*.") Notice that Hecate stays onstage but does not participate in the action for about a hundred lines. This awkward presence without dialogue seems to indicate that her character was a later addition that was not completely integrated into the text. Again, the song the witches sing

does not appear in its entirety in the Folio text. It was common practice in Early Modern dramatic texts to include only the title of a song, because most of the readers of such a text were already familiar with it.

Macbeth seeks a new prophesy

Notice the urgency with which Macbeth addresses the witches. He demands answers to his fearful questions. He now *needs* their information and wants it despite what harm and destruction it causes. He actually invites disorder and the destruction of religion ("pyramids") and political states ("palaces") (57). His villainy seems to be on the verge of madness.

Macbeth is given the choice of hearing the prophecy from the weird sisters or seeing it from their masters, presumably Hecate and the Devil. He chooses to learn his fate directly from the sisters' masters saying, "Call 'em: let me see 'em" (63). Macbeth is unable to process the apparitions alone, so the illusions speak to him as well.

Holinshed's account of this story includes the basic prophetic statements but does not include the apparitions. Deviating from the *Chronicles* allows Shakespeare to further explore the theme of illusion versus reality. The apparitions are at once illusions and representatives of Macbeth's future reality. They speak truthfully, but their words are so carefully chosen that they convince Macbeth that any threat against him is an illusion. He is unable to interpret them accurately, so he cannot distinguish where illusion ends and reality begins. They lull Macbeth into a false confidence.

The addition of the apparitions is also linked to the medium in which Shakespeare wrote, because these "illusions" would have been relatively easy to stage and their presence would add to the spectacle of the play. The presence of a trapdoor on the Early Modern stage would allow the apparitions to ascend and descend. (See the "Introduction to Early Modern England" for a discussion of this theatrical device.)

The first apparition.

The apparitions speak

The first apparition that Macbeth sees is an "armed Head." By *armed,* Shakespeare indicates that the head is probably wearing a helmet. The apparition warns Macbeth to "beware Macduff" (71), confirming Macbeth's fear that Macduff will be his downfall.

Notice how quickly Macbeth dismisses the first prophecy upon hearing the second. A bloody child appears and tells him that no man "of woman born / Shall harm Macbeth" (80–81). Macbeth instantly feels that he has no reason to fear Macduff, saying "[t]hen, live" (82). But Macbeth quickly changes his mind again, saying that he will "make assurance double sure" by eliminating Macduff anyway (83).

Macbeth's responses to the prophecies he receives have been very curious throughout the play. On the one hand, he

The second apparition.

believes the prophecies are true, but on the other, he thinks that he can change or ignore them to suit his ambitions and alleviate his fears. This dual reaction continues here.

The third apparition is a child with a crown who holds a tree. The child declares that "Macbeth shall never vanquish'd be until / Great Birnam Wood to high Dunsinane Hill / Shall come against him" (92–94). Macbeth again takes comfort in the seeming impossibility of a moving forest. He interprets this vision as an indication that he is invincible.

Despite all of the disorder that his actions cause — disorder that he embraces (consider his initial lines in this scene) — Macbeth returns to the natural order of the world when he craves security. He cannot imagine a man who is not born of a woman. He also cannot imagine a forest that can move. Notice how equivocation, which Macbeth previously used for his own advantage, is being used here to dupe him. As we shall see, the statements made by the apparitions are true — from a certain perspective.

A final vision

Despite being thrilled by the "[s]weet bodements" or predictions offered by the first three apparitions, Macbeth is still concerned about Banquo's descendants becoming kings (96). Against the weird sisters' warnings, he demands to know if Banquo's prophecy will hold true.

A final apparition — a procession of eight kings — appears. The glass that the eighth king holds is not a drinking cup but rather a looking glass or a mirror that, Macbeth tells us, reflects the future kings descending from Banquo's line. The eight kings represent the entire history of Scottish kings up through Shakespeare's day. The only omission is Mary, Queen of Scots. Schol-

The third apparition.

ars speculate that Shakespeare may have omitted her because of her gender or her Catholic religion. The eighth king is, of course, James VI and I, King of Scotland and England. The multiple insignia and scepters that Macbeth sees some of them carrying refer to multiple realms. For example, James ruled England and Scotland but also had France in his title (though not really under his control). This procession is clearly meant to be a tribute to James and the entire Stuart dynasty.

This final apparition carries no prophetic statement; it merely confirms the earlier prophecy that the weird sisters gave to Banquo. Macbeth can interpret this vision himself. Because Fleance survived Macbeth's plot to murder him, Banquo's line lives on, and Macbeth's fears are justified.

Damned by trust

When the apparitions disappear, Macbeth denounces them by crying, "Infected be the air wheron they ride, / And damn'd all those that trust them!"

The final apparition.

(138–139). The irony is that Macbeth trusts the prophecies he has received. Shakespeare may be indicating that Macbeth is extremely self-aware; he may know instinctively that his trust of the witches has damned him. The effect of this is to help the audience divide the blame for his actions between Macbeth, who acts out of free will, and the witches, who manipulate and deceive him.

Macbeth learns from Lennox that Macduff has traveled to England. At this point, Macbeth falls headlong into his actions. He resolves to execute these actions before contemplating their consequences. He then orders the murder of Macduff's entire family, even though he earlier assumed (because of the second apparition) that Macduff cannot hurt him. Clearly, he is not certain which apparition to trust, so he determines to defy the first apparition by eliminating the threat of Macduff.

Act IV, Scene 2

Ross and Lady Macduff discuss Macduff's departure for England, which has left his family unprotected. After a pitiful conversation between Lady Macduff and her son, a messenger enters and warns them to flee for their safety. Lady Macduff refuses, and soon murderers enter who kill their son onstage and pursue Lady Macduff off of the stage.

ACT IV, SCENE 2
Fife. Macduff's castle.

[Enter LADY MACDUFF, her Son, and ROSS]

Lady Macduff What had he done to make him fly the land?

Ross You must have patience, madam.

Lady Macduff   He had none:
His flight was madness: when our actions do not,
Our fears do make us traitors.

Ross   You know not
Whether it was his wisdom or his fear.   5

Lady Macduff Wisdom! to leave his wife, to leave his babes,
His mansion and his titles in a place
From whence himself does fly? He loves us not;
He wants the natural touch; for the poor wren,
The most diminutive of birds, will fight —   10
Her young ones in her nest — against the owl.
All is the fear and nothing is the love;
As little is the wisdom, where the flight
So runs against all reason.

Ross   My dearest coz,
I pray you, school yourself: but, for your husband,   15
He is noble, wise, judicious, and best knows
The fits o' the season. I dare not speak much further:
But cruel are the times, when we are traitors
And do not know ourselves, when we hold rumour
From what we fear, yet know not what we fear,   20
But float upon a wild and violent sea
Each way and move. I take my leave of you:
Shall not be long but I'll be here again.
Things at the worst will cease, or else climb upward

NOTES

3–4.   *when . . . traitors:* Macduff had done nothing treasonous, yet fear made him flee to the English court, making him a traitor.

7.   *his titles:* all of his hereditary possessions.

9.   *the . . . touch:* the instinct that prompts all creatures to defend their young.

11.   *in her nest:* therefore, in her charge.

15.   *school yourself:* control yourself.

   for: as for.

17.   *The fits o' the season:* the irregular happenings of the time.

19–20.   *hold rumour . . . we fear:* We're ready to believe rumors that support our fears.

24.   *climb upward:* take a turn for the better.

To what they were before. My pretty cousin,   25
Blessing upon you!

Lady Macduff Father'd he is, and yet he's fatherless.

Ross I am so much a fool, should I stay longer,
It would be my disgrace, and your discomfort:
I take my leave at once. *[Exit]*

Lady Macduff   Sirrah, your father's dead: 30
And what will you do now? How will you live?

Son As birds do, mother.

Lady Macduff   What! with worms and flies?

Son With what I get, I mean; and so do they.

Lady Macduff Poor bird! Thou'dst never fear the net nor lime,
The pit-fall nor the gin.   35

Son Why should I, mother? Poor birds they are not set for.
My father is not dead, for all your saying.

Lady Macduff Yes, he is dead: how wilt thou do
for a father?

Son Nay, how will you do for a husband?

Lady Macduff Why, I can buy me twenty at any market.   40

Son Then you'll buy 'em to sell again.

Lady Macduff Thou speak'st with all thy wit; and yet, i' faith,
With wit enough for thee.

Son Was my father a traitor, mother?

Lady Macduff   Ay, that he was.

Son What is a traitor?

Lady Macduff   Why, one that swears and lies.   45

Son And be all traitors that do so?

Lady Macduff Every one that does so is a traitor,
and must be hanged.

---

25. *My pretty cousin:* Ross turns to speak to the boy.

29. *my disgrace:* to disgrace himself by weeping.

30. *Sirrah:* often (to boys) a playful and affectionate term.

34. *lime:* a sticky substance for trapping birds.

35. *pit-fall:* a kind of trap.

gin: short for engine, used for any contrivance.

36. *they:* the net, trap, etc.

42–43. *Thou . . . thee:* What you say shows but a child's wisdom, yet for a child, your wit is pretty good.

45. *one . . . lies:* one who takes an oath and breaks it. The term was commonly used also for people who, through perjury or equivocation, swore oaths against their convictions. Thus, the audience may assume a topical reference to the gunpowder plot.

Son And must they all be hanged that swear and lie?

Lady Macduff Every one.

Son Who must hang them? 50

Lady Macduff Why, the honest men.

Son Then the liars and swearers are fools, for there
are liars and swearers enow to beat the honest men,
and hang up them.

Lady Macduff Now God help thee, poor monkey! 55
But how wilt thou do for a father?

Son If he were dead, you'd weep for him: if you
would not, it were a good sign that I should quickly
have a new father.

Lady Macduff Poor prattler, how thou talk'st! 60

[Enter a Messenger]

Messenger Bless you, fair dame! I am not to you known,
Though in your state of honour I am perfect.
I doubt some danger does approach you nearly:
If you will take a homely man's advice,
Be not found here; hence, with your little ones. 65
To fright you thus, methinks, I am too savage;
To do worse to you were fell cruelty,
Which is too nigh your person. Heaven preserve you!
I dare abide no longer. *[Exit]*

Lady Macduff Whither should I fly?
I have done no harm. But I remember now 70
I am in this earthly world, where to do harm
Is often laudable, to do good sometime
Accounted dangerous folly; why then, alas!
Do I put up that womanly defence,
To say I have done no harm?
[Enter Murderers]
What are these faces? 75

Murderer Where is your husband?

62. *in your . . . perfect:* I'm aware of your rank.

63. *doubt:* fear.

64. *homely:* of no high rank.

67. *fell:* fierce.

69. *I dare abide no longer.* It would mean death to me if I were discovered giving you information.

72. *sometime:* sometimes.

Lady Macduff I hope in no place so unsanctified
  Where such as thou mayst find him.

Murderer   He's a traitor.

Son Thou liest, thou shag-ear'd villain.

Murderer   What, you egg!
  Young fry of treachery! *[Stabbing him]*

Son   He has killed me, mother: 80
  Run away, I pray you! *[Dies]*

*[Exit LADY MACDUFF, crying 'Murder',
  and pursued by the Murderers]*

79. *shag-ear'd:* The long shaggy hair falling over the
     ruffian's ears reminds the boy of a dog's ears.

80. *fry:* spawn.

COMMENTARY

Despite being cut from most modern productions in order to save time, this scene is very important. The action could have occurred offstage, so it is significant that Shakespeare stages it — particularly the violence that occurs at the end.

Traitorous fear

Lady Macduff's first comments indicate the paranoia that grips Scotland. She notes that her husband is not a traitor in action, but his fear (which caused him to run) makes him one. Her statement is ironic, because Macbeth's fears of Macduff have convinced him that Macduff is a traitor.

Notice that Lady Macduff, like Lady Macbeth, questions her husband's masculinity by accusing him of being a coward for abandoning his wife and children. At the same time Macduff is developing into the "hero" who will save Scotland from Macbeth, he is accused by his wife of being unnatural or out of order because he lacks "the natural touch" to defend his children (9).

The owl that Lady Macduff refers to in line 11 symbolically represents Macbeth. (Recall the frequent references to the owl that surround Duncan's murder in Act II, Scene 2.) The owl also foreshadows the horror at the end of this scene.

Ross provides another picture of the current state of affairs in Scotland. He invokes the cliché that things can get only better because they are currently at their worst.

Ross claims that if he stays, he will weep and disgrace his manhood, as well as make Lady Macduff uncomfortable. Thus, he abandons the Macduff family in the name of masculinity. The effect of this action seems to be a piercing criticism of masculinity, in addition to being another sign of the extent of the disorder in Scotland.

A fatherless son

In line 27, Lady Macduff refers to her son when she says, "Father'd he is, and yet he's fatherless." Consider why Lady Macduff tells her son that his father is dead (in line 30). What purpose does this serve? The audience knows that Macduff is safe in England. The bitter irony, of course, is that Lady Macduff and her family are not safe in Scotland.

Note also Lady Macduff's cynical view of husbands and their widespread availability. When her son asks how she'll get another husband, her response is "I can buy me twenty at any market" (40). She seems to criticize masculinity harshly.

The cynicism that dominates this scene extends even to the small boy. He believes that there is such a disparity between honest men and liars that the liars could easily overrun the honest men. Because equivocation was usually associated with Catholics in Shakespeare's time, this statement may possibly allude to a widespread Catholic underground in England. Subjects under James were required to swear an oath to the English church and king. Equivocation was often presented as a way of taking the oath and remaining Catholic.

"Whither should I fly?"

A messenger arrives to instruct Lady Macduff to flee from imminent danger. She refuses to do so, because she knows that she has done nothing to deserve punishment. But recognizing that innocence does not guarantee her safety, Lady Macduff laments the world in which good and evil have been reversed. Her words echo the witches' sentiment in the first act that "Fair is foul and foul is fair."

It is interesting that the murderer asks Lady Macduff the whereabouts of her husband, even though from the previous scene we know that Macbeth is aware of his location and absence from the castle.

The dramatic presentation of the violence in this scene is significant. Except for Duncan's murder, all of Macbeth's tyrannical violence has been staged. The effect may be to distance the sympathy of the audience from Macbeth or to use that sympathy to implicate the audience in his actions. Either way, it causes us some discomfort. The first violent incident in the play depicted the murder of an innocent man (Banquo). This scene depicts the murder of a child. Notice that he is referred to as "egg" and "[y]oung fry" (79). Earlier, Lady Macbeth claimed that she could kill a child, but Macbeth, through his commands, actually does.

Macbeth's violent actions become steadily more evil and senseless. Duncan's murder, though clearly wrong, provided Macbeth with real and immediate political benefits. Banquo's murder was also committed in the name of political gain, even though he posed no current threat and was innocent. By the time we arrive at the murder of Macduff's family, Macbeth's violence seems to lack any real purpose or goal.

Shakespeare also creates a great deal of suspense by having Lady Macduff flee, pursued by the murderers. It is unclear to the first-time audience member or reader whether or not she escapes. The scene ends without that resolution.

Act IV, Scene 3

Macduff arrives in England and reunites with Malcolm. Suspicious of anyone from Scotland, Malcolm tests Macduff by pretending to be tyrannical. After Macduff passes the test by remaining loyal to Duncan's son, Malcolm speaks of the healing power of Edward the Confessor, England's king, and informs Macduff of England's military support for their impending war against Macbeth. The scene closes with the appearance of Ross, who relates recent events in Scotland, primarily the murder of Macduff's family.

ACT IV, SCENE 3
England. Before the king's palace.

[Enter MALCOLM and MACDUFF]

Malcolm Let us seek out some desolate shade, and there
  Weep our sad bosoms empty.

Macduff   Let us rather
  Hold fast the mortal sword, and like good men
  Bestride our down-fall'n birthdom; each new morn
  New widows howl, new orphans cry, new sorrows   5
  Strike heaven on the face, that it resounds
  As if it felt with Scotland and yell'd out
  Like syllable of dolour.

Malcolm   What I believe I'll wail,
  What know believe; and what I can redress,
  As I shall find the time to friend, I will.   10
  What you have spoke, it may be so perchance,
  This tyrant, whose sole name blisters our tongues,
  Was once thought honest; you have lov'd him well;
  He hath not touch'd you yet. I am young; but something
  You may deserve of him through me, and wisdom   15
  To offer up a weak, poor, innocent lamb
  To appease an angry god.

Macduff I am not treacherous.

Malcolm   But Macbeth is.
  A good and virtuous nature may recoil
  In an imperial charge. But I shall crave your pardon;   20

NOTES

3.   *mortal:* deadly.

4.   *Bestride:* stand over to defend.

6.   *that:* so that.

8.   *Like syllable of dolour:* similar sounds of grief.

10.   *As . . . friend:* when the time seems right.

12.   *sole:* mere.

13.   *honest:* good, honorable, noble.

14.   *I am young; but . . . :* Although I'm young, I can see.

15.   *deserve:* win, earn.

     through me: by betraying me to Macbeth.

     and wisdom: and it is wisdom.

19–20.   *recoil . . . charge:* give way under pressure from a monarch.

That which you are my thoughts cannot transpose;
Angels are bright still, though the brightest fell;
Though all things foul would wear the brows of grace,
Yet grace must still look so.

Macduff   I have lost my hopes.

Malcolm Perchance even there where I did find my doubts. 25
Why in that rawness left you wife and child —
Those precious motives, those strong knots of love —
Without leave-taking? I pray you,
Let not my jealousies be your dishonours,
But mine own safeties: you may be rightly just,   30
Whatever I shall think.

Macduff   Bleed, bleed, poor country!
Great tyranny, lay thou thy basis sure,
For goodness dare not check thee! wear thou thy wrongs;
The title is affeer'd! Fare thee well, lord:
I would not be the villain that thou think'st   35
For the whole space that's in the tyrant's grasp,
And the rich East to boot.

Malcolm   Be not offended:
I speak not as in absolute fear of you.
I think our country sinks beneath the yoke;
It weeps, it bleeds, and each new day a gash   40
Is added to her wounds: I think withal
There would be hands uplifted in my right;
And here from gracious England have I offer
Of goodly thousands: but, for all this,
When I shall tread upon the tyrant's head,   45
Or wear it on my sword, yet my poor country
Shall have more vices than it had before,
More suffer, and more sundry ways than ever,
By him that shall succeed.

Macduff   What should he be?

Malcolm It is myself I mean; in whom I know   50
All the particulars of vice so grafted,
That, when they shall be open'd, black Macbeth
Will seem as pure as snow, and the poor state

21. *tranpose:* transform. My suspicion can't alter the fact of your honor, if you're as you say.

22. *the brightest:* Lucifer (the devil).

23. *the brows of grace:* seeming goodness.

24. *so:* like herself, like virtue.

25. *Perchance . . . my doubts:* This line makes sense if Macduff's hope was to put Malcolm in Macbeth's power (as Malcolm assumes).

26. *rawness:* raw haste.

27. *motives:* incentives to action.

29. *jealousies:* suspicious cares.

30. *rightly just:* perfectly honorable and good.

32. *basis:* foundation.

33. *check thee:* call thee to account.

34. *affeer'd:* legally confirmed. Macbeth's title is established beyond dispute, because Malcolm refuses to contest it.

41. *withal:* also, besides.

43. *England:* the king of England.

44. *but . . . this:* At this point Malcolm's device for testing Macduff begins.

46. *yet:* after all that (spoken emphatically).

49. *What . . . be?:* What worse king could there be than Macbeth?

51. *particulars:* particular kinds, special varieties.

52. *open'd:* The figure is from the opening of a bud, suggested by the word "grafted."

Esteem him as a lamb, being compar'd
With my confineless harms.

Macduff   Not in the legions   55
Of horrid hell can come a devil more damn'd
In evils to top Macbeth.

Malcolm   I grant him bloody,
Luxurious, avaricious, false, deceitful,
Sudden, malicious, smacking of every sin
That has a name; but there's no bottom, none,   60
In my voluptuousness: your wives, your daughters,
Your matrons, and your maids, could not fill up
The cistern of my lust, and my desire
All continent impediments would o'erbear
That did oppose my will; better Macbeth   65
That such an one to reign.

Macduff   Boundless intemperance
In nature is a tyranny; it hath been
Th' untimely emptying of the happy throne,
And fall of many kings. But fear not yet
To take upon you what is yours; you may   70
Convey your pleasures in a spacious plenty,
And yet seem cold, the time you may so hoodwink.
We have willing dames enough; there cannot be
That vulture in you, to devour so many
As will to greatness dedicate themselves,   75
Finding it so inclin'd.

Malcolm   With this there grows
In my most ill-compos'd affection such
A stanchless avarice that, were I king,
I should cut off the nobles for their lands,
Desire his jewels and his other's house;   80
And my more-having would be as a sauce
To make me hunger more, that I should forge
Quarrels unjust against the good and loyal,
Destroying them for wealth.

Macduff   This avarice
Sticks deeper, grows with more pernicious root   85
Than summer-seeming lust, and it hath been
The sword of our slain kings: yet do not fear;
Scotland hath foisons to fill up your will,

55.	*confineless harms:* the boundless injuries that I should do to my people.
57.	*top:* surpass.
58.	*Luxurious:* lewd, lustful.
59.	*Sudden:* violent.
63.	*cistern:* tank, vat.
64.	*continent impediments:* restraining limits.
65.	*will:* desire.
66–67.	*Boundless . . . tyranny:* Boundless intemperance usurps absolute sway over all his other qualities.
69.	*yet:* in spite of all you've said.
71.	*Convey:* manage craftily or secretly.
72.	*time:* the times, the people.
75.	*dedicate:* offer up.
76.	*Finding:* if they find.
77.	*ill-compos'd affection:* character made up of evil elements.
78.	*stanchless:* insatiable.
80.	*his:* this man's.
81.	*more-having:* increase in wealth.
82.	*forge:* devise falsely.
83.	*Quarrels:* charges.
85.	*Sticks deeper:* is less easily uprooted.
86.	*summer-seeming:* befitting only the summertime of life, and therefore not lasting as long as greed.
88.	*foisons:* abundant supplies.

Of your mere own; all these are portable,
With other graces weigh'd.   90

Malcolm But I have none: the king-becoming graces,
As justice, verity, temperance, stableness,
Bounty, perseverance, mercy, lowliness,
Devotion, patience, courage, fortitude,
I have no relish of them, but abound   95
In the division of each several crime,
Acting it many ways. Nay, had I power, I should
Pour the sweet milk of concord into hell,
Uproar the universal peace, confound
All unity on earth.

Macduff   O Scotland, Scotland!   100

Malcolm If such a one be fit to govern, speak:
I am as I have spoken.

Macduff   Fit to govern!
No, not to live. O nation miserable,
With an untitled tyrant bloody-scepter'd,
When shalt thou see thy wholesome days again,   105
Since that the truest issue of thy throne
By his own interdiction stands accurs'd,
And does blaspheme his breed? Thy royal father
Was a most sainted king; the queen that bore thee,
Oft'ner upon her knees than on her feet,   110
Died every day she liv'd. Fare thee well!
These evils thou repeat'st upon thyself
Have banish'd me from Scotland. O my breast,
Thy hope ends here!

Malcolm   Macduff, this noble passion,
Child of integrity, hath from my soul   115
Wip'd the black scruples, reconcil'd my thoughts
To thy good truth and honour. Devilish Macbeth
By many of these trains hath sought to win me
Into his power, and modest wisdom plucks me
From over-credulous haste; but God above   120
Deal between thee and me! for even now
I put myself to thy direction, and
Unspeak mine own detraction, here abjure
The taints and blames I laid upon myself,

89.	*portable:* bearable.
95.	*relish:* trace, taste.
95–96.	*abound . . . crime:* I'm guilty of every possible form of each sin.
99.	*Uproar:* change to tumultuous strife.
104.	*tyrant:* usurper.
107.	*interdiction:* under the ban of the Church; a curse excluding one from the throne.
111.	*Died . . . liv'd:* referring to penances and religious exercises by which the queen renounces the world.
114.	*passion:* strong emotion.
115.	*Child of integrity:* which can proceed only from integrity of character.
118.	*trains:* plots.
119.	*modest wisdom:* wise moderation; prudent caution.
	plucks me: restrains me.
121.	*Deal . . . me:* Be judge between us in the matter.
122.	*to thy direction:* under thy guidance.
123.	*abjure:* deny solemnly, as upon oath.

For strangers to my nature. I am yet   125
Unknown to woman, never was forsworn,
Scarcely have coveted what was mine own;
At no time broke my faith, would not betray
The devil to his fellow, and delight
No less in truth than life; my first false speaking   130
Was this upon myself. What I am truly,
Is thine and my poor country's to command;
Whither indeed, before thy here-approach,
Old Siward, with ten thousand war-like men,
Already at a point, was setting forth.   135
Now we'll together, and the chance of goodness
Be like our warranted quarrel. Why are you silent?

Macduff Such welcome and unwelcome things at once
'Tis hard to reconcile.

[Enter a Doctor]

Malcolm Well; more anon. Comes the king forth,
    I pray you?   140

Doctor Ay, sir; there are a crew of wretched souls
  That stay his cure; their malady convinces
  The great assay of art; but, at his touch,
  Such sanctity hath heaven given his hand,
  They presently amend.

Malcolm   I thank you, doctor.   145

[Exit Doctor]

Macduff What's the disease he means?

Malcolm   'Tis called the evil:
  A most miraculous work in this good king,
  Which often, since my here-remain in England,
  I have seen him do. How he solicits heaven,
  Himself best knows; but strangely-visited people,   150
  All swoln and ulcerous, pitiful to the eye,
  The mere despair of surgery, he cures,
  Hanging a golden stamp about their necks,
  Put on with holy prayers; and 'tis spoken,
  To the succeeding royalty he leaves   155
  The healing benediction. With this strange virtue,
  He hath a heavenly gift of prophecy,

---

125. *For . . . nature:* as being quite foreign to my actual character.

126. *forsworn:* an oath-breaker.

131. *upon:* against.

135. *at a point:* fully prepared.

136–137. *the chance . . . quarrel:* May our chance of success be as good as our cause is just.

142. *stay:* await.

convinces: baffles.

143. *The . . . art:* the utmost efforts of medical science.

146. *the evil:* scrofula or the king's evil, so called because it was thought to be cured by the royal touch.

148. *my here-remain:* my stopover here.

150. *strangely-visited:* afflicted with hideous disease.

152. *mere:* utter.

153. *stamp:* a coin which the king gave to the patient whom he touched.

156. *virtue:* healing power.

And sundry blessings hang about his throne
That speak him full of grace.

[Enter ROSS]

Macduff   See, who comes here?

Malcolm My countryman; but yet I know him not.   160

Macduff My ever-gentle cousin, welcome hither.

Malcolm I know him now. Good God, betimes remove
   The means that makes us strangers!

Ross   Sir, amen.

Macduff Stands Scotland where it did?

Ross   Alas! poor country;
   Almost afraid to know itself. It cannot   165
   Be call'd our mother, but our grave; where nothing,
   But who knows nothing, is once seen to smile;
   Where sighs and groans and shrieks that rent the air
   Are made, not mark'd; where violent sorrow seems
   A modern ecstacy; the dead man's knell   170
   Is there scarce ask'd for who; and good men's lives
   Expire before the flowers in their caps
   Dying or ere they sicken.

Macduff   O! relation
   Too nice, and yet too true!

Malcolm   What's the newest brief?

Ross That of an hour's age doth hiss the speaker;   175
   Each minute teems a new one.

Macduff   How does my wife?

Ross Why, well.

Macduff   And all my children?

Ross   Well too.

Macduff The tyrant has not batter'd at their peace?

Ross No; they were well at peace when I did leave 'em.

159.   *grace:* sanctity, holiness.

162.   *betimes:* speedily.

163.   *The means:* i.e., Macbeth.

165.   *to know itself:* to look its own misfortunes in the face.

167.   *who:* one who.

168.   *rent:* rip or tear apart.

169.   *not mark'd:* ignored because they're so common.

170.   A *modern ecstacy:* a fad.

172.   *flowers:* It was an Elizabethan fashion to wear a flower in the cap.

173.   *or ere:* before, i.e., by violence.

174.   *Too nice:* too minutely accurate.

175.   *That . . . speaker:* Telling dreadful news from an hour ago would get the teller a hissing for bringing stale news.

177.   *well:* intentionally ambiguous; often used in breaking bad news gently. It means not only in good health, but also well off, i.e., in heaven.

Macduff Be not a niggard of your speech: how goes 't?   180

Ross When I came hither to transport the tidings,
Which I have heavily borne, there ran a rumour
Of many worthy fellows that were out;
Which was to my belief witness'd the rather
For that I saw the tyrant's power a-foot.   185
Now is the time of help; your eye in Scotland
Would create soldiers, make our women fight,
To doff their dire distresses.

Malcolm   Be 't their comfort
We are coming thither. Gracious England hath
Lent us good Siward and ten thousand men;   190
An older and a better soldier none
That Christendom gives out.

Ross   Would I could answer
This comfort with the like! But I have words
That would be howl'd out in the desert air,
Where hearing should not latch them.

Macduff   What concern they?   195
The general cause? or is it a fee-grief
Due to some single breast?

Ross   No mind that's honest
But in it shares some woe, though the main part
Pertains to you alone.

Macduff   If it be mine
Keep it not from me; quickly let me have it.   200

Ross Let not your ears despise my tongue for ever,
Which shall possess them with the heaviest sound
That ever yet they heard.

Macduff   Hum! I guess at it.

Ross Your castle is surpris'd; your wife and babes
Savagely slaughter'd; to relate the manner,   205
Were, on the quarry of these murder'd deer,
To add the death of you.

Malcolm   Merciful heaven!
What! man; ne'er pull your hat upon your brows;

182.	*heavily:* sadly.
183.	*out:* in the field, under arms.
185.	*For that:* because.
	power: forces, troops.
	a-foot: in motion, mobilized.
189.	*England:* the King of England.
191.	*none:* there is none.
192.	*gives out:* proclaims.
194.	*would be:* require to be, should be.
195.	*latch:* catch.
196.	*a fee-grief:* one that belongs to him alone.
197.	*honest:* good and honorable.
202.	*heaviest:* saddest.
204.	*surpris'd:* seized, captured.
206.	*quarry:* slaughtered bodies.
208.	*pull . . . brows:* become melancholy and brooding.

Give sorrow words; the grief that does not speak
Whispers the o'er-fraught heart and bids it break. 210

Macduff My children too?

Ross   Wife, children, servants, all
That could be found.

Macduff   And I must be from thence!
My wife kill'd too?

Ross   I have said.

Malcolm   Be comforted:
Let's make us medicine of our great revenge,
To cure this deadly grief. 215

Macduff He has no children. All my pretty ones?
Did you say all? O hell-kite! All?
What! All my pretty chickens and their dam
At one fell swoop?

Malcolm   Dispute it like a man.

Macduff I shall do so; 220
But I must also feel it as a man:
I cannot but remember such things were,
That were most precious to me. Did heaven look on,
And would not take their part? Sinful Macduff!
They were all struck for thee. Naught that I am, 225
Not for their own demerits, but for mine,
Fell slaughter on their souls. Heaven rest them now!

Malcolm Be this the whetstone of your sword: let grief
Convert to anger; blunt not the heart, enrage it.

Macduff O! I could play the woman with mine eyes, 230
And braggart with my tongue. But, gentle heavens,
Cut short all intermission; front to front
Bring thou this fiend of Scotland and myself;
Within my sword's length set him; if he 'scape,
Heaven forgive him too!

Malcolm   This tune goes manly. 235
Come, go we to the king; our power is ready;

210. *Whispers . . . heart:* whispers to the overburdened heart.

212. *And . . . thence!:* spoken in bitter self-reproach.

217. *hell-kite:* hellish bird of prey.

220. *Dispute it:* Resist it; withstand your grief.

225. *Naught:* worthless man.

230. *play . . . eyes:* weep.

231. *braggart . . . tongue:* rant.

232. *intermission:* the time between now and our meeting.

235. *goes manly:* has a manly sound.

Our lack is nothing but our leave. Macbeth
Is ripe for shaking, and the powers above
Put on their instruments. Receive what cheer you may;
The night is long that never finds the day. *[Exeunt]*   240

237. *Our lack . . . leave:* We wait only to take leave of those who will remain here.

239. *Put on their instruments:* encourage or urge forward their weapons, tools, or agents.

COMMENTARY

In addition to being the longest in the play, this scene is the most static. It consists of discussion of past events and future plans. Through this discussion, it lays the foundation for the climactic Act V, where the representatives of good and evil will meet.

This is also the only scene not set in Scotland. Its placement in England helps create a dichotomy between the two countries that will be illustrated more fully as the scene unfolds.

Pay close attention to the increased references to God and Christianity in this scene and throughout the rest of the play. Remember, the play began with the supernatural weird sisters and with Macbeth invoking darkness and evil. In contrast, the characters here invoke goodness and light. Thus, this scene sets up the two sides in opposition religiously as well as politically. Macbeth himself is labeled "black" and "devilish" in this scene (52, 117).

Sidney Lamb logically subdivides this scene into three separate sections: 1) the reconciliation of Malcolm and Macduff; 2) the representation of England and its king, Edward, and 3) a report of recent events in Scotland. The following discussion of the scene will use those divisions.

The reconciliation of Malcolm and Macduff

Though they are on the same "side" against Macbeth, notice the immediate disagreement between Malcolm and Macduff. Malcolm wants to discuss and weep over the past. In contrast to Malcolm's desire for words, Macduff calls for action, asserting that there is no time to waste. Keep this disagreement in mind as the scene closes; consider whether the two men still hold their respective positions at the end of the scene.

For the next 100 or so lines, Malcolm tests Macduff's loyalty. Malcolm is understandably suspicious of anyone from Scotland. Specifically, he fears that Macduff will use him as a tool to win Macbeth's favor.

Duncan's son is concerned about the imperial influence on Macduff. Because the king is considered God's appointed deputy on Earth, any treason (even against a tyrannical king) is a violation of God's will as well as politically unlawful. Notice that Macduff circumvents this by repeatedly noting that Malcolm, not Macbeth, is the rightful king.

Malcolm also echoes his father (I.4.11–14) in his recognition that the face does not always accurately represent the heart. Notice that he adopts a more pessimistic stance and extends it by asserting that all foul things look like grace. The clothing metaphor reappears in Macduff's speech as he speaks of "wear[ing]" wrong (33).

Around line 47, Malcolm starts to test Macduff by pretending to be capable of much worse tyranny than Macbeth. Many scholars and critics are dissatisfied with this interchange and argue that it is out of character for Malcolm and does not make logical sense. It is also quite extensive, consisting of about 70 lines and ending on line 113. This dialogue is taken very closely from Holinshed's *Chronicles* with only minor changes.

Those dissatisfied by this section of the scene seem to be especially bothered by Macduff's unconvincing arguments. Such critics assert that it is not clear why Malcolm's suspicions would be alleviated by Macduff's statements that Scotland has enough willing "dames" and "foisons" (abundant supplies) to satisfy Malcolm's supposed tyranny (73, 88).

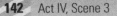

Remember that Malcolm, under the divine right theory of kingship, is the true king. For this reason, whatever tyranny he might inflict would not contradict this because God cannot be wrong. A rightful tyrant would restore the order that a usurping or, in Macduff's terms, an "untitled" tyrant disrupts (104).

Starting in line 114, Malcolm indicates that he is finally convinced of Macduff's loyalty and informs him of the plans to invade Scotland with the help of Old Siward, the Earl of Northumberland and Commander of the English Army. Incidentally, King James was also a descendant of Old Siward, so this plot move deepens the play's tribute to him.

In this speech to Macduff, Malcolm relates his virtues, one of which is his inexperience with women. Chastity was considered a great virtue in men and women.

A representation of England and Edward the Confessor

This section of the scene helps to establish the dichotomy of good versus evil through the contrasting pairs of England versus Scotland and Edward versus Macbeth.

The entrance of the doctor marks the transition to this second section. It is significant that the doctor portrays Edward as a healer. Macbeth, of course, is the exact opposite — a killer.

The tradition of a king's touch being able to heal scrofula, also known as the "king's evil," began with Edward the Confessor (who reigned from 1042 to 1066) and lasted until 1719. Scrofula is an enlargement of the neck glands that is also accompanied by a discharge of pus and scarring. Edward had white hair and an extremely fair complexion, and Lamb even suggests that he may have been an albino. Early Modern audiences may have been aware of his light complexion. Thus, visually, Edward is associated with whiteness, holiness, and purity, and Macbeth, as we have seen, is associated with blackness and unholiness.

Sidney Lamb points out that while Queen Elizabeth I embraced this tradition of healing, James initially perceived it as superstitious and refused to perform it.

Lamb suggests that this mention of the king's touch could be a public recognition of James's willingness to please the desires of his people. Furthermore, there is a symbolic connotation to this portrayal as well, because Edward will literally help cure Scotland of its evil — Macbeth.

Malcolm's description of his time in England and his personal testimony of Edward's healing powers demonstrates the order and peace of England, which stands in contrast to the disorder and mayhem of Scotland. With the help of ordered and peaceful England, Macduff and Malcolm will save their country.

It is significant that these two men are unable to stop Macbeth without the help of the English. James's arrival in England, three years before the composition of *Macbeth*, was accompanied by an anti-Scottish sentiment due to the influx of Scottish nobility into the English court and the different ways in which the affairs of court and state were conducted. It seems unlikely that the portrayal of England as superior to Scotland is coincidental. This portrayal may be part of the implicit criticism of James and kingship that some critics have located in the play.

Recent events in Scotland

The distinction between England and Scotland is brought into sharp view with the arrival of Ross and his account of recent events in Scotland.

Ross's first lines describe Scotland as "poor" and "afraid to know itself" (164–165). Compare the country's lack of self-knowledge to Macbeth's "To know my deed 'twere best not to know myself" (II.2.73) and Ross's "we are traitors / and do not know ourselves" (IV.1.19). What are the implications of fearing to know oneself?

Ross brings the dreadful news of the events at Macduff's castle. Shakespeare draws out the suspense of Act IV, Scene 2 through Ross's reluctance to relate the full events. Though we may initially be consoled by Ross's indication that Macduff's wife is well, his next line claims that Macduff's children are also well. The audience is aware that the latter is not true but cannot be sure of the former.

Ross also equivocates when he tells Macduff that his family was "well at peace when I did leave 'em" (179). This statement is true but misleading. It merely draws out the suspense. Notice that the suspense in the audience is greater than Macduff's, because we know that his son was killed but do not know whether or not the rest of his family escaped. This is a good example of how Shakespeare draws the audience's emotions into the play.

Furthermore, compare Ross's words that equate death with peace to Macbeth's acknowledgment that Duncan can no longer be hurt (III.2.22–26) and Lady Macbeth's assertion that "'Tis safer to be that which we destroy" (III.2.6–7).

This suspense lasts for approximately 30 lines. We finally learn that Macduff's entire household was killed. In Early Modern England, servants were considered part of the family and, therefore, their deaths would have been difficult to hear of as well.

Ross claims that this act was committed as a way of killing Macduff through grief. Imagine how powerful that grief must be and listen for it in the rest of Macduff's lines.

Ross puns on the word "deer" in line 206. Literally, this word refers to the game animal and metaphorically

fits with Ross's use of "quarry." The pun is, of course, on "dear" — all that were "dear" to Macduff were killed.

Once again, grief is associated with being unmanly. Malcolm tells Macduff to "[d]ispute" or resist his grief "like a man" (219). But there seems to be a double meaning in this line; Malcolm could be saying to dispute the murder of his family like a man — that is, by helping to conquer Macbeth.

Macduff's response is interesting in that he acknowledges the need to grieve; he says that he "must also feel it as a man" (221). A few lines later, however, he equates tears with being womanly by saying one of his options is to become a woman with his eyes. The other option is to destroy Macbeth.

Macduff chooses to seek revenge, which Malcolm describes as a "manly" tune (235). This implies that grief is best felt through violence in this definition of masculinity. The need for violence and the inability to cry may be an implicit criticism of that masculinity.

The lengthy discussion of this scene draws to a close with the call to action that will consume the fifth act.

Notes

Notes

Notes

CLIFFSCOMPLETE

MACBETH
ACT V

Macbeth *Out, out, brief candle!*
Life's but a walking shadow, a poor player
That struts and frets his hour upon the stage,
And then is heard no more; it is a tale
Told by an idiot, full of sound and fury,
Signifying nothing.

Act V, Scene 1

A doctor and a gentlewoman witness Lady Macbeth sleepwalking. The gentlewoman indicates that Lady Macbeth sometimes composes a letter in her sleep. On this night, however, she rubs her hands together in an effort to "wash" a spot of blood off. Although the doctor and the gentlewoman realize that her conscience is burdened, they don't understand that it stems from her complicity in Duncan's murder. After Lady Macbeth returns to bed, the doctor commands that precautions be taken to prevent Lady Macbeth from committing suicide.

ACT V, SCENE 1
Dunsinane. A room in the castle.

[Enter a Doctor of Physic and a Waiting-Gentlewoman]

Doctor I have two nights watched with you, but can
perceive no truth in your report. When was it she last
walked?

Gentlewoman Since his majesty went into the field,
I have seen her rise from her bed, throw her night
gown upon her, unlock her closet, take forth paper,　　　　5
fold it, write upon 't, read it, afterwards seal it,
and again return to bed; yet all this while in a most fast
sleep.

Doctor A great perturbation in nature, to receive at
once the benefit of sleep and do the effects of watch-
ing! In this slumbery agitation, besides her walking　　　　10
and other actual performances, what, at any time,
have you heard her say?

Gentlewoman That, sir, which I will not report after her.

Doctor You may to me, and 'tis most meet you should.

Gentlewoman Neither to you nor any one, having
no witness to confirm my speech.　　　　15
[Enter LADY MACBETH, with a taper]
Lo you! here she comes. This is her very guise; and,
upon my life, fast asleep. Observe her; stand close.

NOTES

s.d.:　*a Waiting-Gentlewoman:* a lady of the nobility, companion to the queen (not a servant).

3.　*went into the field:* took arms (see IV.3.185).

10.　*slumbery agitation:* sleepy activity. The doctor's speech is rather wordy, perhaps because of his professional manner.

14.　*meet:* suitable.

15.　*no witness:* These are dangerous times, and the gentlewoman's words may, in the hands of an informer, bring a charge of treason against her.

16.　*guise:* manner.

17.　*stand close:* keep out of sight; hide.

Doctor How came she by that light?

Gentlewoman Why, it stood by her: she has light by
   her continually; 'tis her command.   20

Doctor You see, her eyes are open.

Gentlewoman Ay, but their sense is shut.

Doctor What is it she does now? Look, how she
   rubs her hands.

Gentlewoman It is an accustomed action with her,
   to seem thus washing her hands. I have known her   25
   to continue in this a quarter of an hour.

Lady Macbeth Yet here's a spot.

Doctor Hark! she speaks. I will set down what
   comes from her, to satisfy my remembrance the more
   strongly.

Lady Macbeth Out, damned spot! out, I say! One;   30
   two: why, then 'tis time to do 't. Hell is murky! Fie,
   my Lord, fie! a soldier, and afeard? What need we
   fear who knows it, when none can call our power to
   account? Yet who would have thought the old man
   to have had so much blood in him?   35

Doctor Do you mark that?

Lady Macbeth The Thane of Fife had a wife: where
   is she now? What! will these hands ne'er be clean? No
   more o' that, my Lord, no more o' that: you mar all
   with this starting.

Doctor Go to, go to; you have known what you
   should not.   40

Gentlewoman She has spoke what she should not, I
   am sure of that: Heaven knows what she has known.

Lady Macbeth Here's the smell of the blood still:
   all the perfumes of Arabia will not sweeten this little
   hand. Oh! oh! oh!

Doctor What a sigh is there! The heart is sorely
   charged.   45

27.   *spot:* i.e., of blood on her hand.

28.   *set down:* i.e., in a notebook.

30-31.   *One; two . . . do 't:* a reference to the hour of Duncan's murder, or perhaps the ringing of the signal bell (II.1).

36.   *mark:* notice. This is an exclamation as much as it is a question.

37.   *Thane of Fife:* Macduff.

39.   *my Lord:* Macbeth.
      mar all: spoil everything.

40.   *Go to:* an exclamation indicating shocked amazement.

Gentlewoman I would not have such a heart in my
  bosom for the dignity of the whole body.

Doctor Well, well, well.

Gentlewoman Pray God it be, sir.

Doctor This disease is beyond my practice: yet I   50
  have known those which have walked in their sleep
  who have died holily in their beds.

Lady Macbeth Wash your hands, put on your night-
  gown; look not so pale. I tell you yet again, Banquo's
  buried; he cannot come out on 's grave.   55

Doctor Even so?

Lady Macbeth To bed, to bed: there's knocking at
  the gate. Come, come, come, come, give me your hand.
  What's done cannot be undone. To bed, to bed, to bed.

[Exit]

Doctor Will she go now to bed?   60

Gentlewoman Directly.

Doctor Foul whisperings are abroad. Unnatural deeds
  Do breed unnatural troubles; infected minds
  To their deaf pillows will discharge their secrets;
  More needs she the divine than the physician.   65
  God, God forgive us all! Look after her;
  Remove from her the means of all annoyance,
  And still keep eyes upon her. So, good-night:
  My mind she has mated, and amaz'd sight.
  I think, but dare not speak.   70

Gentlewoman Good-night, good Doctor. *[Exeunt]*

55. *on 's:* of his.

56. *Even so?:* The doctor has heard what amounts to a
confession from Lady Macbeth.

67. *means of all annoyance.* anything she may use to
injure herself.

69. *mated:* baffled, overcome (as when checkmated in
chess).

COMMENTARY

This famous scene depicting Lady Macbeth sleep-walking is original to Shakespeare. It marks a significant change from Holinshed's portrayal of Macbeth's wife.

The doctor's comments at the opening of the scene alert us that this sleepwalking is a recent occurrence. The doctor indicates that this is the third night he has kept watch, at the gentlewoman's request, to witness Lady Macbeth's odd behavior.

The gentlewoman's response not only informs the audience that Macbeth has left to do battle with the English forces but also reconnects Lady Macbeth with writing and, specifically, letters. Recall that when Shakespeare introduced Lady Macbeth in Act I, Scene 5, she was reading a letter from Macbeth. She also uses diction connected to reading and writing in many of her lines.

Because literacy rates were low in Early Modern England, lower in medieval Scotland, and even lower for women during both periods, Shakespeare seems to be stressing Lady Macbeth's learning. How does perceiving Lady Macbeth as literate change our perception of her? Also, consider how this sleepwalking scene changes our perception of her.

Lady Macbeth's transformation

The first sense that a major change has occurred in Lady Macbeth comes when the gentlewoman informs the doctor that Lady Macbeth requires light at all times. Contrast this to her earlier lines, "Come, thick night, / And pall thee in the dunnest smoke of hell, / That my keen knife see not the wound it makes" (I.5.48–50). Earlier, she requested darkness. Now she demands light.

The theme of sleep returns in this scene. Recall that in Act II, Scene 2, Macbeth told his wife of the voices that claimed he would no longer be able to sleep because he had murdered sleep. Lady Macbeth can sleep, but not peacefully; she is haunted by dreams of the evil deeds she and Macbeth have committed.

Lady Macbeth *by Henry Fuseli, 1784.*
Musee de Louvre, Paris/Lauros-Giraudon, Paris/SuperStock

Lady Macbeth dreams that there is a spot of blood on her hands that she is unable to clean. She seems to have reversed roles with her husband. In Act II, Scene 2, immediately after the king's murder, Macbeth believed that he would never be able to wash the blood from his hands. At that time, Lady Macbeth asserted that a "little water" could wash away the blood as well as the guilt. Now, while Macbeth seems to have rid himself of all remorse for his actions, Lady Macbeth realizes that "all the perfumes of Arabia" could not cover the scent of blood on her hands (44).

"What's done is done"

Lady Macbeth's lines recount many of the deeds she and her husband have committed; she seems haunted by memories of Duncan, Banquo, and Macduff's wife. In line 59, she states that "What's done cannot be undone." Compared to her line in Act III, Scene 2 — "What's done is done" — her words here indicate what a complete change has occurred in her conscience. Notice how closely these two lines mirror each other but how significant the slight change in wording is to the meaning of each. Shakespeare often plays upon the subtleties of language to demonstrate how easily meaning can change.

The doctor rightly connects Lady Macbeth's inner turmoil to her actions. He describes both the turmoil and the deeds as "[u]nnatural" (62). This parallels Lady Macbeth's request in Act I, Scene 5 for spirits to make her unnatural by "unsexing" her, or removing her feminine qualities.

The doctor also fears that Lady Macbeth may try to commit suicide, and he orders that "the means of all annoyance" — anything she might use to hurt herself — be removed from her possession (67). His words foreshadow her death.

The doctor and the gentlewoman make frequent references to God and heaven in this scene. But we realize that Lady Macbeth, like her husband, has forsaken God and cannot seek divine aid for her troubled mind. While Macbeth moves from inner turmoil to remorseless determination during the course of the play, Lady Macbeth moves in the opposite direction, which will soon prove fatal.

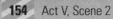

Act V, Scene 2

A group of Scottish thanes enter on their way to Birnam Wood to unite with Malcolm and the English forces. They also indicate that although Macbeth's army still obeys him, it no longer feels loyalty toward the King.

ACT V, SCENE 2
The country near Dunsinane.

[Enter, with drum and colours, MENTEITH, CAITHNESS, ANGUS, LENNOX, and Soldiers]

Menteith The English power is near, led on by Malcolm,
His uncle Siward, and the good Macduff.
Revenges burn in them; for their dear causes
Would to the bleeding and the grim alarm
Excite the mortified man.

Angus   Near Birnam wood   5
Shall we well meet them; that way are they coming.

Caithness Who knows if Donalbain be with his brother?

Lennox For certain, sir, he is not: I have a file
Of all the gentry: there is Siward's son,
And many unrough youths that even now   10
Protest their first of manhood.

Menteith   What does the tyrant?

Caithness Great Dunsinane he strongly fortifies.
Some say he's mad; others that lesser hate him
Do call it valiant fury; but, for certain,
He cannot buckle his distemper'd cause   15
Within the belt of rule.

Angus   Now does he feel
His secret murders sticking on his hands;
Now minutely revolts upbraid his faith-breach;
Those he commands move only in command,
Nothing in love; now does he feel his title   20
Hang loose about him, like a giant's robe
Upon a dwarfish thief.

NOTES

2.   *uncle:* Malcolm's mother was Siward's sister.

3.   *dear:* intense and personal.

4.   *the bleeding . . . alarm:* war.

4–5.   *Would . . . man:* would stir up even a man who had given up worldly action.

11.   *Protest . . . manhood:* show their manhood for the first time.

15–16: *buckle . . . rule:* bring order into his deranged affairs.

17.   *sticking on his hands:* i.e., as blood might.

18.   *minutely:* by the minute, every moment.

Menteith   Who then shall blame
His pester'd senses to recoil and start,
When all that is within him does condemn
Itself for being there?

Caithness   Well, march we on,   25
To give obedience where 'tis truly ow'd;
Meet we the medicine of the sickly weal,
And with him pour we in our country's purge
Each drop of us.

Lennox   Or so much as it needs
To dew the sovereign flower and drown the weeds.   30
Make we our march towards Birnam.

[Exeunt, marching]

COMMENTARY

This short scene begins a segment of six scenes that are all related to the final battle. Here, a number of Scottish noblemen discuss Macbeth (absent from the play since Act IV, Scene 1) and his actions.

Pay particular attention to the references to man and manhood that implicitly place the violence of this battle in the realm of the masculine.

Lennox's reference to Old Siward's son and the "first of manhood," those men who are proving their masculinity in battle for the first time, foreshadows Macbeth's deadly encounter with Young Siward in the last scene (11).

The reference to Birnam Wood in line 5 should raise a signal. Recall that this is the forest that has to move to Dunsinane hill (on top of which stands Dunsinane castle where Macbeth is fortified) in order for Macbeth to be vanquished. Keep in mind that Malcolm and his army know nothing about the witches or the prophecy.

Angus's description of Macbeth defines a significant contrast between this new king and King Duncan. Macbeth's troops follow him because he commands them to; they do not follow him out of love. Recall the love and devotion that Duncan gave and received in the opening scenes of the play.

Notice the reference to robes and clothing again in lines 21 and 22. Angus says that Macbeth now "feel[s] his title / Hang loose about him, like a giant's robe / Upon a dwarfish thief." Macbeth's new title does not fit his character.

Interestingly, there is a note of sympathy in the voices of many of these noblemen for Macbeth's torment and, in particular, his descent into madness. It is important not to lose sight of the fact that despite Macbeth's tyranny, these thanes all seemed to be close friends at the beginning of play.

Act V, Scene 3

Waiting for the battle to begin, Macbeth oscillates between being overly aggressive and confident and being melancholic. Although he provides a glimpse into his inner turmoil by saying that he is "sick at heart," his presentation is balanced by premature calls for his armor and his false confidence in the second group of prophecies.

ACT V, SCENE 3
Dunsinane. A room in the castle.

[Enter MACBETH, Doctor, and Attendants]

Macbeth Bring me no more reports; let them fly all:
  Till Birnam wood remove to Dunsinane
  I cannot taint with fear. What's the boy Malcolm?
  Was he not born of woman? The spirits that know
  All mortal consequences have pronounc'd me thus: 5
  'Fear not, Macbeth; no man that's born of woman
  Shall e'er have power upon thee.' Then fly, false thanes,
  And mingle with the English epicures:
  The mind I sway by and the heart I bear
  Shall never sag with doubt nor shake with fear.   10
  [Enter a Servant]
  The devil damn thee black, thou cream-fac'd loon!
  Where gott'st thou that goose look?

Servant There is ten thousand —

Macbeth   Geese, villain?

Servant   Soldiers, sir.

Macbeth Go, prick thy face, and over-red thy fear,
  Thou lily-liver'd boy. What soldiers, patch?   15
  Death of thy soul! those linen checks of thine
  Are counsellors to fear. What soldiers, whey-face?

Servant The English force, so please you.

Macbeth   Take thy face hence. *[Exit Servant]*
  Seyton! — I am sick at heart
  When I behold — Seyton, I say! — This push   20
  Will cheer me ever or disseat me now.

NOTES

1. *them:* the thanes.

5. *mortal consequences:* the course of human events.

8. *epicures:* lovers of luxury, hence soft men. (From Epicurus, a Greek philosopher who believed that happiness was the goal of life.) The English court was more civilized, cosmopolitan, and luxurious than the Scottish; therefore, the English could be regarded contemptuously as playboys.

9. *sway:* control the state. Ironical in this context.

11. *loon (or lown):* a base and silly person.

15. *patch:* fool.

17. *Are counsellors to fear:* excite fear.

   whey: the watery part of milk.

19. *Seyton:* This family was traditional armor-bearers to the Scottish kings.

   I am sick at heart: It seems most dramatic that these saner and lower-keyed remarks are addressed to the doctor.

I have liv'd long enough: my way of life
Is fall'n into the sear, the yellow leaf;
And that which should accompany old age,
As honour, love, obedience, troops of friends,   25
I must not look to have; but, in their stead,
Curses, not loud but deep, mouth-honour, breath,
Which the poor heart would fain deny, and dare not.
Seyton!

[Enter SEYTON]

Seyton What is your gracious pleasure?

Macbeth   What news more?   30

Seyton All is confirm'd, my Lord, which was reported.

Macbeth I'll fight till from my bones my flesh be hack'd.
Give me my armour.

Seyton   'Tis not needed yet.

Macbeth I'll put it on.
Send out more horses, skirr the country round;   35
Hang those that talk of fear. Give me mine armour.
How does your patient, doctor?

Doctor   Not so sick, my lord,
As she is troubled with thick-coming fancies,
That keep her from her rest.

Macbeth   Cure her of that:
Canst thou not minister to a mind diseas'd,   40
Pluck from the memory a rooted sorrow,
Raze out the written troubles of the brain,
And with some sweet oblivious antidote
Cleanse the stuff'd bosom of that perilous stuff
Which weighs upon the heart?

Doctor   Therein the patient   45
Must minister to himself.

Macbeth Throw physic to the dogs; I'll none of it.
Come, put mine armour on; give me my staff.
Seyton, send out. — Doctor, the thanes fly from me. —
Come sir dispatch. —If thou could'st doctor cast   50
The water of my land, find her disease,

23. *sear:* dry, withered.

25. *As:* such as.

28. *fain:* like to.

35. *skirr:* scour, ride rapidly.

37. *Not so sick:* not so much afflicted with any bodily ailment.

38. *thick-coming fancies:* many hallucinations.

39. *Cure . . . that:* That is the very thing of which I want you to cure her

42. *Raze:* take out, erase.

    written . . . brain: troubles written on the brain, remembered.

43. *oblivious:* causing utter forgetfulness.

47. *I'll none of it:* I'll have nothing to do with it.

48. *staff:* baton (suggesting rank).

And purge it to a sound and pristine health,
I would applaud thee to the very echo,
That should applaud again. — Pull't off, I say. —
What rhubarb, senna, or what purgative drug 55
Would scour these English hence? Hear'st thou of them?

Doctor Ay, my good Lord; your royal preparation
Makes us hear something.

Macbeth   Bring it after me.
I will not be afraid of death and bane
Till Birnam forest come to Dunsinane. 60

Doctor *[Aside]* Were I from Dunsinane away and clear,
Profit again should hardly draw me here. *[Exeunt]*

50.   *dispatch:* make haste.

50–51.   *cast . . . water:* diagnose; a medical figure from urine analysis.

52.   *pristine:* such as was enjoyed in former times.

54.   *Pull't . . . say:* some part of his armor.

56.   *scour:* clear away.

58.   *Bring it after me:* the piece of armor.

59.   *bane:* destruction, ruin.

59–62.   The two rhyming couplets are significant. Each marks an exit: the first, Macbeth; the second, the Doctor.

COMMENTARY

This scene marks Macbeth's reemergence onstage and provides the audience with a glimpse of his state of mind. The audience views a pitiful picture of the once admirable and once tyrannical Macbeth. As Sidney Lamb notes, the presence of the doctor with Macbeth implies his mental illness.

Notice that in accordance with Hecate's wishes, Macbeth suffers from overconfidence as a result of the prophecies. It is apparent, however, that he is torn between this overconfidence and the knowledge that the English army is approaching.

In contrast to his wife, Macbeth now cannot stand anything light or white. He yells at the servant who is, of course, white with fear, wishing that the devil would blacken him.

After the servant departs, Macbeth's behavior changes. Rather than being overly aggressive and confident, he becomes more melancholic. He admits that he is "sick at heart" (19).

Macbeth now realizes that the disjunction between a man's face and his heart that he previously used to his advantage is being used against him. Like Angus's remarks in the previous scene, Macbeth knows that he commands no "honour, love, [or] obedience" and that he is hated instead (25). This realization makes it difficult to hate Macbeth. Shakespeare evokes pity for the fallen man.

Throughout the rest of the scene, Macbeth oscillates between being overly aggressive and confident and being melancholic.

Macbeth's premature calls for his armor indicate his need for action; being static seems only to make him more melancholy. While on one hand Macbeth seems to believe that he cannot be harmed, he also hints that he may actually be looking for death. His frequent declarations that he has nothing to fear begin to ring hollow, especially in light of his sentiment that he has "liv'd long enough" (22).

Here, Macbeth himself makes the connection between Lady Macbeth and writing, describing her insanity as "written troubles" (42). He questions the doctor in lines 40 through 45 about the possibility of curing Lady Macbeth's ills. But the questions he asks apply equally to Macbeth himself.

Notice that in the doctor's response, he does not specify which of the Macbeths he means but does indicate that the patient must treat "himself" (46). Macbeth responds angrily to this answer, repudiating medicine entirely. He realizes that at this point nothing can save him from his guilt.

Macbeth's inquiry to the doctor about whether or not he can cure Scotland and "return it to sound and pristine health" rings ironic, because Macbeth himself is the cause of the destruction of his country (52). This line, however, also creates a bit of sympathy for Macbeth; for the first time, he seems to display a love for his country and a sense of regret for its struggles.

The final lines of the scene illustrate how truly alone and abandoned Macbeth is, because even his doctor indicates a desire to be away from the mad tyrant.

One of the implications of Macbeth's loneliness may be that we understand the important role noblemen play in the happiness of a king. Clearly, Macbeth's ambition to be king has been filled. But, unlike Duncan, Macbeth has no followers. The throne brought Macbeth power and control, but it did not bring him happiness and fulfillment. Wearing the crown merely spurred his descent into tyranny and evil.

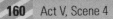

Act V, Scene 4

The Scottish thanes unite with Malcolm and the English forces at Birnam Wood. Malcolm reveals his plan to use tree branches to disguise the approach of the army to Dunsinane Castle. With a large army, this strategy will create the illusion that the woods are moving.

ACT V, SCENE 4
Country near Birnam Wood.

[Enter, with drum and colours, MALCOLM, Old SIWARD and his Son, MACDUFF, MENTEITH, CAITHNESS, ANGUS, LENNOX, ROSS, and Soldiers marching]

Malcolm Cousins, I hope the days are near at hand
That chambers will be safe.

Menteith   We doubt it nothing.

Siward What wood is this before us?

Menteith   The wood of Birnam.

Malcolm Let every soldier hew him down a bough
And bear 't before him: thereby shall we shadow   5
The numbers of our host, and make discovery
Err in report of us.

Soldiers   It shall be done.

Siward We learn no other but the confident tyrant
Keeps still in Dunsinane, and will endure
Our setting down before 't.

Malcolm   'Tis his main hope;   10
For where there is advantage to be given,
Both more and less have given him the revolt,
And none serve with him but constrained things
Whose hearts are absent too.

Macduff   Let our just censures
Attend the true event, and put we on   15
Industrious soldiership.

Siward   The time approaches
That will with due decision make us know

What we shall say we have and what we owe.
Thoughts speculative, their unsure hopes relate,
But certain issue strokes must arbitrate,   20
Towards which advance the war.

[*Exeunt, marching*]

19–20. *Thoughts . . . arbitrate:* Calculations state our reasonable but unsure hopes; only battle will produce results.

21. *Towards which:* towards the result of the battle.

COMMENTARY

In this scene, the Scottish nobles unite forces with Malcolm and the English army. The presence of these nobles dramatically depicts Macbeth's solitude. They also create a spectacular scene on stage, showing the military might of these forces. The "drums" and "colours" referred to in the stage directions provide us with a glimpse of the visual and auditory power of this scene.

The theme of sleep reappears with Malcolm's hope that their chambers or bedrooms will be safe after Macbeth is defeated. In addition to serving as a reminder of the manner in which his father died, this line also refers to

The woods descend on Dunsinane.

the sleeplessness that has gripped Scotland (III.5.34).

The audience discovers how the first prophecy will come true: Malcolm's forces will use tree branches to disguise their numbers as they approach the castle. (Ironically, as we learned in the previous scene, Macbeth already knows their numbers.) This pragmatic use of camouflage stands in stark contrast to the supernatural elements in the play. Here, the audience can also see the equivocation in the witches' prophecies. The woods will not actually move, but then again, they will.

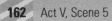
Act V, Scene 5

Preparing for war, Macbeth learns of his wife's death and exhibits little grief. A messenger informs Macbeth of the "approach" of Birnam Wood. Questioning his invulnerability, Macbeth decides that if he is to die, he wants to die in battle.

ACT V, SCENE 5
Dunsinane. Within the castle.

[Enter, with a drum and colours, MACBETH, SEYTON, and Soldiers]

Macbeth Hang out our banners on the outward walls;
The cry is still, 'They come;' our castle's strength
Will laugh a siege to scorn; here let them lie
Till famine and the ague eat them up;
Were they not forc'd with those that should be ours,   5
We might have met them dareful, beard to beard,
And beat them backward home.
[A cry of women within]
                                      What is that noise?

Seyton It is the cry of women, my good lord. *[Exit]*

Macbeth I have almost forgot the taste of fears.
The time has been my senses would have cool'd   10
To hear a night-shriek, and my fell of hair
Would at a dismal treatise rouse and stir
As life were in 't. I have supp'd full with horrors;
Direness, familiar to my slaughterous thoughts,
Cannot once start me.
[Re-enter SEYTON]
                          Wherefore was that cry?   15

Seyton The queen, my Lord, is dead.

Macbeth She should have died hereafter;
There would have been a time for such a word.
To-morrow, and to-morrow, and to-morrow,
Creeps in this petty pace from day to day,   20
To the last syllable of recorded time;
And all our yesterdays have lighted fools
The way to dusty death. Out, out, brief candle!

NOTES

1. *outward walls:* The castle had various walls and fortifications that had to be taken one after the other.

2. *still:* always.

3. *lie:* lie encamped.

4. *ague:* fever.

5. *forc'd:* strengthened, reinforced.

6. *met them:* in the field.

   dareful: boldly.

8. *It . . . women:* Seyton hurries out to learn the reason for the women's shrieks.

9. *forgot the taste of fears:* forgotten what dreadful things are like.

10. *cool'd:* felt the chill of terror.

11. *fell:* scalp, skin.

12. *treatise:* story.

14. *Direness:* horror.

17. *should:* means she inevitably or certainly would have.

18. *such a word:* meaning "death."

21. *recorded time:* time as measured in human history.

Life's but a walking shadow, a poor player
That struts and frets his hour upon the stage,   25
And then is heard no more; it is a tale
Told by an idiot, full of sound and fury,
Signifying nothing.
[Enter a Messenger]
Thou com'st to use thy tongue; thy story quickly.

Messenger Gracious my Lord,   30
I should report that which I say I saw,
But know not how to do it.

Macbeth   Well, say, sir.

Messenger As I did stand my watch upon the hill,
I look'd towards Birnam, and anon, methought,
The wood began to move.

Macbeth   Liar and slave!   35

Messenger Let me endure your wrath if 't be not so;
Within this three mile you may see it coming;
I say, a moving grove.

Macbeth   If thou speak'st false,
Upon the next tree shalt thou hang alive,
Till famine cling thee; if thy speech be sooth,   40
I care not if thou dost for me as much.
I pull in resolution and begin
To doubt the equivocation of the fiend
That lies like truth; 'Fear not, till Birnam wood
Do come to Dunsinane;' and now a wood   45
Comes toward Dunsinane Arm, arm, and out!
If this which he avouches does appear,
There is nor flying hence, nor tarrying here.
I 'gin to be aweary of the sun,
And wish the estate o' the world were now undone.   50
Ring the alarum-bell! Blow, wind! come, wrack!
At least we'll die with harness on our back.

[Exeunt]

23.	*brief candle:* life is compared to a candle flame.
28.	*Signifying nothing:* lacking sense or meaning.
30.	*Gracious my lord:* my gracious lord.
33.	*As I did stand my watch:* while I was on duty.
37.	*mile:* an old form of the plural, meaning "miles."
38.	*I say:* The messenger is courageous: he repeats the terrible message to Macbeth's face.
40.	*Till famine cling thee:* Until you waste away and your skin sticks to your bones.
	sooth: truth.
42.	*pull in:* restrain
43.	*To . . . fiend:* to suspect Satan of ambiguous prophecies.
47.	*avouches:* vouches for, says is true.
	appear: i.e., to our sight.
49.	*gin:* begin.
50.	*estate:* settled order
	undone: returned to chaos.
51.	*wrack:* destruction, wreck, ruin.
52.	*harness:* armor.

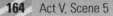
COMMENTARY

Paralleling the last scene, this scene begins with drums and colors in its representation of Macbeth's forces. Notice that Macbeth is the only person of nobility in his procession. The only other named character is one of his officers, Seyton.

The final segment of Act V consists of short scenes with rapid shifts in perspective, moving from one side of the battle to the other. This strategy is typical of Shakespeare's battle scenes and serves to increase the drama of the last scenes as the play pulls closer and closer to the actual battle.

Preparing for a siege

Rather than meet Malcolm's army on the battlefield, Macbeth, whose army has been significantly reduced by deserters, has to resort to forcing his enemies to siege the castle. A siege could occur in two ways: First, the army could try to scale the walls of the castle or force its way through the gates while the army inside could attack from above. This tactic was very costly to the attacking army. The other possibility was to surround the castle and not allow food or water to enter. Depending on the provisions of the castle, this was a slow but effective method. Macbeth's resolve to stay put and let Malcolm attack the castle seems to contradict his earlier urgency to don his armor and begin the battle.

Macbeth claims that a siege would be unsuccessful because his castle is too strong to attack and he has enough provisions to last until the "famine" and "ague" (or fever) consume the opposing army (4).

Lady Macbeth's demise

Macbeth and Seyton hear a woman's cry, and Macbeth's response reveals his deadening emotion — quite a departure from when he was originally consumed by the horror of his deeds. Now he has "almost forgot the taste of fears" (9).

Seyton leaves to investigate the source of the cry and returns to report the queen's death. Macbeth's response to the news about his wife contains one of his most famous passages, in which we can see his desire for death reaching its peak. Modern scholars are particularly interested in these lines because he metaphorically expresses his pessimism about life in terms of the theatre. This metaphor linking theatre to life is not unique to *Macbeth*; compare this speech to the lines "All the world's a stage, / And all the men and women merely players," which appear in *As You Like It* (II.7.138–139).

Upon learning that the woods are moving toward the hill, Macbeth seems to realize that the weird sisters have duped him. Doubting their "equivocation," he now understands that the "fiend" (most likely a reference to Hecate or the devil) "lies like truth" (43–44).

Despite beginning the scene content to let Malcolm and his forces lay siege to his castle, Macbeth's desire for death prompts his attack. He still seems to be concerned with his masculinity, indicating that it would be best to die in armor.

Act V, Scene 6

Nearing Dunsinane, Malcolm orders his army to discard their branches, and Macduff calls for attack.

ACT V, SCENE 6
The same. A plain before the castle.

[Enter, with drum and colours, MALCOLM, Old SIWARD, MACDUFF, etc., and their Army, with boughs]

Malcolm Now near enough; your leavy screens throw down,
And show like those you are. You, worthy uncle,
Shall, with my cousin, your right-noble son,
Lead our first battle; worthy Macduff and we
Shall take upon 's what else remains to do,   5
According to our order.

Siward   Fare you well.
Do we but find the tyrant's power to-night,
Let us be beaten, if we cannot fight.

Macduff Make all our trumpets speak; give them all breath,
Those clamorous harbingers of blood and death.   10

[Exeunt]

NOTES

1.   *leavy:* leafy.

2.   *show:* appear.
     worthy: noble.

4.   *battle:* division.
     we: Malcolm here assumes the royal plural (of the throne) for the first time.

5.   *what:* whatever.

6.   *our order:* the plans already made.

7.   *Do we:* if we do.
     power: forces.

10. *harbingers:* messengers.

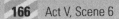

COMMENTARY

Continuing the scene shifts between alternating perspectives, this scene is visually, more than textually, rich and marks the beginning of the actual battle between Macbeth and his enemies.

The theme of disguise appears in Malcolm's order for the army to discard its "screens" and "show like those you are" (1–2). In contrast to the many previous references to characters disguising their inner nature, appearances match reality here — the soldiers show their true selves when facing Macbeth's troops.

Macduff's lines at the end of this scene dramatically represent his grief transformed into anger, recalling Malcolm's advice to Macduff in Act IV, Scene 3.

A scene from the 1971 film version of Macbeth, *directed by Roman Polanski.*
Everett Collection

Act V, Scene 7

Not content to sit safely behind the castle walls, Macbeth engages the enemy on the plain, slaying Young Siward, son of Siward, the Commander of the English Army. Macduff passes over the stage in search of Macbeth. Siward and Malcolm enter. Siward informs Malcolm that Macbeth's army has surrendered the castle.

ACT V, SCENE 7
The same. Another part of the plain.

[Alarums. Enter MACBETH]

Macbeth They have tied me to a stake; I cannot fly,
But bear-like I must fight the course. What's he
That was not born of woman? Such a one
Am I to fear, or none.

[Enter YOUNG SIWARD]

Young Siward What is thy name?

Macbeth   Thou'lt be afraid to hear it. 5

Young Siward No; though thou call'st thyself a
hotter name
Than any is in hell.

Macbeth   My name's Macbeth.

Young Siward The devil himself could not
pronounce a title
More hateful to mine ear.

Macbeth   No, nor more fearful.

Young Siward Thou liest, abhorred tyrant; with
my sword   10
I'll prove the lie thou speak'st.

[They fight and YOUNG SIWARD is slain]

Macbeth   Thou wast born of woman:
But swords I smile at, weapons laugh to scorn,
Brandish'd by man that's of a woman born. *[Exit]*

[Alarums. Enter MACDUFF]

NOTES

1.   *They . . . stake:* a figure from bear-baiting. A bear was tied to a stake and attacked by dogs.

2.   *course:* bout.

Macduff That way the noise is. Tyrant, show thy face:
If thou be'st slain and with no stroke of mine,   15
My wife and children's ghosts will haunt me still.
I cannot strike at wretched kerns, whose arms
Are hir'd to bear their staves: either thou, Macbeth,
Or else my sword with an unbatter'd edge
I sheathe again undeeded. There thou should'st be;   20
By this great clatter, one of greatest note
Seems bruited. Let me find him, fortune!
And more I beg not. *[Exit. Alarums]*

[Enter MALCOLM and OLD SIWARD]

Siward This way, my lord; the castle's gently render'd:
The tyrant's people on both sides do fight;   25
The noble thanes do bravely in the war;
The day almost itself professes yours,
And little is to do.

Malcolm   We have met with foes
That strike beside us.

Siward Enter, sir, the castle. *[Exeunt. Alarums]*

16.   *still:* ever, forever.

17.   *kerns:* lightly armed soldiers.

18.   *staves:* spears, lances.

20.   *undeeded:* unused.

    should'st be: ought to be, to judge by the noise.

21.   *one:* someone.

    note: rank.

22.   *bruited:* reported, proclaimed.

24.   *gently render'd:* surrendered without resistance.

26.   *bravely:* finely, splendidly.

27.   *itself professes yours:* calls itself yours.

29.   *beside us:* so as to miss us.

COMMENTARY

This scene marks the actual start of the battle onstage. Here, Macbeth displays a fierce determination to fight.

In the opening lines, Macbeth refers to bear-baiting, which was a popular sport in Early Modern England. In bear-baiting, dogs attacked a bear that was staked in the middle of an arena. The contest ended with either the bear's death or the death of the dogs. There was a bear-baiting pit extremely close to the Globe theatre (the theatre in which this play originally would have been staged).

Previously, the perspective of each short scene in Act V shifted between one army and another. Here, the perspectives rapidly shift within the scene. Because Shakespeare did not designate scene divisions in this text (such divisions were a development of the Folio), some editors break each shift into a different scene.

In the opening moments of the scene, Macbeth encounters and fights Young Siward. Macbeth wins, of course, because Young Siward was born of a woman. In addition to depicting the death of one of the promising youths participating in the battle (see the commentary for Act V, Scene 2), this struggle increases the suspense in the audience. Because Birnam wood has, in a way, come to Dunsinane, the audience suspects that somehow, there may be a man not born of a woman who will defeat Macbeth. But we do not know yet how that is possible.

The scene's perspective next switches to Macduff, who is looking only for Macbeth. The discussion between Old Siward and Malcolm reveals that Macbeth's army is not resisting Malcolm's forces, thus increasing Macbeth's isolation even further. Even those soldiers who did not desert Macbeth's army purposely

Robin Bailey and Alan Howard in a 1993 National Theatre production. Fritz Curzon/PAL.

miss their targets. Malcolm relates this when he says, "We have met with foes / That strike beside us" (28–29). And the strong castle — the one supposedly able to withstand any siege — has already been surrendered.

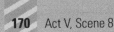

Act V, Scene 8

Macbeth and Macduff finally meet, and Macbeth learns that Macduff was surgically removed from his mother's womb and thus was not born of a woman. Although Macbeth initially refuses to fight, Macduff's plans to make a spectacle of the tyrannical king prompts him to action, and they fight their way off the stage. Siward is informed of his son's death and honorably commends his son's valor without grieving. Macduff reenters with Macbeth's head and declares Scotland free. The play ends with Malcolm and the thanes leaving for Scone where Malcolm will be crowned King of Scotland.

ACT V, SCENE 8
The same. Another part of the plain.

[Re-enter MACBETH]

Macbeth Why should I play the Roman fool, and die
  On mine own sword? whiles I see lives, the gashes
  Do better upon them.

[Re-enter MACDUFF]

Macduff   Turn, hell-hound, turn!

Macbeth Of all men else I have avoided thee:
  But get thee back, my soul is too much charg'd   5
  With blood of thine already.

Macduff   I have no words;
  My voice is in my sword, thou bloodier villain
  Than terms can give thee out! *[They fight]*

Macbeth   Thou losest labour:
  As easy mayst thou the intrenchant air
  With thy keen sword impress as make me bleed: 10
  Let fall thy blade on vulnerable crests;
  I bear a charmed life, which must not yield
  To one of woman born.

Macduff   Despair thy charm;
  And let the angel whom thou still hast serv'd
  Tell thee, Macduff was from his mother's womb   15
  Untimely ripp'd.

Macbeth Accursed be that tongue that tells me so,
  For it hath cow'd my better part of man:

NOTES

1–2. *Why should I . . . sword?:* It was proper for Roman officers to commit suicide rather than surrender.

2. *lives:* those who are living.

4. *avoided thee:* Macbeth is avoiding Macduff not only because of the sisters' prophecy but also because he feels sure that Macduff will fall if they fight, and he still has a drop of the "milk of human kindness" left.

8. *Than . . . out:* than words can describe thee.

9. *intrenchant:* that can't be cut or gashed.

10. *impress:* make an impression.

12–13. *I bear . . . born:* He wants Macduff to yield; he doesn't want to kill him.

14. *angel:* demon, guarding spirit.

18. *my better . . . man:* my courage.

And be these juggling fiends no more believ'd,
That palter with us in a double sense;   20
That keep the word of promise to our ear,
And break it to our hope. I'll not fight with thee.

Macduff Then yield thee, coward,
And live to be the show and gaze o' the time:
We'll have thee, as our rarer monsters are,   25
Painted upon a pole, and underwrit,
'Here may you see the tyrant.'

Macbeth   I will not yield,
To kiss the ground before young Malcolm's feet,
And to be baited with the rabble's curse.
Though Birnam wood be come to Dunsinane,   30
And thou oppos'd, being of no woman born,
Yet I will try the last: before my body
I throw my war-like shield. Lay on, Macduff,
And damn'd be him that first cries, 'Hold, enough!'

[Exeunt, fighting]
[Retreat. Flourish. Reenter, with drum and colours,
MALCOLM, OLD SIWARD, ROSS, Thanes, and Soldiers]

Malcolm I would the friends we miss were safe
          arriv'd.   35

Siward Some must go off: and yet, by these I see,
So great a day as this is cheaply bought.

Malcolm Macduff is missing, and your noble son.

Ross Your son, my lord, has paid a soldier's debt:
He only liv'd but till he was a man;   40
The which no sooner had his prowess confirm'd
In the unshrinking station where he fought,
But like a man he died.

Siward   Then he is dead?

Ross Ay, and brought off the field. Your cause of sorrow
Must not be measur'd by his worth, for then   45
It hath no end.

Siward   Had he his hurts before?

Ross Ay, on the front.

20.   *palter:* deal deceitfully, equivocate.

22.   *I'll . . . thee:* Macbeth feels helplessly abandoned by the Fates.

24.   *gaze:* spectacle.

          time: age.

26.   *Painted upon a pole:* painted on canvas and fastened to a pole (as at a circus).

29.   *baited:* assailed, tormented.

32.   *the last:* i.e., strength and valor, which may yet prove stronger than fate.

33.   *lay on:* strike hard.

s.d.:   *Retreat:* this calls for a trumpet signal indicating the defeat of the enemy and halting further pursuit.

36.   *go off:* die, be lost.

39.   *paid a soldier's debt:* fought until he died.

41.   *The which:* i.e., the fact that he became a man.

          confirm'd: proved.

44.   *cause:* a case as presented in court, therefore any statement of grievances.

Siward   Why then, God's soldier be he!
  Had I as many sons as I have hairs,
  I would not wish them to a fairer death:
  And so, his knell is knoll'd.

Malcolm   He's worth more sorrow,   50
  And that I'll spend for him.

Siward   He's worth no more;
  They say he parted well, and paid his score:
  And so, God be with him! Here comes newer comfort.

[Re-enter MACDUFF, with MACBETH'S head]

Macduff Hail, king for so thou art. Behold, where stands
  The usurper's cursed head: the time is free: 55
  I see thee compass'd with thy kingdom's pearl,
  That speak my salutation in their minds;
  Whose voices I desire aloud with mine;
  Hail, King of Scotland!

All   Hail, King of Scotland!

[Flourish]

Malcolm We shall not spend a large expense of time   60
  Before we reckon with your several loves,
  And make us even with you. My thanes and kinsmen,
  Henceforth be earls, the first that ever Scotland
  In such an honour nam'd. What's more to do,
  Which would be planted newly with the time,   65
  As calling home our exil'd friends abroad
  That fled the snares of watchful tyranny;
  Producing forth the cruel ministers
  Of this dead butcher and his fiend-like queen,
  Who, as 'tis thought, by self and violent hands   70
  Took off her life; this, and what needful else
  That calls upon us, by the grace of Grace
  We will perform in measure, time, and place:
  So, thanks to all at once and to each one,
  Whom we invite to see us crown'd at Scone.   75

[Flourish. Exeunt]

---

47. *God's . . . he:* God has taken him in the performance of his duty, and so I leave him in God's hands.

50. *knoll'd:* tolled.

52. *parted well:* made a good end, owed nothing.

55. *the time is free:* Now we are free (from tyranny).

56. *compass'd:* surrounded.

  pearl: all that's good in the kingdom.

61. *reckon with:* repay.

64. *What's more to do:* whatever else must be done.

65. *Which . . . time:* that the new order of things requires.

68. *Producing forth:* bringing to light or justice.

71. *what needful else:* whatever else is necessary.

72. *calls upon us:* demands my attention.

73. *in measure:* with respectability and good behavior, as opposed to the crude rule of Macbeth.

74–75. *one . . . Scone:* These words make a very good rhyme in the English of Shakespeare's time.

COMMENTARY

The beginning of this concluding scene shows Macbeth rejecting the idea of suicide. This rejection foreshadows the end of the scene, when we finally learn how Lady Macbeth died. Because this rejection comes in the form of a rhetorical question to himself, we can infer that Macbeth has been contemplating suicide prior to the scene's opening. If Macbeth truly believes that "none of woman born" can harm him, as the prophecy indicated, then the extent of Macbeth's torment and madness are even more evident here. What else but torment and madness would prompt him to commit suicide in the face of such a promising prophecy?

Macduff's entrance begins their final encounter. Immediately, Macbeth learns that Macduff was "[u]ntimely ripp'd" from his mother's womb, and the final piece of the prophecy puzzle falls into place (16). Macduff's birth was unnatural; instead of being born naturally, he was forcibly removed from his mother through caesarian delivery.

Macbeth responds to this information by refusing to fight. This refusal adds an interesting twist: If Macduff fulfills his rage by killing Macbeth, he will be killing a defenseless man and, to some extent, will dishonor himself.

In a move reminiscent of Lady Macbeth and her psychological manipulation, Macduff calls Macbeth a coward. He tells him that his army will turn Macbeth into a spectacle and put him on display if he refuses to fight.

Macduff's words provoke Macbeth to action; he once again decides to attempt to defy the prophecy. Calling for a fight to the death, Macbeth and Macduff battle their way offstage.

Malcolm and the other nobles enter. Old Siward informs us that the victory is "cheaply bought," meaning that their army has suffered only light casualties (37). Of course, the vicotry was not "cheaply bought" for Old Siward; he will soon learn that he lost his son to Macbeth.

Shakespeare pulls Old Siward's reaction to the news of his son's death from Holinshed's account of Edward the Confessor. This reaction meshes nicely with the previous discussions of masculinity in the play. Young Siward, we learn, died "like a man" (43). Furthermore, Old Siward's form of grief recalls other expressions of grief in the play, particularly Macduff's in Act IV, Scene 3. Siward chooses not to grieve because his son "parted well" and is, therefore, with God (52).

Stephen Billington in a 1996 Royal Shakespeare Company production. Clive Barda/PAL

Macduff's reentry with Macbeth's head in hand marks the culmination of Macbeth's fall, which not only resulted in his death but the desecration of his body.

Malcolm transforms his thanes (a title that connotes a warrior culture) into earls (a title that connotes increased nobility and, specifically, a connection to England). This change may signal Malcolm's civilizing effect on Scotland. Remember the dichotomy between the two countries that Shakespeare has established. Having lived in England and witnessed its level of civility, Malcolm is able to change Scotland for the better.

Here, Malcolm echoes his father, Duncan. He refers to the processes of restoring order to Scotland as being "planted newly" (65). This line recalls Duncan's statement to Macbeth in Act I, Scene 4 that he has "begun to plant" Macbeth. This suggests that Malcolm's ascension to the throne restores the order that was present during Duncan's reign.

We also finally learn that Lady Macbeth committed suicide. What is the effect of delaying this information until the final lines? How does her means of death alter our perception of Lady Macbeth?

Malcolm's sentiment that things will be performed in their "measure, time and place" is another indication that order has been restored (73).

The play ends with Malcolm's thanks and invitation for everyone to attend his coronation at Scone. These lines, in addition to being a proper ending for the plot, are a fitting end to the play and may have been directed at the audience. Order and happiness have been restored to the kingdom with the restoration of God's appointed deputy.

Notes

Notes

Macbeth

CLIFFSCOMPLETE REVIEW

Use this CliffsComplete Review to gauge what you've learned and to build confidence in your understanding of the original text. After you work through the review questions, the problem-solving exercises, and the suggested activities, you're well on your way to understanding and appreciating the works of William Shakespeare.

SHORT ANSWER

Provide short answers to each of the following questions.

1. Define *equivocation* and give an example.

2. What are the two methods of royal succession presented in the play?

3. List the three apparitions and their corresponding prophecies that Macbeth witnesses in the weird sisters' cavern.

4. Which character kills Macbeth and why is he able to do so?

5. Who is King Duncan's legitimate heir and where does he flee after his father's murder?

IDENTIFY THE QUOTATION

Identify the following quotations by answering these questions:

* Who is the speaker of the quotation? Who (if anyone) is listening?

* What does the quotation reveal about the speaker's character?

* What does the quotation tell us about other characters within the play?

* Where does the quotation occur within the play?

* What does the quotation show us about the themes of the play?

* What significant imagery do you see in the quotation, and how do these images relate to the overall imagery of the play?

1. If good, why do I yield to that suggestion
   Whose horrid image doth unfix my hair
   And make my seated heart knock at my ribs,
   Against the use of nature? Present fears
   Are less than horrible imaginings;
   My thought, whose murder yet is but fantastical,
   Shakes so my single state of man that function
   Is smother'd in surmise, and nothing is
   But what is not.

2. Fair is foul, and foul is fair:
   Hover through the fog and filthy air.

3. Out, damned spot! out, I say! One; two: why then 'tis time to do 't. Hell is murky! Fie, my lord, fie! a soldier and afeard? What need we fear who knows it, when none can call our power to account? Yet who would have thought the old man to have had so much blood in him?

4. So I lose none
   In seeking to augment it, but still keep
   My bosom franchis'd and allegiance clear,
   I shall be counsell'd.

5. There's no art
   To find the mind's construction in the face:
   He was a gentleman on whom I built
   An absolute trust.

6. Come, you spirits
   That tend on mortal thoughts! unsex me here,
   And fill me from the crown to the toe top full
   Of direst cruelty; make thick my blood
   Stop up the access and passage to remorse,
   That no compunctious visitings of nature
   Shake my fell purpose, nor keep peace between
   The effect and it!

7. But 'tis strange:
   And oftentimes, to win us to our harm,
   The instruments of darkness tell us truths,
   Win us with honest trifles, to betray's
   In deepest consequence.

8. Nothing in his life
   Became him like the leaving it; he died
   As one that had been studied in his death
   To throw away the dearest thing he ow'd,
   As 'twere a careless trifle.

9. O! I could play the woman with mine eyes,
   And braggart with my tongue. But, gentle heavens,
   Cut short all intermission; front to front
   Bring thou this fiend of Scotland and myself;
   Within my sword's length set him; if he 'scape,
   Heaven forgive him too!

10. To-morrow, and to-morrow, and to-morrow,
    Creeps in this petty pace from day to day,
    To the last syllable of recorded time;
    And all our yesterdays have lighted fools
    The way to dusty death. Out, out, brief candle!

TRUE/FALSE

1. T F Macbeth encounters three witches who promise him that he shall produce a line of kings.

2. T F Banquo agrees to help Macbeth fulfill his destiny by murdering Duncan.

3. T F Lady Macbeth convinces her husband to kill Duncan by questioning his masculinity.

4. T F In a grief-stricken rage, Malcolm and Donalbain kill Duncan's bloody servants.

5. T F Macbeth orders Banquo and his son Fleance killed because he feels that they pose a threat to his reign and the succession of his line.

6. T F Banquo is killed, but Fleance escapes.

7. T F Duncan's ghost appears at the banquet in Act III.

8. T F Macduff flees to England to join forces with Malcolm in rebelling against Macbeth.

9. T F Macbeth orders Macduff's family executed in retribution for plotting against him.

10. T F Lady Macbeth sleepwalks and dreams that she can't remove a spot of blood from her hands.

11. T F Macbeth revisits the weird sisters, and they show him six apparitions.

12. T F Macduff was "born of woman."

13. T F Birnam Wood moves to Dunsinane Hill because the soldiers carry tree branches.

14. T F Siward, Earl of Northumberland, fights and defeats Macbeth.

15. T F Macduff hails Malcolm as King of Scotland at the end of the play.

MULTIPLE CHOICE

1. Which of the following is NOT a Scottish thane?

   a. Macduff

   b. Banquo

   c. Macbeth

   d. Siward

2. Macbeth and Lady Macbeth have _____ children?

   a. 0

   b. 1

   c. 2

   d. 3

3. What was Banquo's prophecy from the weird sisters?

   a. That he will be king.

   b. That he will die young

   c. That his descendents will be kings.

   d. That Macbeth will murder him.

4. Macbeth informs his wife of the prophecy by what means?

   a. Letter

   b. In person

   c. Messenger

   d. E-mail

5. Whom of the following is NOT in attendance at Macbeth's banquet?

   a. Ross

   b. Lady Macbeth

   c. Lennox

   d. Macduff

6. How many murderers does Macbeth send to kill Banquo and Fleance?

   a. 1

   b. 2

   c. 3

   d. 4

7. Which of the following apparitions does Macbeth see during his second encounter with the weird sisters?

   a. A Scottish thane on horseback

   b. Fleance wearing a crown

   c. A procession of kings

   d. Lady Macbeth sleepwalking

8. Who is the character that first mentions the idea of equivocation?

   a. Macbeth

   b. Porter

   c. Banquo

   d. Lady Macbeth

9. Who is the commander of the English forces?

   a. Macbeth

   b. Banquo

   c. Macduff

   d. Siward

10. Which character does Macbeth NOT kill?

   a. Duncan

   b. Duncan's groomsmen

   c. Siward

   d. Ross

11. Which text was Shakespeare's primary source for the story of *Macbeth*?

   a. Thomas Middleton's *The Witch*

   b. James I's *Daemonologie*

   c. *The First Folio*

   d. Raphael Holinshed's *Chronicles*

12. Who is the ruler of the witches?

    a. Beelzebub

    b. Hecate

    c. Cawdor

    d. Circe

13. Who takes the Scottish throne at the end of the play?

    a. Fleance

    b. Macduff

    c. Malcolm

    d. Siward

14. Macbeth murders Duncan using what weapon?

    a. Dagger

    b. Spear

    c. Sword

    d. Poison

15. The final apparition shown to Macbeth by the weird sisters is a line of how many kings?

    a. 5

    b. 6

    c. 8

    d. 10

FILL IN THE BLANK

1. **Duncan** No more that Thane of Cawdor shall deceive / Our bosom interest. Go pronounce his present death, / And with his former _____ greet Macbeth.

2. **Third Witch** All hail, Macbeth! that shalt be _____ hereafter.

3. **Banquo** New honours come upon him, / Like our strange _____, cleave not to their mould / But with the aid of use.

4. **Lady Macbeth** The sleeping and the dead / Are but as _____; 'tis the eye of childhood/ That fears a painted devil.

5. **Macbeth** Prithee, peace / I dare do all that may become a _____; / Who dares do more is none.

6. **Porter** Faith, here's an _____, that could swear in both the scales against either scale.

7. **Lady Macbeth** Had he not resembled / My _____ as he slept, I had done 't.

8. **Macbeth** Thou canst not say I did it: never shake / Thy gory _____ at me.

9. **Second Apparition** Be bloody, bold, and resolute; laugh to scorn / The power of man, for none of _____ born / Shall harm Macbeth.

10. **Macbeth** Lay on, _____, / And damn'd be him that first cries, 'Hold, enough!'

DISCUSSION

Use the following questions to generate discussion:

1. Compare and contrast the character development of Macbeth and Lady Macbeth. What different stages does each of them go through? How does each react to the crimes they commit? What do the differences in their reactions say about each character? What may these differences indicate about gender roles and how Shakespeare viewed them?

2. Discuss the presentation of masculinity in this play. Are competing definitions of masculinity presented? Are any of the definitions criticized or endorsed? If any are criticized, how does Shakespeare make that criticism evident? How do you think Shakespeare would define an ideal masculinity?

3. Examine the many mentions of sleep in the play. What do the references to sleep and depictions of sleep indicate about the characters, their behavior, and/or the themes of the play?

4. *Macbeth* is often discussed in terms of *dichotomies* (paired opposites). Some of the dichotomies that appear in this play are good versus evil, order versus disorder, reality versus illusions (or appearances), man versus woman, light versus dark, and right versus wrong. Dichotomies often simplify concepts so they are as easy to contrast as black and white. Consider how Shakespeare's presentation of one or more of these dichotomies complicates the opposition so that we are forced to consider the many shades of gray that fall between the two concepts. What is the effect of this complication? How does it change or influence the meaning of the play? How does recognizing a more complex portrayal of these concepts aid our understanding of the tragedy?

5. Let's say that you have been recently hired to produce a modern cinematic production of *Macbeth*, and the budget is unlimited. Decide who you would cast in each of the major roles, and discuss why you would make those particular decisions. Explain why the actors and actresses you name would be the best choices to portray each major character. Make sure to cite specific themes and character traits when justifying your choices.

6. Although *Macbeth* doesn't show you a scene of Duncan's actual stabbing, the play does depict the slaying of Lady Macduff and her son. Consider why we don't see Duncan's death on stage. Why did Shakespeare dramatize Lady Macduff's death? How does Shakespeare make us care about Lady Macduff and her son? Is their death scene necessary?

IDENTIFYING PLAY ELEMENTS

Find examples of the following elements in the text of *Macbeth*:

* **Soliloquy:** A soliloquy is a monologue delivered by a character when he or she is alone. This dramatic technique allows the character to convey his or her inner thoughts and feelings to the audience.

* **Dramatic irony:** This special type of irony occurs when the audience possesses more knowledge than a character, allowing the audience to understand more than the character about what is happening. Dramatic irony often helps an audience anticipate events or behavior that the character(s) can't.

* **Internal stage direction:** This element is a special type of stage direction that occurs when a character indicates through his or her speech that an action has transpired or is transpiring on stage. The character describes for us actions that the playwright does not specify in explicit stage directions.

* **Metaphor:** A metaphor is an object or concept that is identified with and used in place of another object or concept. Metaphors highlight features that the objects or concepts share. For example, in the statement "Love is a rose," *rose* is a metaphor for love that invokes the beautiful (the rose) and painful (the thorns) aspects of love.

* **Apostrophe:** This element occurs when a character speaks directly to a character who isn't on stage or to an inanimate object. Like soliloquies, apostrophes allow characters to convey thoughts and feelings to the audience that they would prefer to be hidden from other characters.

* **Irony:** Irony refers to a marked difference between reality and appearances. It's a deviation from the expected. Verbal irony, a specific form of irony, occurs when a character's speech and his or her thoughts or actions do not match. Verbal irony can also indicate a difference between the literal and implied meanings of a character's speech.

* **Symbol:** A symbol is something (usually an object — a person, place, or thing) that represents something else (often an abstract concept, such as freedom, evil, or love). A symbol is different from a metaphor in that the symbol retains its essential characteristics and also represents something else. In contrast, a metaphor takes the place of the other object or concept.

* **Allusion:** An allusion is a suggested link in the text to something outside of the text. These links can refer to a historical person, a historical event, a literary figure, or even another text.

* **Imagery:** Imagery is the employment of images (textual representations that create "mental pictures") within a work of literature. In many cases, patterns of imagery can lead the reader to a richer understanding of the themes and concepts explored in the text.

* **Aside:** This element is a dramatic convention that finds a character explicitly speaking to the audience while the other characters on stage are not able to hear the speech. Asides can also occur between two characters; in this case, again, the audience is able to hear the conversation but the other characters on stage are not.

ACTIVITIES

The following activities can serve as a springboard for further discussions and projects. Each involves individual work but works best if ideas can be shared in a classroom or group.

1. Pick one scene from *Macbeth* and decide how you, as director, would stage it. Where would the characters stand on stage? How and when would they move? How would they deliver their lines? (Keep in mind that an actor's line delivery has a significant impact on the interpretation of the play.) What types of costumes would the actors wear? What type of scenery would appear on the stage? Consider several answers to each of these questions, and then discuss the impact that each decision would have on the scene's effectiveness. If the resources are available, work as a group to stage the scene under the direction of one person whose ideas seem strong.

2. Memorize one of Macbeth's major soliloquies, making sure to look up all the words that you aren't familiar with. (See, for example, his speeches at the beginning of Act I, Scene 7; at the end of Act II, Scene 1; and in the middle of Act V, Scene 5.) Practice reciting the soliloquy aloud, paying special attention to how you deliver the lines. In a group, take turns reciting the soliloquies and discuss how various readings impact the meaning of the words.

3. Read a couple of paragraphs from Raphael Holinshed's account of Macbeth in *Chronicles of England, Scotland, and Ireland*. (Most university libraries have a copy of this work.) Read passages from Shakespeare's *Macbeth* that relate to those paragraphs from Holinshed. Write down all the major differences that you can identify between the two texts. As a group, bring your findings together and discuss the alterations Shakespeare made to the story and the characters. Consider what Shakespeare's reasoning might have been for those changes and how the play *Macbeth* would have differed had he followed Holinshed's account more closely.

4. Pick an image or group of images that appears often in the play. Some examples include the owl, clothing, writing and reading, theatre, and sleep. Starting from the beginning of the play, record all the references to the selected image or group of images that you can find. How do these references relate to one another? Can you identify any consistency in the way Shakespeare is using the image(s)? If so, what is the

significance of their use? How does studying this image or group of images enhance our understanding and appreciation of the play?

5. Pick a key issue or concept in the play (for example, gender, religion, evil, and so on). Using your local library and Internet resources, find ten articles or other short works that discuss the selected issue or concept in *Macbeth*. Read each of them and write a short summary of the work. In a group discussion, present your findings, focusing on ways in which various critics / readers agree on the play's handling of that issue or concept and ways in which they disagree. Does Shakespeare seem to leave room for debate about that particular issue? Does your own interpretation of the play fit with any or all of the sources you researched?

ANSWERS

Short Answer

1. Equivocation is a theory that provides a justification for lying, claiming that if a statement can be considered truthful from a certain perspective, it's not actually lying. The prophecy that Macbeth receives concerning Birnam Wood moving to Dunsinane Hill is a good example of equivocation, because although the woods don't actually move, they seem to move when the soldiers disguise themselves with branches. From a purely visual perspective, the prophecy comes true.

2. First, a new king could be elected by other thanes; this method was used in Scotland until the eleventh century. This is the way Macbeth attains the throne in the play. Second, the throne could be gained through inheritance. This is called patrilineal succession through *primogeniture* — the first-born son of the king attains the throne upon his father's death.

3. The first apparition of an armed head says to "beware Macduff." The second apparition of the bloody child says that no man born of a woman can harm Macbeth. The third apparition of the crowned child holding a tree says that Macbeth shall not be vanquished until the Birnam Wood comes to Dunsinane Hill.

4. Macduff kills Macbeth. He is able to do so because he was delivered through caesarian delivery ("c-section"), so he was not born of a woman in a natural way.

5. King Duncan's legitimate heir is Malcolm. He flees to England after his father's murder.

Identify the Quotation

1. Macbeth is speaking an aside to himself which only the audience can hear. He is contemplating the meaning and nature (good or evil) of the initial prophecy the weird sisters gave him. Macbeth wonders how the prophecy can be good, because he's already having "horrible" thoughts, presumably about killing Duncan. This quote's significance lies in demonstrating Macbeth's early ambition and thoughts of murder as well as his inner turmoil. (I.3.135-143)

2. The witches are chanting these lines as they exit the first scene. The lines illustrate the evil nature of the witches, who delight in things foul and find disgust in things fair. The significance of this quote is in the disorder and inversion demonstrated in these lines. (I.1.11-12)

3. Lady Macbeth is speaking these lines to herself, although a doctor and her gentlewoman are listening. She's sleepwalking and dreaming that she can't wash a spot of blood, symbolic of her guilty involvement in Duncan's murder, from her hand. This quotation is significant because it illustrates the inner torment and

guilt that invades Lady Macbeth's sleep. Previously able to think rationally about the crimes she and Macbeth commit, by this scene Lady Macbeth's emotions and conscience have caught up with her. (V.1.31–35)

4. In this quotation, Banquo tells Macbeth that he'll help fulfill the weird sisters' prophecy as long as doing so doesn't compromise his loyalty and allegiance to Duncan. This conversation represents the beginning of the separation between the two friends and is significant because Banquo is able to resist his temptation toward evil while Macbeth is not. (II.1.26–29)

5. In these lines, Duncan is talking to Malcolm about the original Thane of Cawdor. He states that it's impossible to understand a man's inner thoughts and feelings from his face. This quotation is significant because the distinction between a man's face and his heart is a theme that runs throughout the play, especially in relation to Macbeth. (I.4.11–14)

6. Lady Macbeth is speaking to herself, so only the audience can hear. Through a letter from her husband, she has just learned of the witches' prophecy. Knowing that Macbeth is undecided about his course of action, she asks the "spirits" (in the form of this prayer) to remove the feminine attributes of her biological sex so she can take an active role in killing Duncan. This quotation raises the question of what it means to be feminine and masculine. (I.5.38–45)

7. Banquo is talking to Macbeth in these lines. He is expressing caution by saying that the weird sisters may tell them small truths in order to convince them to seek larger things. The passage shows Banquo's insight and caution, which contrasts with Macbeth's immediate, rash contemplation of the murder of Duncan. (I.3.123–27)

8. In this passage, Malcolm is speaking to Duncan about the original Thane of Cawdor, who died a noble death after confessing his treasonous actions. This quotation is important because it shows one of the many different ways the play depicts dying. This statement early in the play presents a good example against which to compare other deaths — especially Macbeth's. (I.4.7–11)

9. Macduff is lamenting the murder of his family in front of Malcolm and Ross. He says that he could cry and rant about his loss, but instead he will seek revenge from Macbeth. This quote is significant in its portrayal of dealing with grief as well as its comments on gender. Macduff indicates that open displays of grief, even with such extreme provocation, are not masculine. (IV.3.230–234)

10. Macbeth speaks these lines after learning of Lady Macbeth's death. His officer, Seyton, is also on stage, but Macbeth seems to be talking to himself. These lines demonstrate Macbeth's pessimism with life and his desire for death. (V.5.19–23)

True/False

(1) F (2) F (3) T (4) F (5) T (6) T (7) F (8) T (9) T (10) T (11) F (12) F (13) T (14) F (15) T

Multiple Choice

(1) d. (2) a. (3) c. (4) a. (5) d. (6) c. (7) c. (8) b.
(9) d. (10) d. (11) d. (12) b. (13) c. (14) a. (15) c.

Fill in the Blank

(1) title (2) King (3) garments (4) pictures (5) man
(6) equivocator (7) father (8) locks (9) woman
(10) Macduff

CLIFFSCOMPLETE RESOURCE CENTER

The learning doesn't need to stop here. CliffsComplete Resource Center shows you the best of the best: great links to information in print, on film, and online. And the following aren't all the great resources available to you; visit **www.cliffsnotes. com** for tips on reading literature, writing papers, giving presentations, locating other resources, and testing your knowledge.

BOOKS, MAGAZINES, AND ARTICLES

Adelman, Janet. "'Born of Woman': Fantasies of Maternal Power in *Macbeth*." *Cannibals, Witches, and Divorce: Estranging the Renaissance.* Ed. Marjorie Garber. Baltimore: Johns Hopkins University Press, 1987. 90–121.

Adelman's article provides a psychoanalytic reading of Shakespeare's text. Adelman asserts that *Macbeth* explores the male fantasy of escaping maternal power. Written to an audience of other Shakespearean scholars, this article is complex and best serves advanced students of Shakespeare and *Macbeth*.

Brooks, Cleanth. "The Naked Babe and the Cloak of Manliness." *The Well Wrought Urn.* New York: Reynal and Hitchcock, 1947. 21–46.

In this important article, Brooks explores the symbols and images in the play and discusses how these literary conventions fit into *Macbeth's* larger themes. Although critical trends have moved away from Brooks's focus in recent years, this article is essential for beginning research on *Macbeth*.

Bushnell, Rebecca W., ed. *King Lear and Macbeth: An Annotated Bibliography of Shakespeare Studies, 1674–1995. Pegasus Shakespeare Bibliographies.* Ashville, NC: Pegasus Press/University of North Carolina Press, 1996.

This is an extremely useful bibliography for students of *King Lear* and *Macbeth* that provides annotations for each entry. The listed materials include various play editions, studies on dating the creation of each text, general criticism, studies devoted to stage performance and history, bibliographies, and concordances. This source is easy to use and provides an excellent starting point for the study of *Macbeth*.

Carroll, William C., ed. *Macbeth: Texts and Contexts.* Bedford Shakespeare series. Boston: Bedford/St. Martins, 1999.

In addition to containing the full text of *Macbeth* and an extensive critical introduction, this edition reprints a wide array of contemporary Elizabethan and Jacobean documents. These documents deal with issues pertinent to the play ranging from historical accounts and political discourse to accounts of witchcraft and gender discourse. This volume contains most of the contextual documents needed to study this play.

Cookson, Linda and Bryan Loughrey, eds. *Critical Essays on Macbeth.* Harlow, Essex: Longman, 1988.

This volume contains ten essays concerning *Macbeth*. The essays cover issues including the treatment of evil, the dramatic structure of the play, tragic ambivalence, and the relationship between Macbeth and Lady Macbeth. The wide range of subject matter covered in the essays makes this collection a valuable starting place for general research on *Macbeth*.

Cox, John, D. and David Scott Kastan, eds. *A New History of Early English Drama*. New York: Columbia University Press, 1997.

Although none of the essays in this volume deals directly with *Macbeth*, this collection of articles is invaluable for its coverage and discussion of drama. The essays approach drama from both historical and cultural perspectives and deal with the performance and publication issues surrounding early English plays.

Doyle, John and Ray Lischner. *Shakespeare For Dummies*. Foster City: IDG Books Worldwide, Inc., 1999.

This guide to Shakespeare's plays and poetry provides summaries and scorecards for keeping track of who's who in a given play, as well as painless introductions to language, imagery, and other often intimidating subjects.

Greenblatt, Stephen. *The Norton Shakespeare*. New York: W. W. Norton and Co., 1997.

This anthology of Shakespeare's work includes a valuable critical introduction that introduces students to Shakespeare as well as to Early Modern England. The text's appendixes include an essay on the Shakespearean stage by scholar Andrew Gurr and pertinent historical documents, such as Robert Greene's famous attack on Shakespeare and Shakespeare's will.

Jaech, Sharon L. Jansen. "Political Prophecy and Macbeth's 'Sweet Bodements.'" *Shakespeare Quarterly*. 34 (1983): 290–97.

This article examines the apparition symbolism in relation to political prophecy in sixteenth and seventeenth century England. As an advanced study, this article best serves students performing in-depth research regarding the play's relationship to contemporary politics.

Kastan, David Scott, ed. *A Companion to Shakespeare*. Oxford: Blackwell, 1999.

This collection of essays is devoted to the study of Shakespeare and Early Modern England. It contains a wide array of articles that deal with subjects such as Shakespeare's life, the culture of Early Modern England, life in London, religion, Early Modern family life, political beliefs, and the theatre. Each essay provides a valuable and insightful starting point for further research in the respective topic.

Kernan, Alvin B. *Shakespeare, the King's Playwright: Theater in the Stuart Court, 1603–1613*. New Haven: Yale University Press, 1995.

This book examines Shakespeare's relationship to the Jacobean court, tackling the question of whether Shakespeare's plays are propaganda for the court or subversive of the court. The author asserts that plays such as *Macbeth* comment on political and social issues relevant to the court, but Shakespeare doesn't deviate from his artistic vision while incorporating his political and social views.

Kinney, Arthur F. "Scottish History, the Union of the Crowns, and the Issue of Right Rule: The Case of Shakespeare's *Macbeth*." *Renaissance Culture in Context: Theory and Practice*. Aldershot: Scolar Press, 1993.

This advanced study examines the relationship between Shakespeare's *Macbeth* and Raphael Holinshed's 1577 edition of *Chronicles of England, Scotland, and Ireland*. The author asserts that *Macbeth* is a warning to James against imperialist and absolutist thought. This article is valuable to students interested in Shakespeare's source for the Macbeth story and the contextual relationship to James I.

McDonald, Russ. *The Bedford Companion to Shakespeare: An Introduction with Documents*. Boston: Bedford/St. Martins, 1996.

This companion contains chapters on Shakespeare's life, questions concerning the authorship of the plays attributed to him, the theatre, Early Modern texts, Shakespeare's influences and sources, dramatic genres, dramatic language, daily life, the family, politics, and religion. The text includes illustrations and contemporary documents.

Rosenberg, Marvin. *The Masks of Macbeth*. Berkeley: University of California Press, 1978.

This is one of the decisive works in *Macbeth* studies. In this comprehensive study of the play, Rosenberg works chronologically through the entire play text to analyze the characters, themes, and imagery. Furthermore, the author draws on the play's extensive stage history, noting the evolution of the play through its performances, to support and elaborate on his analysis.

Sinfield, Alan, ed. *Macbeth: New Casebooks*. New York: St. Martins, 1992.

This casebook excerpts a wide variety of essays devoted to *Macbeth*. Written by some of the best scholars in Early Modern studies, these essays approach the play from a diverse range of critical perspectives.

INTERNET

"Arden Net: The Critical Resource for Shakespeare Studies."
www.ardenshakespeare.com/main/
welcome.html

Although registration is required to access this site, it is free to anyone interested in Shakespeare. Aimed at a wide range of Shakespeare readers and scholars, the services of this site include reviews of links and URLs to other useful sites devoted to the study of Shakespeare, news and reviews of performances, books and films, and a discussion area. All of the site's contents are reviewed by Shakespeare experts to ensure that the information is accurate and valuable.

"The Complete Works of Shakespeare." Ed. Jeremy Hylton.
http://tech-two.mit.edu/Shakespeare/

This Web site contains online texts for all of Shakespeare's dramatic and poetic works. The texts feature hyperlinks for definitions of difficult words and are well spaced on the page to aid in reading. Other notable features of this site include a discussion area that is divided by the major works with a separate area for postings that do not pertain to a single work. A search feature allows you to search Shakespeare's plays to find specific passages, key words, and so on.

"Mr. William Shakespeare on the Internet." Terry Gray.
http://daphne.palomar.edu/shakespeare/

As it states on its main page, this Web site has two goals: to provide a comprehensive annotated bibliography for Internet resources dealing with Shakespeare and his works, and to provide online materials about Shakespeare that are not currently available elsewhere on the Internet. Materials that aren't available elsewhere on the Internet include such works as Rowe's 1709 preface to Shakespeare's works, prefatory materials found in the First Folio, and Charles and Mary Lamb's adaptations, *Tales from Shakespeare*. This site is well detailed and is highly recommended when you are conducting Internet research on Shakespeare and his works.

"Macbeth: An In-depth Analysis."
http://library.thinkquest.org/2888/

This site provides a complete online text of *Macbeth* with hyperlinked glossaries to difficult words and passages. In addition to definitions, these hyperlinks also provide some commentary on the play. Other features of this site include a search function as well as a multimedia section where students can download video and audio clips of play performances. Likewise, the site provides an extensive annotated list of sources that deal with Shakespeare, *Macbeth*, and other aspects relevant to the study of this play, such as witches and Medieval history.

"Shakespeare: Chill with Will."
http://library.thinkquest.org/19539/front.htm
This fun and well-designed Web site is aimed specifically at high school students and presents information on Shakespeare's life and works in a medium that is at once entertaining and useful. This site provides in-depth coverage of four of Shakespeare's tragedies — *Romeo and Juliet, Julius Caesar, Hamlet,* and *Macbeth.* Play coverage includes background discussions, criticism, characters, and film reviews.

FILMS

Macbeth. Dir. Orson Welles. Perf. Orson Welles and Roddy McDowall. 1948.

This classic production features Orson Welles as its director and star. It's a must see for students of *Macbeth.*

Macbeth. Dir. Roman Polanski. Perf. Jon Finch and Francesca Annis. 1971.

Roman Polanski's *Macbeth* is considered controversial because of its depiction of graphic violence and nudity. This dark film is useful for its portrayal of Medieval Scotland.

Macbeth. Dir. Trevor Nunn. Perf. Judi Dench and Ian McKellen. 1979.

This powerful film version stars talented British actress Judi Dench (who portrayed Queen Victoria in *Her Majesty, Mrs. Brown*) and British star Ian McKellen (who starred in the recent film *Gods and Monsters*).

Throne of Blood. Dir. Akira Kurosawa. Perf. Akira Kubo, Toshiro Mifune, Takashi Shimura, and Isuzu Yamada. 1957.

Japanese director Kurosawa transplants the tragic story of *Macbeth* from Medieval Scotland to sixteenth century Japan in this classic adaptation of Shakespeare's play.

Macbeth

CLIFFSCOMPLETE READING GROUP DISCUSSION GUIDE

Use the following questions and topics to enhance your reading group discussions. The discussion can help get you thinking — and hopefully talking — about Shakespeare in a whole new way!

DISCUSSION QUESTIONS

1. Throughout *Macbeth*, you can view many of the characters' actions as based on choice (or *free will*), based on fate (or *destiny*), or influenced by supernatural forces. Which of Macbeth's actions seem to come from free will? Which seem to come from destiny? Which seem guided by unearthly forces? What about the actions of Lady Macbeth? Banquo? Malcolm? Macduff? What relationship between free will, destiny, and supernatural forces does Shakespeare suggest?

2. During Macbeth's monologue prior to killing Duncan, Macbeth utters the famous line "Is that a knife I see before me?" If you were producing a film or stage production of *Macbeth*, would you have a knife float in so the audience can see the knife that Macbeth speaks of? Or would you make the knife a figment of Macbeth's imagination and have the actor pretend to see a knife? What are the pros and cons of showing the audience a real knife? What are the pros and cons of having the actor pretend to see a knife?

3. Without a doubt, Lady Macbeth is one of the most coveted roles for Shakespearean actresses. A wide variety of actresses have played the role with much success. How physically attractive should Lady Macbeth be? Should she be younger or older than Macbeth? What is the effect of having an ugly but regal Lady Macbeth? Likewise, what is the effect of having a young, attractive Lady Macbeth?

4. *Macbeth* is a dark play, and most modern productions highlight this darkness through costumes, lighting, and set design. How did Shakespeare make the play feel dark, given that original performances at the Globe theatre were held in the afternoon and very few props or costumes were used? Which characters, lines, and plot points in the play make *Macbeth* dark without the aid of special effects?

5. Throughout the ages, directors of film and stage productions have gone to great lengths (and often great expense) while producing the witches' scenes. The witches have been represented as beautiful floating ballerinas, sinister shrieking hags, and monotone zombies. How would you cast, costume, and stage the witches? Why do you think these characters are open to so many radically different interpretations?

6. Although most of Shakespeare's audience members believed in the power of witchcraft, far fewer modern audience members do. In fact, some productions of *Macbeth* have cut the witches entirely from the play in an effort to focus on the drama within Macbeth's head. Are the witches necessary for a modern audience? What are the benefits of cutting the witches from the play? What does the play lose if the witches are cut?

7. *Macbeth* features numerous supporting characters. Why did Shakespeare include the characters of Fleance, the porter, Lennox, Donalbain, Seyton, and Ross? What do these characters add to the play? How would the play be different if you removed each of these characters?

8. The first Macbeth/Lady Macbeth scene has been performed many different ways in various productions. Some actors use this scene to show an equal partnership between Macbeth and Lady Macbeth, while other actors show Lady Macbeth as controlling and dominating in subtle ways from the start. Simple acting choices can radically affect your understanding of Macbeth and Lady Macbeth's relationship. How would you stage the scene? When Macbeth enters, should Lady Macbeth bow or curtsy? Should Lady Macbeth and Macbeth touch one another during this scene? Should the touch be romantic, gently loving, or sexually charged? Should they exit together?

9. Film and stage productions of *Macbeth* have been set in many different locations and historical time periods. Select a location or historical time period (medieval Europe, a modern political dictatorship, a corporate boardroom, a futuristic space colony, and so on) and suggest how you would stage the following:

* Macbeth and Banquo's first encounter with the witches

* The murder of Duncan

* Macbeth and Lady Macbeth cleaning up after the Duncan's murder

* The appearance of Banquo's ghost at Macbeth's celebration

* Lady Macbeth's final crazed monologue

10. Malcolm's last speech in the play has puzzled many directors, actors, and readers. Some recent productions have had Malcolm's soldiers disturb the audience during the speech in order to highlight that there's more political and social unrest to come. Likewise, one film of *Macbeth* ends with Donalbain going to the witches' lair, implying that the political ambition and revenge depicted in the play may take place again. How genuine should Malcolm be in his final speech? How does an insincere Malcolm affect the play's meaning?

Notes

Index

(continued)

Notes

Notes

Notes

CliffsNotes™

CLIFFSCOMPLETE

Hamlet
Julius Caesar
King Henry IV, Part I
King Lear
Macbeth
The Merchant of Venice
Othello
Romeo and Juliet
The Tempest
Twelfth Night

Look for Other Series in the CliffsNotes Family

LITERATURE NOTES

Absalom, Absalom!
The Aeneid
Agamemnon
Alice in Wonderland
All the King's Men
All the Pretty Horses
All Quiet on the Western Front
All's Well & Merry Wives
American Poets of the
    20th Century
American Tragedy
Animal Farm
Anna Karenina
Anthem
Antony and Cleopatra
Aristotle's Ethics
As I Lay Dying
The Assistant
As You Like It
Atlas Shrugged
Autobiography of Ben Franklin
Autobiography of Malcolm X
The Awakening
Babbit
Bartleby & Benito Cereno
The Bean Trees
The Bear
The Bell Jar
Beloved
Beowulf
Billy Budd & Typee
Black Boy
Black Like Me

Bleak House
Bless Me, Ultima
The Bluest Eye & Sula
Brave New World
Brothers Karamazov
Call of Wild & White Fang
Candide
The Canterbury Tales
Catch-22
Catcher in the Rye
The Chosen
Cliffs Notes on the Bible
The Color Purple
Comedy of Errors…
Connecticut Yankee
The Contender
The Count of Monte Cristo
Crime and Punishment
The Crucible
Cry, the Beloved Country
Cyrano de Bergerac
Daisy Miller & Turn…Screw
David Copperfield
Death of a Salesman
The Deerslayer
Diary of Anne Frank
Divine Comedy-I. Inferno
Divine Comedy-II. Purgatorio
Divine Comedy-III. Paradiso
Doctor Faustus
Dr. Jekyll and Mr. Hyde
Don Juan
Don Quixote
Dracula
Emerson's Essays
Emily Dickinson Poems
Emma
Ethan Frome
Euripides' Electra & Medea
The Faerie Queene
Fahrenheit 451
Far from Madding Crowd
A Farewell to Arms
Farewell to Manzanar
Fathers and Sons
Faulkner's Short Stories
Faust Pt. I & Pt. II
The Federalist
Flowers for Algernon
For Whom the Bell Tolls
The Fountainhead
Frankenstein
The French Lieutenant's Woman
The Giver
Glass Menagerie & Streetcar
Go Down, Moses

The Good Earth
Grapes of Wrath
Great Expectations
The Great Gatsby
Greek Classics
Gulliver's Travels
Hamlet
The Handmaid's Tale
Hard Times
Heart of Darkness & Secret Sharer
Hemingway's Short Stories
Henry IV Part 1
Henry IV Part 2
Henry V
House Made of Dawn
The House of the Seven Gables
Huckleberry Finn
I Know Why the Caged Bird Sings
Ibsen's Plays I
Ibsen's Plays II
The Idiot
Idylls of the King
The Iliad
Incidents in the Life of a Slave Girl
Inherit the Wind
Invisible Man
Ivanhoe
Jane Eyre
Joseph Andrews
The Joy Luck Club
Jude the Obscure
Julius Caesar
The Jungle
Kafka's Short Stories
Keats & Shelley
The Killer Angels
King Lear
The Kitchen God's Wife
The Last of the Mohicans
Le Morte Darthur
Leaves of Grass
Les Miserables
A Lesson Before Dying
Light in August
The Light in the Forest
Lord Jim
Lord of the Flies
The Lord of the Rings
Lost Horizon
Lysistrata & Other Comedies
Macbeth
Madame Bovary
Main Street
The Mayor of Casterbridge
Measure for Measure
The Merchant of Venice

Middlemarch
A Midsummer-Night's Dream
The Mill on the Floss
Moby-Dick
Moll Flanders
Mrs. Dalloway
Much Ado About Nothing
My Ántonia
Mythology
Narr. …Frederick Douglass
Native Son
New Testament
Night
1984
Notes from Underground
The Odyssey
Oedipus Trilogy
Of Human Bondage
Of Mice and Men
The Old Man and the Sea
Old Testament
Oliver Twist
The Once and Future King
One Day in the Life of
    Ivan Denisovich
One Flew Over Cuckoo's Nest
100 Years of Solitude
O'Neill's Plays
Othello
Our Town
The Outsiders
The Ox-Bow Incident
Paradise Lost
A Passage to India
The Pearl
The Pickwick Papers
The Picture of Dorian Gray
Pilgrim's Progress
The Plague
Plato's Euthyphro…
Plato's The Republic
Poe's Short Stories
A Portrait of the Artist…
The Portrait of a Lady
The Power and the Glory
Pride and Prejudice
The Prince
The Prince and the Pauper
A Raisin in the Sun
The Red Badge of Courage
The Red Pony
The Return of the Native
Richard II
Richard III
The Rise of Silas Lapham
Robinson Crusoe

Made in the USA
Middletown, DE
13 March 2023

26698122R00121